economic policy
and the
great stagflation

[student edition]

economic policy
and the
great stagflation

[student edition]

ALAN S. BLINDER

Department of Economics
Princeton University
Princeton, New Jersey

ACADEMIC PRESS

A Subsidiary of Harcourt Brace Jovanovich, Publishers

New York   London   Toronto   Sydney   San Francisco

ACADEMIC PRESS, INC.
111 Fifth Avenue, New York, New York 10003

United Kingdom Edition published by
ACADEMIC PRESS, INC. (LONDON) LTD.
24/28 Oval Road, London NW1 7DX

LIBRARY OF CONGRESS CATALOG CARD NUMBER: 81-3470

ISBN: 0-12-106162-0
PRINTED IN THE UNITED STATES OF AMERICA

81 82 83 84   9 8 7 6 5 4 3 2 1

To my parents, Morris and Shirley Blinder,
without whom this would never have been written

contents

7 fiscal policy and the great stagflation   141

8 monetary policy and the great stagflation   179

9 the legacy of the great stagflation   203

preface

This is a book both about national economic policy and about economics as a policy-oriented science. (I trust the adjective does not contradict the noun.) Both experienced a kind of trial by fire during the Great Stagflation of the mid 1970s; and while neither escaped unscathed, it is my contention that economic policymaking fared much worse than did economic science.

It is simply not feasible to purge "political" issues from a book on economic policy, and I do not pretend to have done so. Rather than try to write in the style of a political eunuch, I have not hesitated to stake out positions on controversial issues where that seemed warranted. Though this is a book with a point of view, I think the positions taken here are not extreme ones. During the 3 years in which this book was taking shape, most of these positions were bounced off a number of my professional colleagues, and in the process of bouncing many of them were modified and moderated. In discussing these matters with colleagues both to my left and to my right, my own positions have doubtless become more centrist. I hope the outcome is not just milquetoast. I think it is not.

Why would an ivory tower economist like me write a down-to-earth book like this? I think I know the reason. In my judgment, the makers of national economic policy made several grievous errors during the years covered by this book (1971-1976). If we are not to repeat the same mistakes—a possibility that looks all too likely as this is penned—the story of this period needs to be told and retold, and the lessons learned.

Actually, I did not set out to write a book at all. This monograph had its origins in 1976 in a paper I agreed to prepare for a Brookings Institution conference on "Stabilization Policies in Industrialized Countries, 1972–1976," held in Rome from May 30 to June 3, 1977. It was Gardner Ackley, the organizer of that conference, who persuaded me, against my better judgment, to undertake an interpretive economic history of an episode so recent that the ink was not yet dry on the data. As it turned out, a book—not a paper—was necessary to do justice to the policy errors of the 1970s. As is, I suppose, inevitable in writing history with so brief a time perspective, many of the ideas—and certainly all of the data!—have changed considerably since the original paper prepared for that conference. But I think the basic message of this volume is the same as it was in the conference paper—that U.S. policymakers, faced with a difficult situation in 1973–1975, made a bad job of it.

Acknowledgments

Just as a stone gathers moss if it fails to roll, a manuscript like this gathers intellectual debts as it matures. My biggest one is certainly to Burton Malkiel who, first as a discussant at the Rome conference and second as a colleague back at Princeton, ignored the constitutional prohibition on double jeopardy and put himself through the rigors of two complete drafts of this work. While the two of us have not agreed on all issues, his good judgment was always welcome and his influence is manifested in many places throughout the book. I thank him sincerely.

At the Rome conference, a number of useful suggestions were offered by George Perry, and by Franco Modigliani, one of our profession's best discussants at large. While the overgrown "paper" was being transformed into a book, I benefited from a host of useful comments from Jeffrey Perloff and Albert Ando. The life cycle of a research assistant being what it is, quite a few Princeton students contributed to the preparation of this work. I hope I am not leaving anyone out when I name David Card, Suzanne Heller, Robin Lindsey, Robert Marshall, and especially William Newton, and thank them all. Phyllis Durepos did her usual fine job in typing the manuscript.

Mention should be made of Otto Eckstein's book, *The Great Recession* (North-Holland, 1978), which appeared after this monograph had gone through several drafts. The two books overlap considerably, though each takes up a number of topics not dealt with by the other. Where they overlap, they seem not to contradict one another. Several references to Eckstein's book will be found in the text; but I have not attempted a detailed point-by-point comparison.

Fortunately, economic researchers normally do not do their work while starving in a garret—romantic as that may seem. Several benefactors have supported this research, including the Ford Foundation, which financed the Rome conference; the Brookings Institution, which commissioned the original paper; the Institute for Advanced Studies in Jerusalem, where I worked on this project for half a year; and the National Science Foundation, which helped finance two econometric spinoffs of this project (reported in Chapters 6 and 7).

As it happened, during the 3-year gestation period of this book I was also working on a textbook. All praise is due my wife, Madeline, for putting up with this rare conjunction of events. She says it was not easy. My two sons, Scott and William, retarded progress on this book as only little boys can—thereby imbuing the work with the wisdom that only the passage of time can impart. By coincidence, I suppose, William's birth corresponded almost exactly with that of this manuscript. If only the latter had progressed as much as the former in the ensuing years!

1 introduction

Stagflation is a term coined by our abbreviation-happy society to connote the simultaneous occurrence of economic *stag*nation and comparatively high rates of in*flation*. While the coexistence of these two maladies is in fact not quite as unique as was originally thought, there is no question that the virulence of the stagflation that afflicted us in the mid 1970s was unprecedented. This book aims to summarize what economists do and do not know about the inflation and recession that beset the U.S. economy during the years of the Great Stagflation, so that we may understand better what policymakers did, why they did it, and what effects their actions had.

1. Historical Perspective

At least by postwar historical standards, inflation was a rather new problem for American policymakers, while recession was not. Of all the years between 1948 and 1968, only 1951 would be considered "inflationary" by current standards. During the 11 years from 1953 to 1964, for example, the U.S. generally operated a low-pressure economy, and inflation (as measured by the GNP deflator) averaged only 1.9% per annum, exceeding 2% in only 4 years. Recessions and unemployment, however, are nothing new. During those same 11 years, there were recessions in 1953–1954, 1957–1958, and 1960–1961. According to the Council of Economic Advisers' (CEA) revised estimates of potential Gross National

1

Product, GNP was below potential in every year from 1954 through 1964 except 1955.[1] Similarly, unemployment averaged 5.4% during those years, and was below 5% only during 1955–1957. Even given the redefinition of the "full employment unemployment rate" to account for changes in the demographic composition of the labor force, unemployment was substantially above full employment in every year but these 3.[2]

A sea change in the nature of America's macroeconomic problems appears to have occurred around 1965 (see Figure 1-1), and has been widely attributed to the political decision to finance the Vietnam War without a tax increase. The 5 years from 1965 through 1969 saw a high-pressure economy with no recessions,[3] and an unemployment rate that averaged only 3.8%—substantially lower than the adjusted full employment target. Similarly, except for 1965 (when they were virtually identical) GNP consistently exceeded its potential. Inflation always exceeded 2% per annum during these 5 years, and averaged 3.6%—roughly double the average rate of 1954–1964.

The 1970s have been characterized by the worst of both worlds. High inflation and low levels of activity have become the norm. During the 8 years from 1969 to 1977, inflation averaged 6.4%, and was below 5% only under price controls in 1972. The gap between potential and actual GNP was positive in 7 of these 8 years, and averaged $41 billion (in 1972 dollars). The cumulative gap amounted to over 3 months' production at 1973 rates. Unemployment never fell below 4.9% (as a yearly average) during these years, and averaged 6.3%. The 9% overall unemployment rate recorded in May 1975 was the highest in the postwar period, and even after 2 years of recovery the rate remained above 7%.

2. Preview of Things to Come

This book chronicles the nature and causes of this dramatic worsening of the economic picture. But, to a much greater extent, it is about how policymakers responded to this adversity and whether their actions exacerbated or ameliorated the problems. While the study focuses on the events of 1973–1975, the story must begin in 1971, both because of the

---

[1] See *Economic Report of the President*, 1978, Table 10, p. 84. Potential and actual GNP were less than 1% apart in 1955 and 1956. It should be remarked that the measurement of potential GNP is a matter of some controversy these days.

[2] The estimates of the moving full employment target are also those of the CEA. The rate rises from 4.0% to 4.3% during this period.

[3] A very mild recession started in the last quarter of 1969.

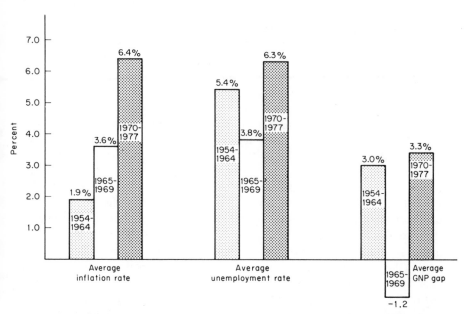

Figure 1-1. Indicators of inflation and recession. This figure shows the behavior of the inflation rate and two different indicators of recession—the unemployment rate and the GNP gap—during three different periods: 1954–1964, when both inflation and resource utilization were low; 1965–1969, when inflation was higher but resource utilization was much higher; 1970–1977, when inflation was very high but resource utilization was very low. The inflation rate is measured by the yearly average GNP deflator; the unemployment rate is measured by the yearly average overall unemployment rate; and the GNP gap by the gap between potential and actual GNP in 1972 dollars, expressed as a percentage of potential. (*Sources: Economic Report of the President,* 1978 and 1979, and *Survey of Current Business,* July 1978.)

lags in monetary and fiscal policy and because of the importance during this period of the New Economic Policy that President Richard M. Nixon inaugurated in August 1971.

Before getting into these important matters, however, the next chapter seeks to provide a conceptual framework for the entire book by presenting a fairly simple and general theory of stagflation. While this is the one chapter in the book that is ''theoretical,'' the analysis to be found there certainly is not very technical.

Chapters 3–5 contain a rather interpretive, but I hope only slightly idiosyncratic, history of the Great Stagflation. The first of these chapters provides a fairly broad overview, treating some topics in reasonable detail, but necessarily moving rapidly over several aspects of the economic history of the 1970s that merit much closer scrutiny. The next two chapters remedy some of these deficiencies by taking a closer and more detailed look at the two phenomena whose conjunction seems to merit the name "Great Stagflation." Chapter 4 profiles the economic collapse that took place from 1973 to 1975; and Chapter 5 dissects and analyzes the remarkable burst of inflation that came at roughly the same time.

The next three chapters are about the three major varieties of economic policy that played important roles in shaping the Great Stagflation. Chapter 6 discusses wage-price controls—a policy which, I argue, contributed more to the Great Stagflation than is commonly realized. With price controls now once more on the national agenda, a look at what happened in 1971–1974 and after may give us pause. Chapters 7 and 8 turn to the more traditional tools of stabilization policy—fiscal policy (Chapter 7) and monetary policy (Chapter 8). In each case, I summarize the policies that were actually followed, explain the reasons for these decisions, and appraise the good or harm these policies may have done. The overall conclusion, to anticipate things a bit, is that the policymakers did not exactly cover themselves with glory.

Finally, a concluding chapter summarizes the major arguments of the book, seeks to ferret out the lessons for contemporary policymaking, and against this backdrop briefly discusses the economic events of 1977–1979.

The Great Stagflation, like the Great Depression, may with the passage of time prove to be *sui generis*—an unhappy episode caused by a rare conjunction of events. However, there is every reason to think that stagflation, which has been with us before, will be with us again. It is said that those who fail to learn from their mistakes are condemned to repeat them—a cliché, no doubt, but one that captures very well the reason for writing (or reading!) a book such as this.

2 understanding stagflation: some basic concepts

Everything should be made as simple as possible, but not more so.
—Albert Einstein

During and since the mid 1970s it has been widely claimed by journalists, politicians, and even by many economists that the phenomenon of stagflation perplexed economists, ran counter to all of our most cherished theories, and generally made the policy advice we offered at best useless and at worst downright dangerous. If repetition implied veracity, these claims would by now be beyond dispute.

Fortunately, however, though economists were certainly perplexed by the events of the mid 1970s, the puzzlement was mainly over what to do about stagflation, not about understanding why it was occurring. Nor, as will be seen in this chapter, does the existence of stagflation require that we jettison contemporary macroeconomic theory, for that theory can indeed explain what has happened. When it comes to policy recommendations, however, more circumspection is appropriate. No economist had then, or has now, a perfect or even a halfway decent cure for stagflation. But this does not imply that the performance of policymakers could not have been improved. After all, though it may be quite difficult to extricate oneself from 4 feet of quicksand, there is still something to be gained by going in feet first rather than head first.

A major theme of this book is that government policies coped rather poorly with the Great Stagflation—that while there was no way that things were going to be very good, they could have been a great deal better than they were. A wide variety of data, models, statistical methods,

5

and documentary evidence will be used to buttress this view, but any counterfactual statement such as this ultimately relies on some theory. The principal purpose of this chapter is to make this theory explicit. The chapter seeks to explode two widespread myths about stagflation: first, that stagflation is a mystery that economic theory cannot explain; and second, that because of stagflation policymakers no longer face a trade-off between inflation and unemployment. In the process, it will become clear why there is no remedy for stagflation, at least not within the conventional litany of policy tools.

This is the first and only chapter of the book that is mainly about economic theory. Readers who have little patience for such matters can proceed directly to the brief summary on page 23 where, however, they will have to accept the conclusions as bold-faced assertions, lacking the supporting arguments that are presented in the chapter.

1. Aggregate Supply and Demand Analysis

It may be helpful to begin by reviewing the basic organizing framework that most macroeconomists use nowadays in thinking about aggregative issues like inflation, unemployment, and stagflation. Borrowing the oldest tool of economic analysis, the economy as a whole is thought of as a giant market; and its various aspects are divided into those pertaining to "aggregate demand" and those pertaining to "aggregate supply."

AGGREGATE DEMAND

During the 1950s and 1960s, and continuing even into the early 1970s, the greatest controversies among macroeconomists revolved around the specification of aggregate demand; Keynesians and monetarists argued whether aggregate demand was more usefully obtained by *adding* consumption, investment, and government purchases or by *multiplying* the money stock times velocity. There was a long debate over whether monetary policy mattered (much?) for aggregate demand, followed by an equally long debate over whether fiscal policy mattered (much?).

By now this is largely behind us, and it is widely recognized that the same sort of aggregate demand curve—a downward sloping relationship between the volume of real demand and the price level—can be derived from either a monetarist or a Keynesian approach, and can be shifted by either fiscal or monetary policy.[1] Figure 2-1 depicts such a curve. It is

[1] The two approaches, while they differ in style, are essentially equivalent except in some extreme cases, which each side now disavows.

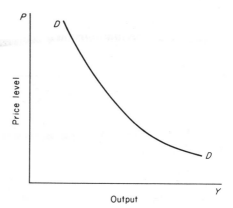

Figure 2-1. An aggregate demand curve.

worth briefly enumerating some of the reasons for its negative slope, because these reasons play a role in the analysis of stagflation that follows.

1. At higher price levels, research has shown, the demand for money is proportionately higher because the same number of transactions require more dollars to finance them. Thus, for a given supply of money, a higher price level brings forth a "tighter" situation in the money markets. Typically, this financial stringency manifests itself in higher interest rates, which have deleterious effects on business investment and, especially, on mortgage financing and residential construction.[2] In this respect, a higher price level acts much like a reduction in the money supply: it raises interest rates and, because of this, reduces aggregate demand.

2. Much consumer wealth is held in the form of assets whose values are fixed in money terms. The purchasing power of such assets declines as the price level rises. Money itself is the clearest example; but all of the many varieties of time and savings accounts share this attribute with money and are much more important quantitatively. Government and corporate bonds also decline in real value when prices rise. Finally, recent research has suggested that even common stocks, which used to be thought of as a hedge against inflation, can often behave much like nominal assets. For all these reasons the real wealth of consumers falls when prices rise, and this loss of purchasing power puts a damper on consumer spending.

3. Our personal income tax system is *progressive*, and tax liabilities are defined in *nominal* terms. In combination, these two features mean that during inflationary periods each rise in the price level leads to a

---

[2] Higher interest rates may also reduce consumption and state and local government spending, but these effects are likely to be minor.

more than proportional rise in nominal tax receipts, so the real value of taxes increases automatically *even if real incomes are not changing.* A variety of features of the tax code combine to produce this result; the most obvious of these, though probably not the most important, is that many taxpayers are pushed into higher tax brackets as nominal incomes rise. This unlegislated tax increase that inflation produces drains consumer purchasing power, and cuts into aggregate demand.

4. Domestic inflation raises the prices of the goods we sell abroad. Quite obviously, this normally will be damaging to the demand for our exports. At the same time, domestic inflation encourages Americans to import more in order to take advantage of lower foreign prices. Since *net* exports (that is, exports minus imports) are a component of U.S. aggregate demand, higher prices dampen demand on both counts.

AGGREGATE SUPPLY

As the controversies over aggregate demand subsided, monetarists and Keynesians regrouped for a new battle, and the most heated debates in macroeconomics these days are over the specification of *aggregate supply*. It would be foolhardy for me to try to present a consensus view of the aggregate supply mechanism, since no such consensus exists. Instead, I will offer one consistent—and not terribly partisan—view of aggregate supply, and hope that the eventual consensus bears a close resemblance to it.

The question here is this: How does the aggregate volume of production respond to changes in the price level? Since producers in the U.S. economy are mainly motivated by profit, it is at once clear that the answer depends largely on what is simultaneously happening to production costs. It is hardly a surprising notion that output will rise vigorously if costs are held constant while selling prices increase, but may not respond at all if every item of cost rises proportionately with prices. For this reason the analysis of aggregate supply is conducted in the market for factors of production and in particular in the market for the most important factor, labor.

In the very short run, labor and other inputs normally are available at constant costs. There are many reasons for this. Labor, like other factors, may be supplied under long-term contracts that stipulate fixed money wages. Failing this, firms and their workers may have entered into implicit agreements under which the firms are entitled to purchase whatever labor they want (within limits) at set wage rates. Or, when there is unemployment, there may be many available workers who can be hired at the going wage. Whatever the reason, the short-run stickiness of money wages, and to a lesser extent of other factor prices as well, seems a well-established fact.

One implication of this fact is that when demand increases firms can meet the higher demand profitably without raising prices because their marginal costs are relatively fixed.[3] Beyond this, there may be further reasons why prices remain fixed even if costs escalate. Just as firms have agreements, implicit or explicit, with their employees, so do they also have agreements with their customers. Catalogs and price lists may have been circulated; deals may have been struck at agreed upon prices; long-term purchase contracts may have been made. Perhaps even more important, firms simply may be reluctant to change their prices at every little vacillation of demand. Before they increase prices, they may want evidence that the increase·in demand has staying power.

I conclude that, in the very short run, prices in the industrial sector of the economy are basically determined by costs, and do not respond to demand. Within limits, any increase in demand can be met without increases in prices, as is illustrated by the horizontal supply curve SS in Figure 2-2(a).

As time passes, however, this happy situation begins to melt away. Increasing input scarcities drive prices higher. Workers must be paid overtime premiums to elicit longer hours of work. Implicit agreements setting fixed wages and prices start to become unstuck, and at least some long-term buying and selling contracts expire and are renegotiated at higher rates. In this "intermediate run," firms find their costs increasing with their production levels and consequently are willing to meet the higher levels of demand only at higher prices, However, at these higher selling prices, they are happy to produce more because some elements of fixity in their costs remain. Not all their input purchase agreements have been escalated to reflect the higher prices, so "real costs" of production (that is, marginal costs divided by the selling price) are reduced. The relationship between output supply and price in the intermediate run is precisely the one we have been accustomed to since Adam Smith: at higher prices, more is produced as illustrated in Figure 2-2(b).

But this positive relationship between output and prices is unlikely to last forever. As more and more time elapses, fewer and fewer of the firm's inputs remain supplied at fixed prices. Contracts are renegotiated; and with prices of outputs higher, prices of inputs are bound to follow suit. Indeed, there are both theoretical and empirical reasons to believe that wages ultimately rise in full proportion to the increase in prices, so

---

[3] Indeed, in the very short run, they can normally meet any such surge in demand by drawing down inventories.

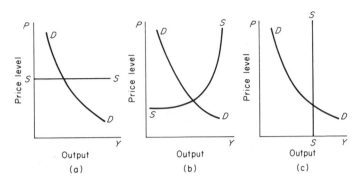

Figure 2-2. Aggregate supply and demand analysis: (a) the short run; (b) the intermediate run; (c) the long run.

that real unit labor costs are no lower than they were prior to the increase in demand. In this case, there is no reason to believe that firms will want to supply any more output than they did previously. Here we have the basic insight behind the celebrated theory of the "natural rate" of employment (or output): in the very long run, output is completely supply determined. As indicated in Figure 2-2(c), total production is independent of the level of aggregate demand, which serves only to determine the price level at which this fixed amount of output can be marketed.

Several remarks need to be made about this conclusion. The first is an expression of the modesty of economic theory. The conclusion is not that economic theory *proves* that the aggregate supply curve is *exactly* vertical in the long run. Rather we conclude that there are good reasons to believe that a vertical long-run supply curve is a good approximation.

Second, the time dimension of the analysis merits further comment and emphasis. The *long run,* as defined here, is a period sufficiently lengthy so that none of the firms' inputs are committed at previously agreed upon prices. In the case of labor, for some firms this may be a period of 3 years or more. For some other inputs, contract lengths can go even longer. The case of energy is particularly germane to this book. Since late 1973, the Organization of Petroleum Exporting Countries (OPEC) has been providing oil to the oil consuming world at a monopoly price which it has set *in terms of dollars.* This pricing method means that, at least for American firms, oil is a factor of production supplied at a price fixed in *nominal* terms. As long as OPEC sticks to this policy, we never reach the truly "long" run where all input prices adjust proportionately to the price level. Thus the supply curve retains some upward slope even in the long run.

To recapitulate briefly, in the very short run the supply curve is horizontal; thus aggregate demand determines output and (relatively fixed) production costs determine prices. Over a somewhat longer run, production costs and selling prices lose some of these elements of fixity. The supply curve is upward sloping so that higher demand calls forth both greater production and higher prices. Over the very long run, when all elements of fixity have evaporated, all factor prices move more or less in proportion to output prices. Consequently, the aggregate supply curve is vertical and production is independent of demand; supply determines output and demand determines price.

RESOURCE UTILIZATION AND AGGREGATE SUPPLY IN THE INTERMEDIATE RUN

I take it for granted in this book that our greatest concern, both for policymaking and analysis, is with the intermediate run—a period of time that may stretch anywhere from 2 to 4 quarters to 3 or more years. Over this "run" the shape of the aggregate supply curve is of primary interest because, as Figure 2-2(b) indicates, this shape governs how any increase in aggregate demand gets apportioned between an increase in real output and an increase in the price level.

One factor relevant to this division has already been discussed: the amount of time involved. Over very short periods of time, the supply curve looks little different from the horizontal curve in Figure 2-2(a); so demand stimulation leads mainly to higher output and lower unemployment. Over very long periods of time, the supply curve resembles Figure 2-2(c); so the effect of greater aggregate demand is mainly to raise prices.

During the lengthy and amorphous "intermediate run," however, the degree of resource utilization is a principal determinant of the shape of the aggregate supply curve. Around the trough of a business cycle, with labor markets slack, product demand weak, and capacity utilization low, firms are likely to respond to an upsurge in demand by bringing their unused capital and labor resources back into production. They will find it neither necessary nor advisable to raise prices; the supply curve is relatively flat. Conversely, during a boom period in which both labor and product markets are tight, firms will find it difficult or impossible to increase output without increasing costs. Price increases will thus be indicated from the cost side, and will not be resisted very forcefully by consumers on the demand side. The supply curve will be relatively steep.

2. Explanations for Stagflation

The basic organizing framework of aggregate demand–aggregate supply analysis, then, is this. Macroeconomic equilibrium is determined by the intersection of a downward sloping aggregate demand curve and an aggregate supply curve that is rather horizontal in the short run, probably upward sloping over "intermediate" runs, and may or may not be vertical in the long run (see Figure 2-2). This equilibrium determines both national income and the price level. Both the rate of inflation and the rate of real economic growth are fundamentally determined by the relative growth rates of aggregate supply and demand. If aggregate demand races ahead of aggregate supply, inflation will result. On the contrary, the economy can expand without inflation if aggregate supply grows in balance with aggregate demand. Finally, any retardation in the growth of aggregate supply will tend to produce both an acceleration of inflation and a slow-down in real economic growth.

Within this broad framework there are two basic explanations for stagflation, though each comes in many variants. The first explanation is based on *overshooting* caused by the sluggish adjustment of wages and prices to changes in aggregate demand, and has been around long enough to command something close to universal assent. Unfortunately, while it explains well some earlier and milder bouts with stagflation, it does not seem to account very well for the Great Stagflation of the 1970s. The other explanation—based on *shifts in aggregate supply*—is newer and less widely accepted, but far more descriptive of what happened in this country in 1972-1976.

DEMAND INFLATION AND STAGFLATION

Let us first consider how a surge in aggregate demand can bring a period of stagflation in its wake. As a simple example, consider a hypothetical economy in which aggregate demand and supply are expanding in balance, so that there is no inflation. Now let there be a one-time increase in aggregate demand, after which demand resumes its normal growth rate. Such an increase could be caused, for example, by an increase in the money supply, a tax cut, or a change in private spending habits. How will prices and output react to this shock?

As I have already suggested, prices are basically fixed in the very short run, and hence will show no immediate reaction. The increase in demand manifests itself entirely in greater real output. After a while, however, the increase in demand leads to depleted inventories and higher production costs; at this point prices begin to rise while the expansion of real output continues. As more time passes, however, more and more factor prices are adjusted upward and inflationary pressures intensify. The resulting higher prices for goods and services depress demand for reasons discussed earlier. Thus output begins to fall back toward its "natural" level while prices continue to rise. Finally, since we have assumed the

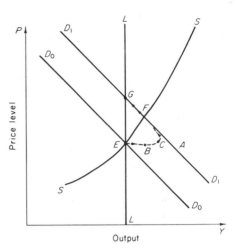

Figure 2-3. The "overshooting" explanation of stagflation.

demand stimulus was a one-shot event, output returns to its natural rate and inflation returns to zero.[4]

There are thus three characteristic phases of an inflation fueled by excessive aggregate demand, and Figure 2-3 is a convenient way of depicting them. (In the figure, the increase in aggregate demand is represented by the shift from demand curve $D_0 D_0$ to demand curve $D_1 D_1$; curves SS and LL are, respectively, the intermediate-run and long-run supply curves. The short-run supply curve would just be a horizontal line through point E, and is omitted to avoid cluttering the diagram.)

Beginning from an initial equilibrium at point E, where demand curve $D_0 D_0$ intersects both SS and LL, the economy expands without inflation to point B. This is the first phase of growth without inflation.

Next, however, costs and prices begin to rise as the aggregate supply curve begins to acquire some slope. In the second phase, depicted by the path from point B to point C, both output and prices are rising.

The third phase is the stagflationary phase. Over a longer period of time, the aggregate supply curve becomes quite steep and perhaps even vertical. As costs catch up to prices, the incentive to produce beyond the natural rate diminishes. Consequently, output falls while prices continue to rise—as indicated by the path CFG in Figure 2-3.[5]

The basic reason for stagflation in this model is common to most

---

[4] In the case of a *continuing* stimulus to aggregate demand, the rate of inflation would not return to zero.

[5] The portion of the path from C to F illustrates that the existence of stagflation does not in any way rely on the validity of the natural rate theory. Even if SS were the long-run supply curve, stagflation would still occur.

theoretical approaches to macroeconomics: because wages and prices move sluggishly, real output must overshoot its eventual position.[6] As output and prices adjust to equilibrium, stagflation occurs.

There is relatively little theoretical controversy over this mechanism for stagflation, and its basic outlines have received strong empirical support. The scenario seems roughly descriptive, for example, of the U.S. economy in 1965–1970 when an inflationary recession (1969–1970) followed on the heels of an explosion in aggregate demand (1965–1968). Unfortunately, it is doubtful that this analysis helps us very much in understanding what happend to our economy in the mid 1970s. First, unlike the stagflationary period of 1969–1970, the Great Stagflation did not follow as the aftermath of a non-inflationary boom.[7] Second, the Great Stagflation was much longer and deeper than can be accounted for by "overshooting." Third, it is very doubtful that the natural rate of output was unaffected by what happened in the 1970s.

In sum, we seem to need an alternative model of stagflation.

SUPPLY INFLATION AND STAGFLATION

Let us, therefore, consider the other possibility: that inflation is initiated by an adverse shift in the aggregate supply curve. Such a supply shock could be caused by any of a variety of unpleasant events: a natural disaster (e.g., flood, drought, earthquake) could lead to a scarcity of agricultural products or of some other commodity; labor might suddenly become more aggressive and demand higher wages; a monopoly in control of some natural resource (such as OPECs control of crude oil) could raise its price.

A food shortage caused by bad weather is the simplest case to deal with since, we may assume, it has no permanent effect on the long-run supply curve.[8] It is also quite germane to the events of the 1970s.

As is well known, the markets for foodstuffs and feedstuffs are characterized by rather inelastic supply and demand. As a consequence, reductions in supply kick off large price increases. These higher prices for raw agricultural products represent cost increases to the industrial sector. This is obvious in the case of industries that process, distribute, and merchandise food; but is also true of industries that use agricultural

---

[6] If wages and prices jumped immediately to their new equilibrium values, the economy would jump abruptly from point E to point G. There would be no temporary surge in output, and no stagflationary phase.

[7] The economy did, however, produce beyond potential GNP in 1973—way beyond according to Perloff and Wachter (1979).

[8] This assumes that crop failures are temporary things, not permanent reductions in world agricultural productivity.

products (e.g., fibers) as inputs into industrial processes. Such cost increases are promptly incorporated into product prices since, as I have argued earlier, prices are largely cost determined in the short run. Over the intermediate run, now that costs are higher firms will be willing to continue to supply their old levels of output only at higher prices: the aggregate supply curve shifts to the left.

Figure 2-4 depicts this chain of events. (The vertical long-run supply curve is omitted from the diagram since it is assumed to recover to its original position before the long run is reached. The horizontal short-run supply curves are again omitted for clarity.) The short-run movement of the economy in this case is mostly vertical: prices rise quickly before output has had a chance to fall. Thereafter the higher prices take their toll on aggregate demand, and the economy moves toward point B (the intersection of the new supply curve $S_1 S_1$ and the unchanged demand curve DD) with prices rising and output falling; that is, there is stagflation.

The stagflation in this case is one that we have every reason to believe should be temporary: poor harvests in one year should be followed by normal or good harvests in succeeding years. Let me then turn to a more lasting supply shock: the case of OPEC in 1973–1974.

The same diagram can be used for this purpose, though its interpretation is different. With the OPEC cartel fixing the price of oil in dollars, the long-run supply curve will retain some slope since the *real* cost of oil declines as the price level rises. The supply curve will, of course, be steeper in the long run than in the intermediate run; but to keep the diagram simple let me work with just one set of curves ($S_0 S_0$ and $S_1 S_1$ in

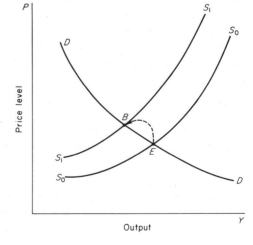

Figure 2-4. The "supply shock" explanation of stagflation.

Figure 2-4). The higher cost of oil raises production costs and thus prices (that is, it shifts the supply curve upward). Since aggregate demand is lower at higher prices, the equilibrium level of output subsequently falls (the movement from E to B in Figure 2-4); and, importantly, stagflation occurs throughout the adjustment period. Moreover, there is no reason to expect the stagflationary shock to be reversed. This would happen only if the OPEC cartel broke up or rescinded its price hike.[9] In the absence of these events, the higher prices and lower output are with us forever.[10]

There are several important respects in which the supply shock explanation for stagflation differs from the overshooting explanation. First, there is no particular reason to think the drop in output must be only temporary. In some cases (e.g., a crop failure) the adverse shift in supply is temporary, but in others (e.g., OPEC) it may be permanent. True enough, a large change in the price of, say, energy relative to labor and capital will, in the very long run, induce factor substitution as entrepreneurs seek new cost-minimizing input combinations. Such reactions will cushion the blow somewhat. But it is not likely that the possibilities for factor substitution are so bountiful that the reduction in supply can be escaped completely, even in the very long run.

Second, the sequence of adjustment is likely to be the reverse of what it is in the demand inflation case. Under a supply shift, as just noted, prices are likely to rise quite promptly (leaving wages lagging) as firms follow a markup pricing policy.[11] The attempt of labor to make up for these losses ensures that the initial burst of inflation is followed by a long wage–price spiral because: (a) workers, feeling cheated by the burst of unanticipated inflation, seek compensation in their next contract round; or (b) the increase in the inflation rate raises the expected rate of inflation, and this in turn raises nominal wage demands. With rising prices, the aggregate quantity demanded must be falling. So output subsequently declines. But, as compared with the overshooting explanation, the roles of the chicken and the egg have clearly been reversed: it is the rising prices that cause the drop in output.

---

[9] If OPEC set its price in real terms, that is, indexed the price of oil to the U.S. price level, the long-run supply curve would be vertical and would be shifted to the left by an increase in the (real) monopoly price. The analysis is much the same, with the supply shock now reducing the natural rate of output.

[10] What happens to employment in the long run depends mainly on what the scarcity of oil does to the marginal product of labor. If the marginal product is reduced, as seems likely, employment falls. However, it is doubtful that this effect is very large.

[11] An obvious exception to this will be if the supply shock consists of an autonomous upward push on wages. In this case, wages will lead the wage–price spiral and prices will lag.

Third, and very briefly, there are no particular reasons to suspect episodes of supply-induced stagflation to happen only when unemployment is low, or to follow a noninflationary boom, or to be of short duration.

In all of these respects, the supply shift explanation of stagflation fits the facts of the mid 1970s better than the overshooting explanation. So it is no surprise that in recent years this alternative explanation of stagflation based on supply side shocks has become increasingly popular. Admittedly, it smacks a little bit of being an *ex post facto* rationalization of what in fact happened. However, economists need not be too apologetic about this. (We should, I suppose, be a *little* apologetic.) The aggregate demand–aggregate supply framework was, after all, widely accepted for many years before OPEC. The simple fact was that macroeconomic fluctuations in earlier years were dominated by movements in aggregate demand along an aggregate supply curve that shifted more or less passively to the right year after year. So until the mid 1970s, the idea of an economy buffeted by exogenous shocks to the supply curve seemed a theoretical possibility with virtually no empirical counterpart. It is little wonder, then, that economists were lulled into thinking that macroeconomic fluctuations *were* fluctuations in aggregate demand.

The world crop failures of 1972–1974 and the solidification of OPEC in 1973–1974 disabused us of these notions. Fluctuations in economic activity, we now know, not only *can* be initiated from the supply side, but sometimes actually *are* so initiated. Given the sledgehammer manner in which the world learned this lesson, it is not likely that it will soon be forgotten.

INCOME REDISTRIBUTION AND AGGREGATE DEMAND

There is one other important aspect of the supply shocks of the 1970s that can hardly escape our attention. The huge realignment of relative prices necessitated by both the OPEC cartel and the poor harvests led to a massive redistribution of real income away from urban workers and toward farmers and oil producers. In the case of food prices, it has been well known for many years that farmers have unusually high propensities to save, so the redistribution surely reduced consumer demand.

In the case of oil producers, there were two principal classes of beneficiaries. First, there were the governments of the OPEC countries. One obvious point is that any redistribution of income from Americans to foreigners will lead to a reduction in U.S. aggregate demand because foreigners have a lower marginal propensity to spend on U.S. goods than do Americans. But beyond this it is well documented that the OPEC nations, at least in the short run, spent rather little of their largesse. Thus, this income redistribution caused a drop in consumption that was only slightly offset by a minor increase in exports.

Second, there were the domestic oil companies or, more accurately, the stockholders of these companies. An obvious side effect of OPEC's quadrupling of the price of crude oil was to hand a windfall gain to these oil companies. Part of their swollen profits were, perhaps, paid out in dividends to stockholders. Another part probably was plowed back as investments in the companies. But a substantial part, and probably most of it in the short run, was simply retained by the companies as corporate saving. Thus this redistribution caused a drop in consumption that was offset very little by an increase in investment. However, of all the redistributions considered here, this one was no doubt the smallest because price controls on domestically produced oil limited profits.

When we tote up the score, it is clear that the supply shocks of the 1970s had very important effects on aggregate demand—reducing demand in every case. In terms of the aggregate supply and demand analysis, the leftward shift of the supply curve was accompanied by a leftward shift of the demand curve (because of the redistribution from spenders to savers). This latter effect compounded the severity of the recession, but had little mitigating effect on the inflation at first because prices are insensitive to demand in the short run. As we look toward the longer run, however, it is likely that the drop in demand helped hold down price increases somewhat.

Finally, it should be pointed out that the demand-reducing effects of the supply shocks are probably not permanent. The farmers who do the high saving are probably accumulating the means to finance subsequent investments in their farms, not to add to their estates. Oil companies will not sit on top of a pile of cash for long. They will either pay it out in dividends (to stockholders who will then spend it), spend it on additional investment goods, or use it to finance internally some investment projects that would otherwise have been financed externally.[12] Like the oil companies, the OPEC nations too cannot be expected to allow the massive buildup of liquid assets to continue indefinitely. Gradually, these countries can be expected to find more and more ways to spend their oil earnings, thus returning demand in the form of exports to the countries that lost demand in the form of consumption. Indeed, there have been reports that some OPEC nations (e.g., Iran) embarked on such ambitious development programs that their spending plans exceeded their projected oil revenues.

---

[12] In the last case, reduced corporate borrowing puts downward pressure on interest rates, with a consequent stimulus to the interest sensitive components of aggregate demand.

The conclusion is that the demand-reducing effects of the relative price shocks of the 1970s should not be expected to last forever, and indeed may by now (mid 1979) be mostly dissipated in the United States. For the long run, we have only the permanent shift of the supply curve to contend with.

3. The Trade-off between Inflation and Unemployment

One apparently innocent victim of the Great Stagflation has been the celebrated trade-off between inflation and unemployment. Since about 1974, the death of this trade-off has been announced, with suitable fanfare, in virtually every newspaper and magazine that cares enough about economic affairs to comment on such events. The obituaries, however, were quite premature.

To understand why the trade-off is alive and well and living in Paris, Washington, and other capitals, it is necessary to distinguish between the Phillips curve and the trade-off itself. The Phillips curve is an empirical regularity, an observed relationship between unemployment and inflation (actually, the rate of change of nominal wages; but never mind that). Specifically, the conventional Phillips curve states that, when certain "other things" are held constant, there is a *negative* correlation between unemployment and inflation.[13] It is a factual statement about empirical data that can be confirmed or denied by direct appeal to experience. In fact, it held up rather well from about 1860 to about 1970, but has fared rather poorly since.

Even if the Phillips curve is already dead and buried (a point I am by no means sure of—see below), this in no way inters the trade-off between inflation and unemployment that has long plagued policymakers. Two facts will explain why. The first is that the Phillips relation works well only so long as macroeconomic fluctuations come predominantly from the *demand* side, for only in that case are inflation and output growth positively correlated, The second is that policymakers' ability to manipulate the macroeconomy is almost exclusively limited to demand management. Thus, even if the sweep of world events includes many supply side fluctuations (so that no "Phillips curve" is observed), policymakers still face this fundamental trade-off: expansionary stabilization policy measures that *temporarily* reduce the rate of unemployment are likely to lead to *temporary* accelerations of inflation. Conversely, contractionary

[13] The vertical Phillips curve notes that one of these "other things" is the expected rate of inflation, and that when this is set equal to the actual rate, rather than being held constant, the Phillips curve becomes vertical.

measures that *temporarily* increase unemployment are likely to lead to *temporary* decelerations of inflation.

Notice the frequent use of the word "temporary." This adjective is required if the theory of the natural rate of unemployment is valid, so that *in the long run* unemployment always converges to its natural rate regardless of the stabilization policy that is followed. While the natural rate theory is by now widely accepted, it in no way vitiates the usefulness of stabilization policy because the "long run" that it envisions may be very far in the future so that these "temporary" gains or losses are quite long lived. All that is needed for there to exist a short-run trade-off between inflation and unemployment for policymakers to contend with is that there be a positively sloped aggregate supply curve *in the intermediate run.*[14]

Furthermore, the fixity of a nominal resource price, such as the price of oil, provides a rationale for a positively sloped long-run supply curve. In such a world, changes in demand lead to *permanent* changes in real output. The trade-off lives, then, so far as policymakers are concerned, certainly in the short run, and perhaps also in the long run.

Things are less clear with respect to the life expectancy of the Phillips curve. If, in the future, demand shocks return to their dominant position as determinants of economic fluctuations, then the data will once again display a predominantly negative relationship between inflation and unemployment (a positive relationship between changes in inflation and changes in economic growth). On the other hand, if supply shocks prove more important, the typical correlation between inflation and unemployment will be positive—an upward sloping Phillips curve. A mixture of these may, of course, continue to produce data on inflation and unemployment that have essentially no correlation—inviting the disparate interpretations that either the Philips curve is vertical (so that accelerations of inflation do not produce real effects on employment) or that it is horizontal (so that changes in unemployment do not affect the rate of inflation).

The important point to stress once again is that, regardless of what type of statistical Phillips curve the data for the years 1980–2000 actually produce, the policymakers' trade-off between inflation and unemployment will persist until someone finds a reliable way to manipulate aggre-

---

[14] There are dissenters from this widely accepted proposition. The rational expectations school believes that the supply curve is essentially vertical, even in the very short run, at least where anticipated policy actions are concerned. At the other extreme, another group of economists believes that the supply curve is horizontal, that is, that aggregate demand has only a negligible effect on prices. Recent events seem more favorable to the latter group than to the former. It should be clear that I have tried to steer a middle course in this chapter—no doubt a foolish strategy that will invite scorn from both sides.

gate supply. The limited capability of policy to influence supply poses a particularly vexing problem in a stagflationary world since any stabilization policy adopted in response to stagflation is bound to aggravate one of the problems even as it helps cure the other. Such is the policy dilemma of stagflation.

4. An Eclectic Word on Monistic Monetarism

Just as *mono*theists believe there is only one God, *mone*tarists believe there is only one cause of inflation: increases in the supply of money. Milton Friedman's categorical statement that "inflation is always and everywhere a monetary phenomenon" is well known and widely cited. Yet I have just outlined a model where inflation is caused by adverse developments on the supply side of the economy *with no change in the money stock*—a model that many monetarists would call, with evident disdain, a "special factors" theory of inflation. Can these two views be reconciled? I believe they can be, once we understand the qualifications that must be made to Friedman's dictum.

In the first place, it is necessary to distinguish between *steady continual inflation* and *one-time bursts of inflation.* It is the former that Friedman has claimed can only be caused by steady printing of money, and rightly so. Data covering centuries of history and spanning much of the globe display an impressive correlation between growth of the money supply and the rate of inflation *in the long run.*

The aggregate supply and demand analysis helps us understand why this is so. From simple manipulation of the supply and demand graphs, it is apparent that *steady* inflation can occur only if aggregate demand is shifting outward more rapidly than aggregate supply, year after year. In most times and places, the long-run growth of aggregate supply is quite smooth. The natural rate of output (if there is one) grows more or less steadily because its main constituents—the size of the labor force and productivity (output per worker)—grow at roughly constant exponential rates. This leaves differences in inflation among countries and epochs to be explained mainly by differences in the behavior of aggregate demand; and the growth rate of the money supply is the major factor accounting for these differences. One need not accept the extreme (and by now outmoded) monetarist proposition that money is *the* determinant of aggregate demand to concede this point, as most Keynesians now do. The principle, however, is not that only money has the mystical power to propel aggregate demand steadily upward faster than aggregate supply. It is just that, in practice, it is the only variable that actually does this steadily over long periods of time. For example, if government purchases rose faster than potential GNP year after year at a more or less steady rate, then inflation would become a "fiscal phenomenon." Steady velocity growth would replace steady money growth. The plain truth, however, is that excessive government spending (*without* money creation) has never been the source of a sustained inflation, and probably never will be.

So we may accept the notion that *steady inflation* is always a monetary phenomenon as a correct empirical proposition, though not deduced in any neat way from economic theory.[15] One-shot inflation, however, is a bird of a different feather. Anything that makes *either* the aggregate demand curve *or* the aggregate supply curve veer from its normal course can cause a temporary upward or downward "blip" in the inflation rate. And such things often occur.

For example, in 1966–1968 the U.S. government decided to finance sizable wartime defense expenditures without raising taxes, despite the fact that we were producing close to capacity. The resulting fiscal stimulus to aggregate demand was tremendous and, despite monetary restrictions strong enough to bring on a "credit crunch" in 1966, inflation was on its way. Monetarists may point out (correctly) that this kind of government spending can cause *steady* inflation only if defense purchases keep growing faster than potential GNP year after year, which was not the case after 1968. But a one-time step increase in federal spending does cause a one-time step increase in the economy's *equilibrium price level,* as can be seen by shifting an aggregate demand curve outward along a fixed aggregate supply curve. And because of the lags in price and wage setting, such a step increase in the equilibrium price level leads to a period of *inflation* (i.e., of rising prices) as the economy moves toward its new equilibrium. An inflation of this type is, of course, self-liquidating unless the "special factor" that initiated it is repeated. But the proverbial man in the street can be forgiven for failing to distinguish between this sort of one-shot inflation and the steady inflation that is "always and everywhere a monetary phenomenon." To him it is all the same: prices are rising, plain and simple.

The supply shift explanation of inflation that I have outlined already, and that I will be documenting in subsequent chapters, is precisely of the "special factor" variety. Quadruplings of the price of oil do not happen every year, nor even every few years. Nor are crop failures perpetual repeating events. But any event like these, by shifting the aggregate supply curve abruptly inward, can jack up the economy's equilibrium

---

[15] One proviso should perhaps be added. If the rate of productivity growth diminishes, and the rate of growth of aggregate demand is not reduced accordingly, steady inflation can result. Monetarists, however, may still want to call this a "monetary phenomenon" because the growth rate of money is now inappropriately high.

price level. And an inflationary spiral is the economy's way to adjust to such a shock. Further, because of the lags we have spoken of already, the adjustment period can be quite protracted. One-shot changes in the equilibrium price level may lead to years of inflation.

5. Summary

The analysis of this chapter leads to several conclusions that are important for the subsequent discussion of the Great Stagflation.

First, aggregate demand declines as the price level rises for a number of reasons. One consequence of this fact is that a supply shock that forces prices upward will have a contractionary influence on aggregate demand. And the particular sort of supply shocks that we suffered through in the 1970s had important redistributive effects (shifting purchasing power from spenders to savers) that siphoned off demand still more.

Second, the aggregate supply mechanism that translates changes in demand into changes in prices and in output operates very differently in the short, intermediate, and long runs. In the very short run, prices are relatively fixed; so a demand stimulus calls forth mainly greater sales and production. In the intermediate run, there is a mixture of higher output and higher prices. And in the long run, the principal effect of an increase in demand is to raise the price level.

Third, contemporary economic theory has two basic explanations for stagflation—one based on the normal aftermath of a surge in aggregate demand, and the other based on a restriction of aggregate supply caused, for example, by the scarcity of some resource. Of the two explanations, there is little doubt that the latter is far more descriptive of what happened in the 1970s.

Fourth, the fact that both inflation and unemployment were higher in the mid 1970s than they were in the early 1970s in no way repeals the trade-off between inflation and unemployment. While there were many voices arguing during the Great Stagflation that we could reduce unemployment without exacerbating inflation, or that we could stop the inflation without raising unemployment, the weight of the evidence suggests that both groups were whistling in the dark.

Fifth, and finally, the monetarist dictum that only printing money can cause inflation is correct only if we are prepared to look at rather long periods of time—decades, say. Over shorter periods, all sorts of things like government spending, food shortages, oil cartels, and so on can—and do—cause inflation.

3 the turbulent economic history of 1971-1976

If anything can go wrong, it will.
—Murphy's Law

The 1970s have been an incredible decade for the U.S. economy—years in which Murphy's Law replaced Okun's Law as the most reliable empirical regularity in macroeconomics.[1]

The saga of the seventies began, not with a whimper but with a bang, when President Nixon announced his "New Economic Policy" in August 1971, borrowing the name, one assumes unknowingly, from Lenin. The cornerstones of the New Economic Policy were two stunning departures from previous U.S. economic policy: mandatory wage-price controls in peacetime, and the suspension of the free convertibility of the dollar into gold, which unilaterally abolished the Bretton Woods system. The aftershocks of both of these events were felt for much of the decade, and play a significant role in explaining the Great Stagflation.

1972 was both an election year and a boom year for the economy—a conjunction of events that many claim was no coincidence. That same year also saw the beginning of a series of bad harvests all over the world, which sent food costs spiraling upward. In 1973 it was almost all bad news. The natural scarcity of food continued, and OPEC added a contrived scarcity of oil late in the year, especially during and after the Arab–Israeli war in October. The worst recession of the postwar period also began about then, although this was not nearly so apparent with foresight as it is with hindsight.

[1] Okun's Law is the rule of thumb that associates each 1 percentage point rise in the unemployment rate with a 3 percentage point rise in the GNP gap.

25

The epicenter of the Great Stagflation was 1974, with inflation sky-rocketing into the "double digit" range for a sustained period and the recession gathering momentum. Coincidentally, this was also the year that the American polity endured a traumatic change of presidents. The second half of the 1970s can be aptly characterized as the period in which the U.S., and indeed the entire world, sought to recover from these body blows—a recovery that is still in progress as this is written.

1. The New Economic Policy: Wage–Price Controls

The economic scenario of the late 1960s followed a classic textbook pattern: an economy that had become overheated by an excessive dose of aggregate demand (stemming from the Vietnam War) was reined in by restrictive monetary and fiscal policies. A made-in-Washington recession, one that most economists conceded to be necessary, began in the closing months of 1969 and lasted throughout 1970. Its aim was to reduce the rate of inflation, which was progressing at rates that were considered intolerably high at the time (5 to 6%).

As is so typically the case, however, the dampening of aggregate demand had its earliest and most pronounced effects on real economic activity, not on inflation. While inflation inched downward ever so slowly (from 6.1% during 1969 to 5.5% during 1970, according to the Consumer Price Index), unemployment marched noticeably and ominously upward. The overall unemployment rate, which had fallen as low as 3.3% in February 1969 and was still only 3.9% in January 1970, climbed to 6% by January 1971. The public was clearly growing impatient with the progress of the "old time religion," and this naturally meant that both Congress and a politically astute President were also growing impatient. Ironically, however, only a bit more patience might have done the trick. From January to July 1971, the annual inflation rate was only 4.4%.

As the President sought a new "game plan" (to use his own phrase) during the summer of 1971, his problem was to find a way to increase output and employment without worsening inflation. Aggregate demand policy, at least by itself, would clearly not accomplish this. So the obvious solution was to stimulate the economy while at the same time putting a lid on inflation through the use of mandatory controls over prices and wages—using the authority Congress had given him, perhaps on a dare, a year earlier. This bold stroke was taken on August 15, 1971.

The controls program began with a 90-day freeze on almost all wages and prices in the economy—a hiatus that gave the administration some time to work out the details of the nation's first experiment with peace-time price controls. The controls evolved through four further "phases" (including a second freeze in the summer of 1973), and were gradually dismantled in late 1973 and early 1974.

I argue in Chapter 6 that price controls *reduced* the rate of inflation slightly for most of the period during which they were in effect. But then the end of controls *raised* the rate of inflation in 1974 as prices held down by controls snapped back to equilibrium levels. Furthermore, since this extra "catch up" inflation was a one-shot phenomenon, not a reason for continued steady inflation, the controls program also helps explain why inflation fell so rapidly in 1975. All of this is made more precise, and backed up with econometric evidence, in Chapter 6.

If this analysis of the effect of controls on the price level is approximately correct, then there is a related effect on real output that must be accounted for. It will be recalled from Chapter 2 that prices are mostly cost determined in the very short run, and that the (almost exogenous) price level is, in turn, a determinant of real aggregate demand and output.

Specifically, autonomous upward (downward) pushes on the price level depress (stimulate) aggregate demand for several reasons that were enumerated in Chapter 2 and will be reviewed later in this chapter (see pages 37–39). Consequently, since they held prices down, the controls program probably added to aggregate demand during the 1972–1973 boom. Then, by pushing prices up faster than they would otherwise have grown, the end of controls probably siphoned off aggregate demand as things began to deteriorate seriously in 1974. In this sense, the controls program turned out to be a *procyclical* demand–management policy.

2. The New Economic Policy: Devaluing the Dollar

The Bretton Woods system of fixed exchange rates based on the free convertibility of the U.S. dollar into gold, which had been showing signs of strain for many years, came apart entirely on August 15, 1971. President Nixon's announcement that the U.S. would no longer sell gold at $35 per ounce effectively set the dollar afloat. By December 1971, the dollar had fallen about 6% relative to a multilateral trade weighted average of currencies, as the world groped for a new international monetary system.[2]

In an attempt to restore the old system of fixed exchange rates, representatives of the major trading nations of the world met at the Smithsonian Institution in Washington in December 1971, and agreed upon a new set of currency parities. Despite the hyperbole with which they were announced by President Nixon and other leaders, the Smithsonian agree-

---

[2] The exchange rate series used here and in the following paragraph is reported in *Economic Report of the President*, 1979, Table B-96, p. 293.

ments were destined soon to take their place among the Smithsonian's other dinosaurs. While exchange rates were stabilized for about a year, the agreements became unglued in the early months of 1973. Massive capital flows from the United States to Europe and Japan forced what came to be called the "second devaluation" of the dollar. From December 1972 to March 1973, the dollar fell about 9% relative to a trade weighted average, and from March to June 1973 it lost about another 3.5%, for a cumulative devaluation since June 1971 of 19%.[3]

This devaluation of the dollar affected prices and output in the U.S. through a number of channels that have by now become quite standard. An obvious arithmetical effect, if we measure inflation by the increase in consumer prices, is that imported consumer goods became more expensive in terms of U.S. dollars.[4] The inflationary impact of this event can be measured quite simply as the product of the percentage devaluation of the dollar times the fraction of consumer goods that are imported. The volume of imported U.S. consumer goods can be estimated from trade statistics showing the composition of imports. Using 1972 data, I have estimated this fraction to be only 4.4%.[5] In a world of floating rates there is no unique way to measure the percentage devaluation of the dollar. Using the abovementioned 19% to measure the devaluation between mid 1971 and mid 1973, I conclude that devaluation raised the consumption (PCE) deflator by only .8%, which means that it added only about .4% to the annual rate of inflation over this period.

But this calculation gives merely the *direct arithmetical effect,* before any prices (other than the exchange rate) or quantities have had a chance to adjust. To appraise these further reverberations, a complete model of the balance of payments and the macroeconomy is necessary. In a model constructed by Peter Kenen *et al.* (1978), the exchange rate affects the U.S. domestic price structure through the following channels (apart from its effects on aggregate demand via changing the balance of trade). A rise in the price of foreign exchange (i.e., a devaluation) increases the dollar price of internationally traded spot commodities. This increase in raw materials prices pushes up wholesale prices in the U.S., which in turn

---

[3] The value of the dollar rose in the fourth quarter of 1973, so that the net devaluation from June 1971 to December 1973 turned out to be only about 15%.

[4] As GNP is domestic value added, the GNP deflator is not affected directly. But it is affected as import-competing goods rise in price.

[5] The following items (data from *Survey of Current Business*, June 1977) were classified as consumer goods for purposes of this calculation: foods, feeds, and beverages; passenger cars; other consumer merchandise; travel; passenger fares; private payments for other services. Together, these amounted to $32 billion in 1972, whereas total consumer expenditures were $733 billion.

feed into various deflators for components of GNP. At least in principle, this empirical model adds to the *direct* effects of the devaluation on import prices the *indirect* effects through price increases of import-competing goods and other tradables. It also allows any initial shock to the price level to be magnified through a standard wage–price spiral.

Based on this model, devaluation of the dollar from 1971:1 to 1973:2 (which was 16.6% in the index Kenen uses) raised the PCE deflator for 1973:2 by 2.4%. This is about triple the direct effect, and amounts to about 25% of the total inflation during that period.[6] Most of this occurred in the year between 1972:2 and 1973:2, meaning that devaluation added over 2 percentage points to that year's inflation rate—more than enough to account for the acceleration in inflation over the previous year.

Even this number has to be raised somewhat to make allowance for the fact that the consequent improvement in the trade balance adds to aggregate demand. Peter B. Clark (1974) has estimated that the 1971–1973 devaluations raised real net exports in 1973:2 by some $3.3 billion in 1963 dollars. A rough translation to 1972 dollars makes this about $4.3 billion. As this is only about one-third of one percent of real GNP, the inflationary effects through aggregate demand are probably small enough to be ignored. However, it should be noted that neither the wage–price adjustment nor the trade balance adjustment was complete by 1973:2. Current wage–price models suggest very protracted periods of adjustment following exogenous shocks to the price level, so that the inflation rate is affected for years to come.[7] And the so-called "J-curve" phenomenon in world trade—the notion that the balance of trade first deteriorates and then improves following a devaluation—implies that very little of the ultimate effect of the devaluation on aggregate demand would have been felt by 1973:2. In sum, a 3–4% final effect on the domestic price level seems a prudent estimate.

3. Monetary and Fiscal Actions:
A Destabilization Policy for 1972–1973

One of the alleged dangers of wage–price controls is that policymakers, thinking that controls have "taken care of inflation," will be induced to pursue overly stimulative aggregate-demand policies.[8] This hypothesis

---

[6] Kwack's (1974) estimate that each 1% devaluation raises the Consumer Price Index by 2% would imply an even larger effect: 3.3%.

[7] More details on this, and an explicit example, are provided in Chapter 5. See especially Table 5-1.

[8] See, for example, Kosters (1975, pp. 102–103).

predicts an aggressive fiscal and monetary policy in the U.S. in 1971–1972, perhaps even carrying over into 1973.

Another major influence over fiscal (perhaps also monetary) policy decisions in 1971–1972 was the proximity of the November 1972 presidential election. A substantial body of recent research by both political scientists and economists suggests that many democratic countries have a built-in political business cycle, wherein politicians cause the nation's economy to dance to the tune of its electoral cycle.[9]

The existence of a potential political business cycle is due to two apparent facts, one economic and the other political. The relevant economic fact has already been mentioned in Chapter 2: when aggregate demand is stimulated (say, by fiscal policy) output and employment react much more promptly than do prices and wages. The relevant political fact concerns voting patterns, and was first documented by Kramer (1971) and has since been verified by Fair (1978) and others: when they go to the polls, voters have short memories. They apparently care most about the growth rate of real disposable income during the 1 year before the election. In conjunction, these two facts give election minded politicians the following temptation. By stimulating aggregate demand approximately 18 months to 1 year before an election, they are likely to face reelection during an exuberant economic boom but before the inflationary price tag has shown up. The latter is conveniently postponed until after the election.

Does this actually happen in the United States? Political scientist Edward Tufte (1978) claims that, except for the two Eisenhower administrations, it generally does. For example, of the 11 elections held between 1948 and 1976 (excluding the 4 in which Eisenhower was the incumbent President), real disposable income accelerated eight times. By comparison, of the 10 years during the same period with no election, real disposable income accelerated only three times. Perhaps even more dramatically, economic policy was managed to "cheat" the trade-off between unemployment and inflation by achieving reductions in *both* variables simultaneously in 4 of the 8 presidential election years since 1946—a feat it has managed in only 2 of the 24 years without presidential elections!

Note that the theory of the political business cycle predicts that stabilization policy would be used in late 1971 and through most of 1972 to boost disposable income before the election. Then, starting in very late 1972 and early 1973, we would expect a sharp reversal of policy toward restraint in an effort to hold down the burgeoning inflationary tendencies.

---

[9] For a convenient summary of some of this research, see Frey (1978).

Thus, theorizing based both on attitudes toward wage–price controls and on political business cycles predict that policy should have been aggressively stimulative during 1971–1972, and the latter theory also predicts that policy should have turned restrictive in 1973. What, then, actually happened?

FISCAL POLICY

The most popular measure of the thrust of fiscal policy is the change in the high employment surplus. According to the Council of Economic Advisers' new series, the high employment surplus declined moderately (about $6–7 billion per year) during 1970 and 1971, and then slightly further in 1972 to a deficit of $11.8 billion. By this measure, then, fiscal policy was stimulative during 1971–1972. It then turned moderately toward restraint in 1973. However, there are many problems with the high employment surplus,[10] so a superior measure is desirable.

Fortunately, better measures are available for the 1971–1973 period. Using the old version of the MIT–Penn–SSRC (MPS) econometric model of the U.S. economy, Stephen Goldfeld and I (Blinder and Goldfeld, 1976) have devised new measures of both fiscal and monetary policy that obviate all of the problems of the high employment surplus.[11] Since these measures will be used both here and again in Chapters 7 and 8, let me take some time to explain precisely what they mean. Simulations of the MPS model with and without particular policy changes are used to assess the effect of *each quarter's* fiscal policy on the real GNP of subsequent quarters. Specifically, the series we call $F^j(t)$ measures the effect of the fiscal policy actions of quarter t on the real GNP of quarter $t+j$. But since past fiscal policies also influence GNP in quarter $t+j$, we also constructed a series $T^j(t)$ which includes that portion of the lagged effects of previous fiscal policies that is not already incorporated in the GNP of quarter t. A concrete example should make the definitions clear. For 1971:3 F^3 is $7.6 billion (in 1958 dollars) and T^3 is $23.5 billion.[12] The interpretation of these numbers is that fiscal policy actions taken in 1971:3 are estimated to have raised the real GNP of 1972:2 (3 quarters later) by $7.6 billion, while *all* fiscal policy actions of 1971:3 *and earlier quarters* are estimated to have added $23.5 billion to the *growth* of real GNP between 1971:2 and 1972:2.

[10] For a discussion of these problems, see Blinder and Solow (1974, pp. 14–20).

[11] However, our measures introduce one new problem: they are dependent on the model of the economy that is used in their construction. For a full discussion, see Blinder and Goldfeld (1976).

[12] In Blinder and Goldfeld (1976), the T measures have a subscript which indicates the truncation procedure used in their derivation. The series referred to here is $T^3_6(t)$.

Based on these definitions, I can look for a shift in fiscal policy around the time of the controls by comparing the 5 quarters prior to the New Economic Policy (1970:2 through 1971:2) with the 5 quarters after the controls were announced (1971:4 through 1972:4). When I do this, I find that the F^3 series *rises* sharply from an average of $.4 billion before controls to an average of $5.1 billion in the period after controls began. However, the T^3 series, which includes also the "overhang" from past policy actions, *declines* from $19 billion before controls to $14.5 billion after.[13] There is a terminological question, then, about whether we want to say that fiscal policy became more stimulative after August 1971. There is no question, however, that policy was very stimulative between late 1971 and late 1972—precisely the period indicated by the theory of the political business cycle. The levels reached by the T series are the highest in the entire 1959–1973 period, eclipsing even the Vietnam War episode (see Figure 3-1).

Are we to attribute this to mistaken attitudes about controls, or to the dictates of the political business cycle? Unfortunately, motivation is not the sort of thing that can be established by econometrics, and the facts stubbornly refuse to "speak for themselves." But this amateur psychologist is tempted to blame it more on the proximity to the November 1972 elections than on the controls. Indeed, like many others, I wonder whether the controls program would ever have been started were it not for the looming elections. I will have more to say about this issue in Chapter 7's detailed examination of fiscal policy, where it will be seen that both the actions and the words of the Nixon administration point toward the political explanation.

MONETARY POLICY

In the case of monetary policy, growth rates—especially that for M_1— are the most common indicator, though others prefer to look at interest rates. Quarterly growth rates in M_1 certainly do not exhibit any break around the time that the controls program was initiated.[14] Quarterly

---

[13] The T^3_B series cited here is constructed by forcing fiscal effects on real output to reach a steady state of zero after 3 years. An alternative assumption that the steady state reached after 3 years is nonzero leads to a different series [called $T^3_?$ in Blinder and Goldfeld (1976)] that rises sharply from the precontrols period to the controls period. Thus the statement in the text is based on the strong assumption that the "natural rate hypothesis" is roughly correct over a 3-year horizon.

[14] The growth rates referred to here and throughout the book are from the average of one quarter to the average of the next quarter. Others prefer to compute growth rates from the last month of one quarter to the last month of the next. My choice normally gives a much smoother series.

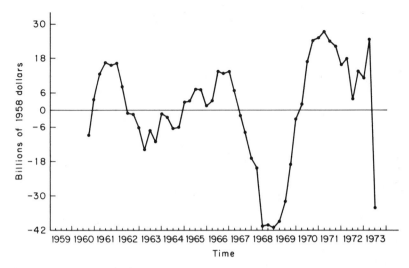

Figure 3-1. Effect of fiscal policy on real GNP (*Source:* Blinder and Goldfeld, 1976.)

growth in the money supply averaged 7% (annual rate) from 1970:2 until 1971:3 and 7.2% from 1971:3 until 1972:4. By most standards, these growth rates were quite high, so it seems that we should characterize monetary policy as quite expansive throughout this period. Beginning with 1973:1, however, the growth rate of M_1 begins a steady decline.

Interest rates tell a rather different story about timing. Short-term rates, which had climbed sharply during 1971:2, began falling at a fairly rapid rate in about mid 1971, and continued to fall until early 1972. This corroborates the view that money was very easy. At this point, however, interest rates began a protracted climb that carried Treasury bill rates, for example, up about 5 percentage points by the summer of 1973. So interest rate data suggest an earlier turn to restriction than do money growth rates.

According to the Blinder–Goldfeld series on the influence of monetary policy on real GNP, *current* monetary policy was quite stimulative throughout 1970–1972, but the *cumulative* effect was much stronger in the period after August 1971. Our series on the thrust of current monetary policy reaches a clear trough in 1971:4, and increases from an average of $7.6 billion in the 5 quarters prior to controls to an average of $11.5 billion in the first 5 quarters after the New Economic Policy. The broader measure, which includes also the lagged effects of the expansionary monetary policies of 1970, does not show any clear break around 1971:3,

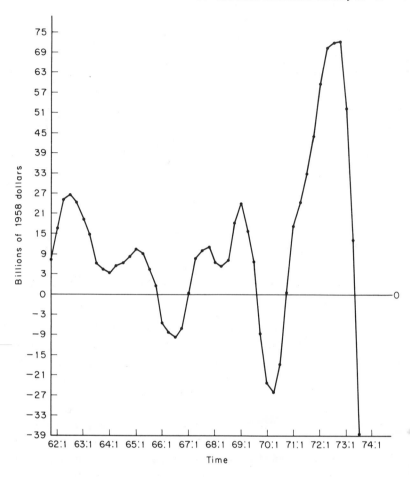

Figure 3-2. Effect of monetary policy on real GNP. (*Source:* Blinder and Goldfeld, 1976.)

but merely continues its remarkably rapid ascent (see Figure 3-2). It averages $63.9 billion in the 5 quarters 1971:4–1972:4 as compared to −$.3 billion in the 5 quarters 1970:2–1971:2.[15] It then declines precipitously from its 1972:4 peak of $73.6 billion to −$38.2 billion in 1973:3.[16] The interpretation, to repeat, is that the monetary policy of 1972:4 and earlier quarters *added* $73.6 billion (in 1958 dollars) to the growth of the economy from 1972:3 to 1973:3, while the policies of 1973:3 and earlier

[15] The specific series referred to are called M_4^3 and S_D^3 in Blinder and Goldfeld (1976).

[16] This is the last quarter of the S_D^3 series. The S_D^0 series, which continues into 1974, continues to fall.

subtracted $38.2 billion from the growth between 1973:2 and 1974:2—a swing of over $110 billion in 1958 prices (or about $170 billion in 1972 prices) in only 3 quarters.

Once again, there are a variety of possible motives for this behavior. One hypothesis is that the Fed was deluded by the efficacy of controls, and believed that more aggregate demand stimulus was appropriate. Under this hypothesis, it realized the error of its ways after the election, and stepped (too hard) on the brakes. A second hypothesis is that the Fed was assisting the administration in engineering a political business cycle—either by design or by inadvertence.[17] A third hypothesis is that the explosion in world currency reserves that followed the advent of floating exchange rates and the devaluation of the dollar loosened the "balance of payments constraint" on monetary policy, and encouraged excessive stimulus—a stimulus that was later counteracted by contractionary measures in 1973.

I leave it to the reader to select his or her own favorite hypothesis. Since all three events take place at about the same time, there is no way for econometric investigation to adjudicate the issue.

HINDSIGHT VERSUS FORESIGHT

One further point about stabilization policy in 1971–1972 is worth making here. The very expansive monetary and fiscal policies of 1971–1972 were formulated with a rather different view of the gap between actual and potential GNP than we have now. In 1971, for example, the estimates of potential GNP suggested a GNP gap of about $62 billion (in 1972 prices); the revised figures place this gap at only $38 billion. The difference is even more dramatic for 1972, where the old data showed a gap of nearly $46 billion, while the new data show a gap of only $15 billion—little more than 1% of GNP.[18] This raises yet another explanation for the stimulative policies of 1972: overestimates of potential GNP and corresponding underestimates of capacity utilization. It must be admitted that hindsight is better than foresight in labeling the policies of 1971–1972 as "too expansionary." And it must also be pointed out that many Democrats were calling for stimulative policies at the time.

---

[17] To the extent that the central bank is trying to stabilize interest rates—a policy it has often followed—any upward pressure on interest rates engendered by expansionary fiscal policy will force the Fed to follow suit.

[18] Perloff and Wachter (1979) have argued that even the new CEA series seriously overstates potential GNP.

4. The Origins of Stagflation, 1973–1974

The years 1973 and 1974 can be characterized as the years of the great exogenous price shocks. After rising at a rate of 3.4% per annum during both 1971 and 1972, the Consumer Price Index (CPI) accelerated to 8.8% during 1973 and to a phenomenal 12.2% during 1974. Three principal events accounted for this acceleration, each of which will be examined in detail in Chapters 5 and 6.

First, the poor harvests that began in 1972 started to have their effects at the retail level in the early months of 1973. Food prices soared at a 20% annual rate during 1973, as compared to a rate under 5% during 1972. This item alone accounts for most of the 1972–1973 acceleration in inflation. For example, if we consider the 9-month period from December 1972 to September 1973, the CPI as a whole rose at the rapid annual rate of 8.7%. But the CPI excluding food rose at a rate of only 4.4%—not much above its 1972 rate of increase.

Second, OPEC's actions started the prices of oil and other energy resources skyrocketing in the last few months of 1973. The retail price of gasoline and motor oil, for example, surged upward by 39% between September 1973 and May 1974.

Third, wage and price controls ended in the spring of 1974, leading to a burst of "catch-up" inflation.

While the inflation was accelerating, the nation enjoyed a prosperous year in 1973. Real GNP increased 5.5% over 1972, unemployment fell from 5.6 to 4.9%, and production actually exceeded the CEA's new estimate of potential GNP by about $8 billion. But all this conceals the fact that 1973 was a year of significant slowdown in the pace of economic activity. As the first column of Table 3-1 clearly shows, the exuberant (and unsustainable) real growth rates of 1972 continued only through 1973:1, and then fell rather abruptly. This pattern is even more vivid in real final sales (see the middle column of Table 3-1), which were unchanged between 1973:1 and 1973:4.

The last quarter of 1973, of course, was disrupted by the Arab oil embargo and the beginnings of the OPEC price hikes. Economic activity in the U.S., as elsewhere, deteriorated quite badly during 1974, as Table 3-1 shows. For the year as a whole, real GNP fell 1.4% over 1973, though the last half of the year was much worse than the first half. Real final sales dropped more slowly, falling .7% below their 1973 level. The unemployment rate rose to a yearly average of 5.6%, which might not be much above the natural rate; but by year end it was already 7.2%. The gap between potential and actual GNP was $46.4 billion for the year as a whole, and widening rapidly at year end.

TABLE 3-1
Quarterly Growth (at Annual Rates) of Real GNP and Real Final Sales, 1972-1974[a]

| | Percentage growth of: | | Change in business |
Quarter	Real GNP	Real final sales[b]	inventories[c]
1972:1	7.6	7.2	4.8
2	7.9	5.9	10.1
3	5.3	4.6	12.1
4	8.5	9.0	10.8
1973:1	8.8	8.4	11.7
2	0.2	−0.3	14.8
3	2.7	2.5	14.1
4	1.4	−2.2	25.4
1974:1	−3.9	−0.9	13.9
2	−1.8	0.2	9.2
3	−1.5	−0.7	2.0
4	−5.5	−8.6	6.8

[a]Source: Survey of Current Business.
[b]GNP less change in business inventories.
[c]In billions of 1972 dollars.

One basic argument of this book is that there were plenty of warning signals of the coming recession, which, for whatever reasons, were not heeded. The food price increases at the retail level during 1973 and 1974 were clearly presaged by the crop failures and wholesale price increases of 1972 and 1973. While perhaps no one could have foreseen the Arab oil embargo and the consequent strengthening of OPEC, by early 1974 all this was a *fait accompli*. And the third major exogenous shock to the price level—the dismantling of controls—was not just predictable, it was in fact a carefully considered government decision. The first two of these constituted a monumental supply shock of the kind considered in Chapter 2. The last, while qualitatively different, had much the same effects in the short run because output is basically demand determined over short periods. I argued in Chapter 2 that these sorts of autonomous increases in prices have contractionary effects on demand for several reasons.[19]

First, if the central bank does not provide enough new cash to meet the increased demand for money caused by the higher prices, interest rates are pushed up and this depresses real demand. The effect is exactly the same as if the money supply had fallen.

Second, because our income tax system is progressive and not indexed,

[19] The mechanism by which autonomous cuts in the price level stimulate demand is obtained by reversing each of these.

the real burden of personal income taxation increases automatically during inflation as taxpayers with unchanged real incomes are pushed into higher tax brackets. This is a feature of our tax system that is a welcome automatic stabilizer when there are demand shocks, but a serious contributor to stagflation when there are supply shocks such as those of 1973–1974.

Third, since so much household wealth is held either in assets that are explicitly nominal (e.g., bank accounts, government bonds) or that behave like nominal assets (e.g., common stocks), price shocks destroy a substantial amount of private sector wealth, and consequently have deleterious effects on consumption.

Fourth, the oil price shock was quite obviously harmful to our balance of foreign trade. This was also true of the catch-up inflation that followed the end of price controls, though to a much smaller extent. Fortunately, the food price shock improved rather than harmed our trade balance because of America's position as a major exporter of foodstuffs.

On top of these direct effects of the adverse shifts in the aggregate supply schedule,[20] I mentioned in Chapter 2 that supply side shocks very often cause major redistributions of income. Since these redistributions played such a major role in the Great Recession, it is worth examining this mechanism in somewhat greater detail.

Suppliers of a good whose price suddenly rises (food, oil, or goods in general in the case of decontrol) will increase their share of total income if (and only if) demand for their product is *inelastic*. In this case, consumers will be spending more on the good that has risen in price and, if policy holds *nominal* income roughly constant, will have to spend less on other products. This is the celebrated "excise tax" analogy that has been used so much with reference to higher oil prices. In the short run, however, *all* price elasticities are fairly low, so *any* price hike can be viewed as an excise tax. What matters, of course, are

1. How low the short-run elasticity is. Price hikes are more contractionary if they are concentrated on goods with very low short-run price elasticities.
2. How fast consumers adjust, thereby approaching the long-run price elasticity, and how large this elasticity is. Again, low elasticities and slow adjustments give price hikes more powerful real effects.
3. Who receives the "tax revenue." In the short run, the food price increases redistributed income in favor of farmers, the energy price increases redistributed income in favor of OPEC and domestic en-

---

[20] This list of four factors describes the movement up the demand curve that is caused by the inward shift of the supply curve.

ergy producers, and the end of price controls redistributed income in favor of corporate profits in general.

I observed in Chapter 2 that each of these redistributions would be expected to reduce aggregate demand because the groups "collecting" the "excise taxes" have lower propensities to spend than the groups "paying" the "taxes."

Certainly these distribution effects will be mostly transitory because price elasticities for most commodities build up over time, because farmers eventually invest their savings, because OPEC eventually will spend its earnings, and because corporate saving will filter through the financial markets causing interest rates to fall and spurring investment. But this hardly makes them unimportant. In a world where the natural rate hypothesis is approximately valid, the real effects of most macroeconomic shocks are "merely" transitory.

In sum, while I do not mean to exaggerate the ease with which the magnitude of the coming debacle could have been predicted—the poor economic forecasts of 1974 bear ample witness to that—the basic causes of the Great Recession were quite apparent by, say, early to mid 1974. These include rising food prices, the turn toward contractionary monetary and fiscal policies, rising oil prices, and the end of wage–price controls. Yet, despite all this, concern about inflation led policymakers to stand idly by as the slide into recession progressed.

5. Recession and Recovery, 1975–1976

While GNP for 1975 as a whole was 1.3% below the level of 1974, the economy seems to have hit bottom around March 1975, and rather rudely at that. As Table 3-2 indicates, the last 3 quarters of 1975 were clearly quarters of recovery, although the recovery in real final sales was weaker than that of GNP.

Inventory investment played a major role both in the late stages of the slide into recession and the early stages of recovery. As can be seen in Tables 3-1 and 3-2, the behavior of real final sales during 1975:1, while poor, was better than it had been in many quarters since 1973:2. The debacle that did occur was caused by the collapse of inventory investment, a phenomenon that I will investigate in some detail in the next chapter. Apparently, many firms suddenly decided to cut production and wear off their unwanted inventory stocks, so real inventory investment plummeted from $6.8 billion in 1974:4 to -$19.4 billion in 1975:1—a swing of $26.2 billion, which accounts (in an arithmetical sense) for almost the entire $28.1 billion drop in GNP in this quarter.

TABLE 3-2
Quarterly Growth (at Annual Rates) of Real GNP and Real Final Sales, 1975–1976[a]

	Percentage growth of:		Change in business inventories[c]
Quarter	Real GNP	Real final sales[b]	
1975:1	−9.1	−0.6	−19.4
2	6.4	5.3	−16.7
3	10.5	3.8	2.1
4	2.6	5.1	−5.2
1976:1	10.7	5.8	8.9
2	2.6	2.3	9.7
3	3.1	4.1	6.7
4	3.5	5.4	1.1

[a]Source: Survey of Current Business.
[b]GNP less change in business inventories.
[c]In billions of 1972 dollars.

Inventory disinvestment continued at nearly this rapid rate during 1975:2, so the rather strong recovery of final sales (5.3% annual growth rate) translated to a slightly larger rise in GNP. But things were much different in 1975:3 when the cessation of inventory decumulation made an ordinary 3.8% growth rate of final sales look like an exuberant boom (10.5% growth rate of real GNP). This kind of support for the recovery from inventory investment was available in only one further quarter (1976:1), when GNP rose at a 10.7% rate despite a 5.8% growth rate of final sales. In the other quarters of 1975–1976 (1975:4, and the last 3 quarters of 1976), inventory change did not prop up the recovery, and the growth rates of real GNP averaged merely 2.9%—a bit below the growth rate of potential output. The recovery in final sales, in a word, was anemic.

Unemployment and the GNP gap reflected this lackluster performance. The $46.4 billion GNP gap of 1974 exploded to $99.8 billion (8.3% of GNP) in 1975, and receded only to $68.1 billion in 1976. The overall unemployment rate began 1975 at 7.9%, reached a peak shortly after the recession trough (in May 1975) at 9.0%, and ended 1975 at 8.3%. A large downtick in January 1976 brought unemployment to 7.8%; but it was still at that rate when 1976 ended.

Inflation declined markedly in 1975 and fell still further in 1976. The "double-digit" inflation rate in the CPI during 1974 (12.2%) dropped to the more manageable 7.0% during 1975, and slipped to only 4.8% during 1976. I will show in Chapters 5 and 6 that virtually all of the deceleration in inflation in 1975 can be accounted for by the fact that the quadrupling of oil prices and the demise of wage–price controls did not occur again. The further deceleration during 1976 can probably be attributed to the low rate of increase of food prices and to the continued slack in the economy.

It seems safe to say that fiscal policy did little to support economic activity during the 1974–1975 slide into recession. Federal government purchases of goods and services, for example, actually declined very slightly in real terms from 1973 to 1974, continuing a downward trend from their 1968 peak, and rose very slightly from 1974 to 1975. Due to the unlegislated tax increases caused by inflation that I have already mentioned, the high employment *deficit* of about $8 billion in 1973 turned into a high employment *surplus* of about $3 billion in 1974 with no important change in discretionary policy. This permanent swing of $11 billion implies that half of the $22 billion temporary tax cut that was finally enacted in March 1975 merely served to offset fiscal drag.[21]

When antirecession action finally was taken, the principal vehicle was a series of *temporary* decreases in taxes and increases in transfer payments. Many economists have argued that changes in disposable income that result from legislation that is explicitly temporary are heavily discounted by consumers who spend on the basis of their permanent income. Others have objected that this is an *a priori* theoretical assertion that is not supported by the facts. In Chapter 7 I try to provide a tentative answer to this question through a new econometric study of the consumption function.

It is hard to know what succinct statement to make about monetary policy during 1974–1976. While it is easy enough to scrutinize the growth rates of the money *supply,* the well-documented gyrations in the money *demand* function during this period make it difficult to know which growth rates constitute "expansionary" monetary policy and which are "contractionary." I reserve discussion of this issue to Chapter 8; but it must be admitted that much of this is only educated guesswork.

As 1976 ended, the inflation problem seemed to be quite similar to what it had been before the price controls: a stubborn, but manageable, baseline rate of inflation of 5–6% that would recede only very slowly due to the inertia of inflationary expectations. But economic activity was a far cry from what it had been in 1969–1971. The GNP gap during those 3 years averaged $19.5 billion (in 1972 dollars), or 1.8% of GNP. At the close of 1976 it was $68 billion, or 5.3% of GNP. The unemployment rate averaged 4.8% during 1969–1971, and stood at 7.8% in December 1976.

---

[21] It is worth noting that contemporary estimates of the swing in the high employment surplus placed it closer to $20 billion.

Whatever the ultimate historical verdict on the stabilization policies of 1972–1976 turns out to be, it is undeniable that the economy was in far worse shape as it entered 1977 than when it left 1971. I argue in this book that policymakers must shoulder a good deal of the blame.

6. Summary

Four major inflationary shocks buffeted the U.S. economy during 1973 and 1974: devaluation of the dollar; rising prices of food on world markets; OPEC's quadrupling of the price of oil; and the end of wage–price controls. All of these can be considered "exogenous" in the sense that economists normally use the word, though two of them were clearly policy decisions of the U.S. government.

Except for the devaluation, which is potentially expansionary due to its long-range favorable effects on the balance of trade, there is no doubt that each of these inflationary shocks also served to siphon off aggregate demand. That is, these were *stagflationary* shocks, and very large ones at that.

Monetary and fiscal policy helped create boom conditions in 1972 and early 1973, thereby losing ground in the battle against inflation; and then turned abruptly restrictive in 1973, thereby helping to bring on a slowdown in economic activity. Thereafter, there was rather little activist stabilization policy of any kind during either the downswing of 1974–1975 or the upswing of 1975–1976. As will be seen in Chapters 7 and 8, it was fear of rekindling inflation that prevented the monetary and fiscal authorities from taking any decisive actions to prevent, or even to cushion, the deterioration in economic activity caused by the stagflationary shocks. Instead, policymakers sat idly by as the worst recession of our postwar history gathered momentum. Murphy would have been proud.

4

the anatomy of the great recession

This poll shows that 74 percent believe we are already in a recession. The other 26 percent are on the Council of Economic Advisers.

—caption on a cartoon published in 1974

The downturn in business activity that began in late 1973 was the most severe one in this country since the Great Depression. The passage of time makes it all too easy to forget how serious the contraction was, and how concerned people became in late 1974 and early 1975 about where it would all end. Furthermore, the recovery that began in the spring of 1975 was pallid by comparison with the severity of the downswing. Even 3 years after the trough of the recession, neither the unemployment rate nor capacity utilization had recovered to their levels of late 1973. All in all, the period certainly merits the appellation "Great Recession."

This chapter documents and interprets what happened to real economic activity during the years 1973-1976. Because of its spectacular fluctuations around the trough and in the early stages of the recovery, I devote particularly close attention to inventory investment. However, a more fundamental view of the cycle must consider the behavior of the components of final sales, especially consumer spending and fixed investment. This discussion points to the sharp drop in consumer spending in late 1974 as one of the major unsolved puzzles of this period. Finally, when the relationships among output, employment, and productivity are examined, an even deeper mystery emerges: Why did productivity fall so sharply in 1974? Given the poor productivity performance of the U.S.

43

economy since then, the question is of much more than academic interest.

1. The Interplay of Inventories and Final Sales

The inventory cycle, a favorite topic of macroeconomists during the 1950s, was all but forgotten during the stable growth decade of the 1960s. But the stunning events of 1973–1976 thrust it back into the limelight with a vengeance. The basic profile of the recession is altered quite radically by purging inventory investment from GNP and looking instead at real final sales. To cite just a few rather incredible numbers, when real GNP at annual rates fell by $28.1 billion during the worst quarter of the recession (1975:1), the swing in inventory investment accounted for $26.2 billion of the fall. Final sales were virtually flat. Then during the best quarter of the recovery (1975:3), when real GNP surged by $30.1 billion, $18.8 billion was a swing in inventory investment. Final sales grew roughly at the growth rate of potential GNP.

Figure 4-1 and Table 4-1 show data on the differing business cycles as seen in real GNP versus real final sales, and also the inventory behavior that accounted for these divergences. The number in parentheses under the title of each item in Table 4-1 is meant to give a rough indication of

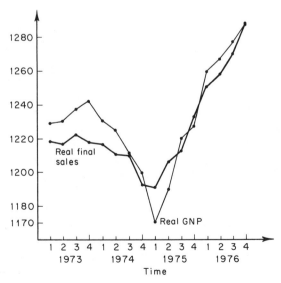

Figure 4-1. The 1973–1976 business cycle in GNP and final sales.

TABLE 4-1
Changes in Real GNP and Components, 1973–1976 [a,b]

Quarter	Real GNP (11)	Real final sales (11)	Real inventory investment (0)	Level of real inventory investment (10)
	Absolute change from previous quarter in:			
1973:1	+27.6	+26.8	+ 0.9	11.7
2	+ 1.3	− 1.8	+ 3.1	14.8
3	+ 5.2	+ 5.9	− 0.7	14.1
4	+ 6.3	− 5.0	+11.3	25.4
1974:1	−12.4	− 1.0	−11.5	13.9
2	− 5.7	− 0.9	− 4.7	9.2
3	− 7.6	− 0.4	− 7.2	2.0
4	−17.2	−22.0	+ 4.8	6.8
1975:1	−28.1	− 1.9	−26.2	−19.4
2	+18.3	+15.5	+ 2.7	−16.7
3	+30.1	+11.4	+18.8	+ 2.1
4	+ 7.9	+15.2	− 7.3	− 5.2
1976:1	+31.6	+17.5	+14.1	+ 8.9
2	+ 7.9	+ 7.1	+ 0.8	+ 9.7
3	+ 9.7	+12.6	− 3.0	+ 6.7
4	+11.0	+16.7	− 5.6	+ 1.1

[a] Source: Survey of Current Business.
[b] In billions of 1972 dollars, at annual rates.

what the average quarterly changes in GNP, final sales, and inventory investment (and also the level of inventory investment) would have looked like in an economy of this size along a steady growth path. Thus, in a loose sense, when the numbers in the table are smaller than these trend guidelines, growth was "weak," and conversely, when they are larger, growth was "strong."

In the briefest possible outline, the GNP data for the recession show a sluggish economy in the last 3 quarters of 1973 (an annualized real growth rate of 1.4%) followed by a 5 quarter downswing starting with the 1973:4 peak and culminating in a true debacle in 1975:1. The total decline in real GNP was 5.7%. But the recession looks much different when viewed from the perspective of final sales. Here the weakness in the last 3 quarters of 1973 was more serious: there was no growth at all. The peak seems to come earlier (in 1973:3); and the downswing lasts longer (6 quarters) and is less severe (a total decline of only 2.6%). The only substantial drop in final sales came in 1974:4, and this quarter remains a bit of a mystery (see below). Thus inventory movements masked the weakening economy in 1973, and then gave an exaggerated impression of the contraction.

The recovery in GNP also differs substantially from that in final sales. The GNP data exhibit a sawtooth pattern with good growth in the first quarter of recovery (a 6.4% annual rate in 1975:2), spectacular spurts in 1975:3 and 1976:1 (annual growth rates of 10.5 and 10.7% respectively), and only trend increases or less in the remaining quarters. The final sales data make the recovery look far smoother and rather unspectacular, with only slightly more than normal trend growth after 1975:2.

The inventory investment series obviously accounts for these discrepancies. Inventory accumulation was abnormally large throughout 1973 and especially in 1973:4. Its return to more normal levels in the first two quarters of 1974, and then to a very low level in 1974:3, caused declines in GNP despite virtually none in final sales. The sharp drop in inventory investment in 1975:1 and the surge in 1975:3 have already been mentioned, and there was another burst in 1976:1 when inventory liquidation was replaced by a near-normal rate of accumulation. In a word, much of the "action" in the GNP series is contained in the inventory investment data, so it behooves us to take a closer look at inventory behavior.

The first question raised by Figure 4-1 is: Why was there so much inventory investment in 1973? The best available data on inventories are the Commerce Department's series on real inventories and sales of industries in the manufacturing and trade sectors. While this sector does not cover the whole economy, it does account for over 80% of inventory investment.[1] The ratio of inventories to monthly sales in the entire sector is shown in Figure 4-2, along with a trend line fit to data from 1959:1 to 1977:4.[2]

While the naive assumption that firms shoot for a target inventory-sales ratio that grows linearly with time is hardly the most sophisticated model of inventory holdings that can be imagined, the only up-to-date

---

[1] Omitted are farms, certain non-farm industries that are neither manufacturers nor wholesalers nor retailers, and so-called "non-merchant" wholesalers. For a detailed list, see *Survey of Current Business*, May 1976, p. 11, footnote 1.

[2] The line comes from the following linear regression:

$$R_t = 1.54 + .00094T_t \qquad R^2 = .15 \qquad \text{standard error} = .051$$
$$\quad (.01) \quad (.00027)$$

where R_t is the inventory–sales ratio, T is a quarterly time trend beginning at 1 in 1959:1, and standard errors are in parentheses.

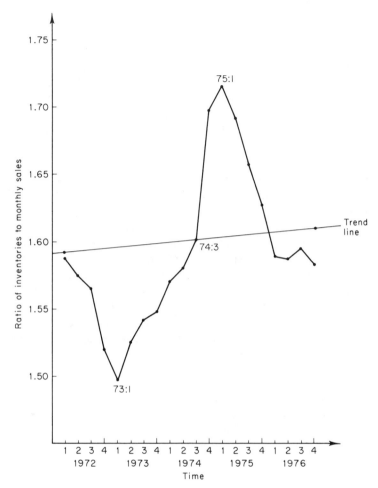

Figure 4-2. Inventory-sales ratio: manufacturing and trade. (*Source:* Bureau of Economic Analysis.)

empirical study of inventories that is relevant to this issue seems to give far less satisfactory results.[3]

Feldstein and Auerbach (1976) have offered a "target adjustment" model for inventories of manufacturers of durable goods wherein firms are always very close to their "desired" inventory stocks, but these

[3] Recent empirical work by Bryant (1978) and Maccini (1977) is not useful in this context because it contains no real notion of a target level of inventories. This may, of course, be a virtue rather than a vice of these studies.

desired stocks adjust very slowly to the long-run "target" stocks. From their estimated coefficients, it is possible to compute these targets, quarter by quarter, and compare them to actual inventory levels. This is done in column (1) of Table 4-2. In column (2) the desired stocks implied by a simple trend regression are compared with the actual stocks. If we are to believe the Feldstein–Auerbach results, manufacturers of durables (this includes auto makers) had an incredible inventory shortfall of $13 billion in 1974:1, were still short by $8 billion even after the sales debacle of 1974:4, and had not succeeded in ridding themselves of unwanted inventories (a $6 billion excess) as late as the end of 1976:1. By contrast, the simple trend regression estimates the inventory shortage in 1974:1 to have been only $3.2 billion, says that there was a $3.3 billion inventory *excess* at the end of 1974:4, and indicates that inventory balance was virtually restored by 1976:1. I find this story much the more plausible.

The simple trend line in Figure 4-2 already helps us understand why inventory investment was so strong in 1973 despite the weakness in final sales. In the first quarter of 1973, there apparently was a tremendous inventory shortfall, amounting to just over $14 billion—more than 6% of actual inventories. For this reason, firms were happy to produce more than they sold, and this remained true even into 1974. By this rough measure, at least, inventory equilibrium was achieved only in 1974:3,

TABLE 4-2
Actual Minus Desired Inventories in Durable Goods Manufacturing[a,b]

Quarter	(1) Based on Feldstein–Auerbach targets	(2) Based on targets from trend regression
1974:1	−12.9	−3.2
2	−11.0	−3.0
3	−12.6	−1.5
4	− 8.0	+3.3
1975:1	+ 4.8	+9.4
2	+12.5	+9.5
3	+ 8.4	+6.4
4	+ 5.4	+5.1
1976:1	+ 6.1	+0.5

[a]*Sources:* Column (1), computed by the author from coefficients and data in Feldstein and Auerbach (1976); column (2), residuals from a regression of the inventory–sales ratio against time. (*Note:* The "actual" data are different in the two cases since Feldstein and Auerbach did not have the latest revised data.)
[b]End of quarter, in billions of 1972 dollars.

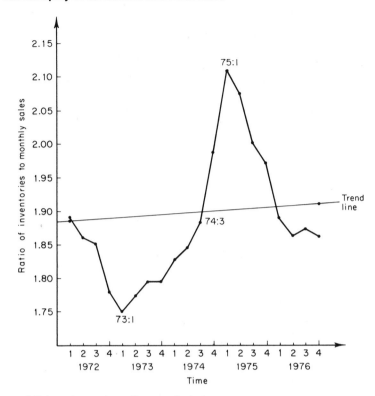

Figure 4-3. Inventory-sales ratio: manufacturing.

only to turn into a massive excess of inventories when sales collapsed in 1974:4.

We can learn more by disaggregating the manufacturing and trade sector into its three major components: manufacturers (roughly 60% of inventories), merchant wholesalers (roughly 15%), and retailers (roughly 25%). Figures 4-3 through 4-5 display the inventory-sales ratios for each of these sectors, with a fitted time trend for each.[4] These diagrams suggest that all three sectors had very large "shortages" of inventories in early 1973, and that only the retailers were able to rectify the imbalance quickly. Apparently strong orders from retailers prevented manufacturers and wholesalers from replenishing their stocks. Then a combination of falling sales and rising inventories in 1973:4 pushed retail inventories way above trend, while wholesalers and manufacturers were still seeking to build their inventories.

---

[4] It is perhaps worth mentioning that the time trend does not fit terribly well ($R^2 = .10$) for manufacturing or retailing ($R^2 = .17$), but fits quite well ($R^2 = .52$) for wholesalers.

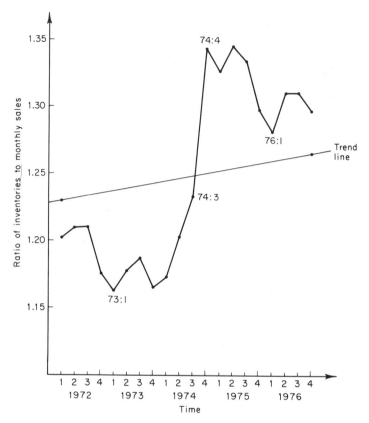

Figure 4-4. Inventory-sales ratio: merchant wholesalers.

While both manufacturers and wholesalers were able to reach approximate inventory equilibrium by 1974:3 poor sales performances prevented retailers from wearing off their unwanted stocks. Then, with the sharp decline of final sales in 1974:4, inventory-sales ratios in all three sectors rose to unusually high levels. Retailers succeeded in unloading their excess stocks rather quickly in 1975:1 and were, in fact, rather low on inventories by 1975:2. But wholesalers and manufacturers were much less successful. Manufacturers' inventories were, in fact, virtually unchanged between 1974:3 and 1975:1 despite an 11% drop in sales.

2. Dynamics of the Recession

If we put these inventory data together with the GNP and final sales data of Table 4-1, a fairly coherent picture of the dynamics of the recession emerges. When the economic boom ended in 1973:1, inventories were low almost everywhere. In fact, time trends fitted to the inventory-sales ratios of all 20 detailed industries included in the Commerce Department's breakdown show that 18 of them had ratios below trend, many decidedly so. The exuberance of the boom may be enough to explain these large inventory gaps, though price controls may also have contributed—either by reducing one of the incentives for holding inventories (price appreciation) or by making it difficult to acquire inventories of materials in short supply. Whatever the reasons, there is no mystery why production held up much better than sales during the last 3 quarters of 1973.

The drop in sales itself probably can be explained with no difficulty by the switch to contractionary monetary and fiscal policies and the deleterious effects of higher food prices on demand. As was seen in Table 4-1, final sales were flat during the last 3 quarters of 1973. The economy clearly was cooling off very rapidly; but this development was viewed as a healthy sign in many quarters—not at all an outlandish view, since the CEA's new estimate of potential GNP shows that actual output was slightly above potential for 1973 as a whole.

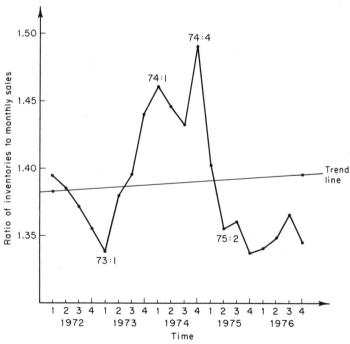

Figure 4-5. Inventory-sales ratio: retail trade.

Then, in 1973:4, the first part of the oil price shock hit the U.S. economy—the Arab oil embargo and the first few hikes in the price of oil. Final sales dropped by $5 billion. Inventory investment accelerated markedly in this quarter, and manufacturers, wholesalers, and retailers all shared in the rise. The preceding diagrams suggest that while manufacturers and wholesalers were happy to replenish their depleted stocks, much of the inventory accumulation at the retail level was unwanted. This supposition is buttressed by the fact that the largest rise was registered by automobile dealers.

From 1973:4 to 1974:1, though final sales hardly changed, GNP dropped sharply owing to the large fall in inventory investment. During 1974:2 and 1974:3, with final sales remaining roughly constant, GNP fell further because inventory accumulation declined (see Table 4-1). Price controls also ended in 1974:2, and this dampened demand.

A full explanation for what happened in 1974:4 is not at hand. Final sales dropped by a staggering $22 billion, despite an improvement in the balance of trade. And the fall in GNP would have been worse yet were it not for the cushion provided by an increase in inventory investment. Given what was happening to sales, and given what we learned in Figures 4-3 through 4-5, it seems safe to say that this inventory accumulation ($6.8 billion at annual rates) was mostly unintended.

The collapse of final demand in 1974:4 will be studied more carefully as this chapter progresses, but whatever the explanation, the result was clear—inventories became alarmingly high in almost every industry. According to the trend regressions, 16 of the 20 detailed industries had excessive inventories by the end of 1974:4. Retail automobile dealers accounted for a major portion of the total inventory accumulation during the quarter. Surprisingly, however, manufacturers of automobiles managed to keep their inventory levels constant despite a sharp drop in sales.

This buildup of unwanted inventory stocks obviously set the stage for a massive liquidation in 1975. Retailers led the way in the first quarter and manufacturers followed. A crude estimate of the excess inventories in manufacturing and trade at the end of 1974:4, based on the trend regression, is about $21 billion. The inventory selloff in the first half of 1975 amounted to about $9 billion; so manufacturers and wholesalers apparently still had substantial excess inventories after it was over. In any case, the downswing in inventory investment in 1975:1 transformed a small decline in final sales into a disaster in terms of GNP. Then a swing from sharp decumulation to slight accumulation of inventories in 1975:3 made a rather ordinary quarter in terms of final sales look like a boom quarter in terms of output.

3. The Predictability of the Recession

With the advantages of hindsight, the interplay between inventories and final sales seems perfectly coherent, and there is nothing terribly surprising about the behavior of the 1973–1975 economy except the sudden drop in spending in 1974:4. But this does not mean that everything was easy to predict *ex ante*. Indeed, we know that the economic forecasts of early 1974 were wide of the mark. Were the forecasters foolish? Was the severity of the contraction easy to predict from inventory behavior?

I believe not. The fact that GNP was growing substantially faster than final sales throughout most of 1973 was not an obvious warning of trouble on the horizon because most industries probably wanted to accumulate inventories. The sharp deterioration in final sales in 1973:4 could easily have been interpreted as a transitory effect of the oil embargo, which it may well have been. The steady inventory accumulation during the first 3 quarters of 1974 was, again, probably desired by most firms other than retailers; and inventory levels (again, except in retailing) were more or less in line as late as 1974:3. It was the suddenness of the drop in sales in 1974:4 that led to massive inventory imbalances and, as we shall see, this collapse is quite hard to explain *ex post*, much less to have anticipated *ex ante*. Once it had happened, it was probably too late to prevent a very severe drop in output.

I conclude, then, that while the ultimate causes of the recession were all visible by early 1974, and while the fact that the U.S. economy was in a recession was obvious enough through most of 1974, the sharpness of the spasm in late 1974–early 1975 could not have been predicted in advance from inventory behavior, even given the data on hand today. With the older and inferior data available at the time, the task would have been more difficult still.

I turn now to the behavior of final sales, and especially to the declines registered in 1973:4 and 1974:4.

4. The Harried Consumer

Consumer spending typically accounts for about 70% of final sales, so it is a logical place to start. The period was not a particularly happy one for the consumer: 1973 and 1974 were years of extraordinarily high inflation and falling stock market prices; 1974 and 1975 were years of declining real disposable income. The whole period is widely agreed to have been one of extreme economic uncertainty and pessimism, as is apparent from the drop in the index of consumer sentiment to all-time low levels in 1974:4 and 1975:1.

Our look at final sales data suggested three basic questions: Why were final sales so weak in the last 3 quarters of 1973, and especially in 1973:4? What accounts for the stunning collapse of demand in 1974:4? Which components of aggregate demand buoyed the recovery in 1975–1976? Table 4-3 presents data relevant to answering each of these questions. The first two columns show the quarter-to-quarter changes in consumer spending and its principal determinant, disposable income, both in billions of 1972 dollars. (As with Table 4-1, the numbers in parentheses are rough indications of what normal growth would have looked like.) The third column shows the personal saving rate, while the fourth shows the saving rate that is predicted from an estimated consumption function that will be described in Chapter 7.[5]

We quickly notice one remarkable fact. Despite the extraordinarily reliable relationship between disposable income and consumption in the long run, spending and income actually moved in *opposite* directions in 6 of the 16 quarters shown in the table. More to the point, these 6 reversals in direction all occurred within a 10-quarter period starting in 1973:2 and ending in 1975:3. This is most unusual behavior, to say the least.[6]

However, the timing of changes in consumption in response to changes in disposable income is complex, and variables other than income also affect consumption, so we must do more than look at the current change in income if we are to judge whether consumer spending was "normal" or "abnormal" in any particular quarter. The predicted saving rates in the last column of Table 4-3 are intended to provide the necessary benchmark. They come from an estimated equation explaining consumer spending by a distributed lag on disposable income, lagged consumer net worth exclusive of the stock market, and a distributed lag on stock market wealth.[7] Thus normal reactions to changes in disposable income, the stock market, and non-stock-market wealth are embodied in the predicted

---

[5] The equation described there actually predicts the average propensity to *consume* (APC). Consumption and saving do not quite exhaust disposable income. There are also interest payments to business and transfer payments to foreigners. However, these two miscellaneous items account for a remarkably stable fraction of income (2.4%). So the predicted saving rates reported in the last row of the table are obtained by adding the residuals in the equation that predicts the APC to the actual saving rates given in the third row.

[6] A regression of the change in consumption on the change in disposable income over these 10 quarters yields a slope coefficient of only .24 and an R^2 of .01.

[7] The equation also includes the after tax real interest rate, but its impact is trivial.

TABLE 4-3
Consumer Spending and Related Data

| Quarter | Absolute change[a] in: | | Personal savings rates[b] | |
	Real consumption expenditures (7)	Real disposable income (7.7)	Actual	Predicted[c]
1973:1	+14.9	+18.0	6.8	6.6
2	− 0.9	+ 7.6	7.8	7.0
3	+ 3.6	+ 5.5	7.9	7.8
4	− 4.5	+ 3.9	8.7	7.9
1974:1	− 4.3	−15.4	7.7	7.9
2	+ 0.1	− 3.6	7.3	7.5
3	+ 4.9	− 0.1	6.7	7.0
4	−13.7	− 7.9	7.5	6.2
1975:1	+ 4.3	− 5.3	6.4	7.1
2	+13.0	+44.3	9.7	10.0
3	+ 9.5	−11.0	7.5	8.0
4	+11.4	+ 8.6	7.1	7.4
1976:1	+16.2	+11.4	6.4	7.0
2	+ 7.2	+ 4.6	6.1	6.2
3	+ 9.5	+ 5.7	5.6	5.6
4	+12.4	+ 9.9	5.2	5.7

[a] In billions of 1972 dollars.
[b] In percentage points.
[c] As explained in text.

savings rates which, as can be seen, do fluctuate quite a bit from quarter to quarter. Unexplained changes in consumer behavior show up as discrepancies between actual and predicted saving rates, and it is clear right away that we have three rather large ones to clear up: 1973:2; 1973:4; and especially 1974:4.

WHY DID CONSUMER SPENDING SAG IN 1973?

Saving the deepest mystery for last, let me start by investigating the poor consumption performance in the last 3 quarters of 1973. As Table 4-3 shows, we can account for very little of this by weak growth in disposable income. That growth was only a little bit below trend in these quarters, yet saving rates were very high—averaging 8.1%. Certainly the plummeting stock market can account for some of this. The Standard & Poor's composite average of 500 stocks declined more or less continuously throughout the year, and at especially rapid rates in the second

TABLE 4-4
Changes in Consumer Expenditures[a,b]

Item	From 1973:1 to 1973:2	From 1973:3 to 1973:4
Total consumer expenditures	−0.9	−4.5
Durable goods	−1.9	−3.1
Motor vehicles and parts	−2.7	−3.9
Other	+0.8	+0.8
Nondurable goods	−3.1	−2.6
Food	−3.0	−3.3
Other	−0.1	+0.7
Services	+4.1	+1.0

[a]Source: Survey of Current Business, July 1976.
[b]Absolute change in billions of 1972 dollars, at annual rates.

and fourth quarters. Yet the estimated equation shows that the declines in consumer spending went well beyond what can be accounted for by the stock market. The equation overestimates spending in all 4 quarters of 1973.

In an effort to provide a better explanation, Table 4-4 breaks down the observed decline in consumption in 1973:2 and 1973:4 into its principal constituent parts. With this disaggregation, it becomes clear that the whole story is told by spending on automobiles and on food.[8] In this context, we would do well to remember that 1973 was the year in which retail food prices began to skyrocket. The CPI for food, which increased 4.7% during 1972, rose at annual rates of 26.6, 17.4, 26.3, and 10.4%, respectively, during the 4 quarters of 1973. It appears, then, that high food prices discouraged consumption (meaning, presumably, that consumers substituted cheaper foods for dearer ones), and that this drop in spending was saved rather than spent on non-food items.

For automobiles, the decline in spending in 1973:4 is very easy to explain. The Arab–Israeli war in October 1973 and the ensuing temporary oil embargo (which was more publicized than effective) must have frightened away many potential car buyers. In fact, George Perry (1975a) estimated a negative effect on auto sales of $6 billion,[9] somewhat larger than the actual decline. The decline in spending on autos in 1973:2 is less easy to explain, though fortunately it is also smaller. In its 1974 report, the Council of Economic Advisers (CEA) speculated that "there was

[8] The reader may wonder whether these same declines were registered in 1973:3 as well. They were for motor vehicles and parts, but not for food.

[9] Perry (1975a, p. 92) estimated $4.3 billion in 1958 dollars using the automobile demand equation of the Michigan model. In 1972 dollars, this is about $6 billion.

some softening in auto demand from the exceptionally high levels of sales
. . . reached in the first quarter, although reports were common in the
spring and early summer that shortages of parts were holding back production and sales of automobiles.''[10] As with food, it appears that the
decline in spending on autos led to more *saving*, not to more consumption
of other goods—a view that accords well with expectations (which the
case of food does not).

In sum, the oil and food price shocks seem to explain the (rather large)
part of the decline in consumer spending in 1973 that cannot be accounted
for by the deceleration of real disposable income and the decline of the
stock market.

THE UNSOLVED MYSTERY OF 1974:4

It is much less easy to account for the astounding $13.7 billion decrease
in consumer spending in 1974:4. As Table 4-3 revealed, historical patterns
called for a *decline* in the saving rate of .8 percentage points, owing
mostly to the sharp drop in real incomes. Instead, the saving rate *increased* by .8 percentage points. The residual for this quarter is the
largest in the 100-quarter sample, and by a large margin. Clearly, something was amiss.

Table 4-5 offers the same disaggregated detail for 1974:4 that the previous table offered for the 2 quarters of 1973. Unfortunately the resolution
of the mystery does not pop off the page this time. The decline in
consumption, we see, was very broadly based. Autos once again accounted for a major share of the drop (more on this below), and spending
on food fell yet again. However, non-food non-auto purchases of goods
also declined precipitously. In a regression of consumer spending on
nondurable goods and services on its own lagged value, reported by
Robert Hall (1978), 1974:4 stands out as the largest residual in 117 quarters. Only the services component of consumer spending, a series whose
trend seems almost unshakable, managed to register an advance.

We have no oil embargo or similar event to explain the collapse of
spending on automobiles in 1974:4. In trying to account for this behavior
in its 1976 report, the CEA claimed that ''some of the sharpness of the
decline in late 1974 reflected a concentration of auto sales in the third
quarter of 1974, when consumers increased purchases of 1974 models to
avoid large price increases announced for the 1975 models.''[11] However,
much as explaining spending fluctuations by intertemporal substitution
effects accords with economists' predilections, the explanation simply

---

[10] *Economic Report of the President,* 1974, p. 55.
[11] *Economic Report of the President,* 1976, p. 66.

TABLE 4-5
Changes in Consumer Expenditures from 1974:3 to 1974:4$^{a, b}$

Item	Change
Total consumer expenditures	−13.7
Durable goods	−11.3
Motor vehicles and parts	− 8.3
Other durables	− 3.1
Nondurable goods	− 4.1
Food	− 1.4
Other	− 2.7
Services	+ 1.8

^{a}*Source: Survey of Current Business,* July 1977.
^{b}Absolute change in billions of 1972 dollars, at annual rates.

will not wash. The rise in real consumer spending on motor vehicles and parts in 1974:3 was only $1.6 billion, whereas the fall in 1974:4 was $8.3 billion.

Another popular explanation for the weakness of consumption in 1974:4 is the stock market. While the fact seems not to be widely appreciated, in real terms the stock market crash of 1973-1974 (which bottomed out in December 1974) was almost exactly equal in severity to the legendary crash of 1929-1933—and it happened in about half the time! Yet, the stock market, volatile as it was, cannot match the volatility of consumer spending in late 1974. The Standard & Poor's average declined about 8% during 1974:4, but it had declined about twice as much during 1974:3 while consumer spending was rising. Less impressionistically, the normal historical reactions to falling stock prices are embodied in the equation I have used to generate "predicted" savings rates. And yet the equation misses 1974:4 quite badly.

What we do know is that the index of consumer sentiment dropped sharply in the last half of 1974, probably because of heightened concern over inflation and fear of job losses as unemployment burgeoned. I am dubious, however, that it is in any sense meaningful to say that this deterioration in consumer sentiment "caused" the decline in spending. Rather, both seem to be manifestations of the same malaise: consumers were plainly worried.[12]

---

[12] An equation developed by Mishkin (1977), which highlights the effects of consumer indebtedness, seems to track 1974:4 very well; but, in fact, it does so only by badly underestimating spending in 1974:3. Like other equations, it fails to predict the sharp drop in spending between 1974:3 and 1974:4.

Once the trough was passed, consumer spending became the main engine of economic recovery. During the 7 quarters from 1975:2 through 1976:4, the increase in consumer spending amounted to 82% of the increase in final sales. Consumption was, of course, buoyed initially by the income tax cuts passed in March 1975 and taking effect in May and June. Of the astounding $44.3 billion increase in real disposable income recorded in Table 4-3 for 1975:2, fully $37.8 was attributable to one-time payments from the Tax Reduction Act. This episode will be examined with some care in Chapter 7, but even a cursory look at the data suggests that a preponderant share of the income tax rebate of 1975 was saved rather than spent. We see in Table 4-3 that consumer spending rose by only $13 billion while income rose by more than $44 billion; the saving rate ballooned to 9.7%.[13] Nor does it seem to be the case that the rebates, being received so late in the quarter (most taxpayers received their check in June), were spent in 1974:3 instead. The saving rate for that quarter was a healthy 7.5%.

I will argue in Chapter 7 that most of the additional disposable income that taxpayers received from the Tax Reduction Act of 1975 was spent much more slowly than is normally the case. Notice the extraordinary behavior of the consumer in 1976. In each quarter the change in consumer spending *exceeded* the change in disposable income and the saving rate fell, reaching exceptionally low levels in late 1976 (and early 1977). The analysis of temporary taxes presented in Chapter 7 implies that this behavior was, at least in part, the mirror image of the high saving rates of mid 1975. Disposable income gained from the Tax Reduction Act was spent in 1976 rather than in 1975. Thus, somewhat ironically, while fiscal policy failed to give the economy much of a boost around the business cycle trough, the lagged effects of the tax cut helped stretch the recovery out and may have prevented it from being still-born.

5. The Worried Investor

The weakness of investment demand during the entire 1973–1976 period, and indeed continuing into 1977 as well, has by now become almost legendary. The basic data on investment and its principal components during the cyclical contraction and expansion are presented in Table 4-6.

---

[13] Readers may be wondering how the estimated consumption function manages to track behavior in 1975:2 so well while most consumption functions substantially overestimate spending in this quarter. The answer lies in the special treatment accorded to temporary tax changes that will be explained in Chapter 7.

TABLE 4-6
Changes in Real Fixed Investment and Its Components, 1973–1976[a]

	From 1973:4 to 1975:1	From 1975:1 to 1976:4
	Percentage changes	
Fixed Investment (186.4)	−17.4	+13.4
Residential (54.0)	−32.8	+43.5
Business (132.4)	−11.1	+ 4.1
Equipment (86.7)	− 7.6	+ 5.0
Structures (45.7)	−17.7	+ 2.1
	Absolute changes[b]	
Fixed Investment	−32.4	+20.6
Residential	−17.7	+15.8
Business	−14.7	+ 4.8
Equipment	− 6.6	+ 4.0
Structures	− 8.1	+ 0.8

[a]Source: Survey of Current Business
[b]In billions of 1972 dollars.

The number in parentheses next to each title is the level of that series in 1973:4.

The table reveals the dominant role played by residential construction in the 1973–1976 cycle. While homebuilding normally accounts for between one-quarter and one-third of fixed investment, the decline in residential investment accounted for more than half of the decline in fixed investment during the business cycle downturn and for most of the rise in investment during the first 7 quarters of the cyclical upswing.[14]

This strongly procyclical behavior of residential construction was unusual and significant for understanding why the recession was so deep. The typical pattern in previous recessions was for a rise in homebuilding to cushion the downswing as declining demands for money and credit eased financial conditions and made mortgage money flow freely. Conversely, credit restrictions would typically put a damper on residential construction when the economy was booming. Quite the opposite happened in 1973–1976.

The reasons for the decline in housing investment are quite clear and

---

[14] If the downswing is dated from 1973:1—the quarter in which fixed investment peaked—homebuilding accounts for nearly three-quarters of the total decline.

well known. First, 1972 was an unprecedented boom year for housing: housing starts reached 2.4 million units, a level not attained before or since. This level of homebuilding was not sustainable and some over-building, which had to be corrected later, no doubt occurred. Second, inflation and other factors sent interest rates soaring to historic highs in 1974, and this applied the usual "double whammy" to construction. Regulation Q ceilings on the interest rates that thrift institutions are permitted to pay caused a massive outflow of funds from these institutions while, at the same time, usury ceilings on mortgage interest rates made home mortgages unattractive investments relative to, say, corporate and government bonds. Consequently, mortgage financing for residential construction virtually dried up, and housing starts fell to only about 1.2 million units in 1975.

After housing bottomed out in 1975:1, it began a fairly impressive rebound, which by 1976:4 had brought it almost back to its level of 1973:4.[15] Thus the consumer was the driving force behind the recovery in fixed investment as well as in consumption. As Table 4-6 shows, the recovery in business fixed investment was anemic: almost $15 billion was lost from cyclical peak to cyclical trough, but less than $5 billion was gained back from trough to 1976:4.

Closer examination of the table reveals that the weakness in business fixed investment came mainly in structures rather than in equipment. Despite the fact that investment in structures is normally about half as large as investment in equipment, the absolute decline from cyclical peak to cyclical trough was greater for structures. Perhaps even more significantly, whereas equipment spending showed some signs of life after bottoming out in 1975:4 (growing 12.7% over the next year), the recovery in spending on structures was virtually nonexistent.

Why did spending on industrial plant fall so much and then rise so little? There is as yet no professional agreement on this question, though several hypotheses have been offered.[16] One obvious reason was the precipitous decline in sales and capacity utilization during the recession. For example, the Federal Reserve Board's index of capacity utilization, which rose as high as 88% in July 1973, fell to an all-time low of 69.6% in March 1975.

A second hypothesis is that low rates of profit deterred investment spending. But in fact, when corrected for the effects of inflation, corporate profit rates were not abnormally low in the years 1975-1976—even

---

[15] This still left it, however, well below its 1973:1 peak.

[16] For clear discussions of this issue see *Economic Report of the President,* 1978, pp. 66–72, or Malkiel (1979).

without making any correction for the normal cyclical behavior of profits.[17] Furthermore, while both cash flow and corporate liquidity (however measured) deteriorated badly in 1974, both indicators of the financial soundness of corporations improved rapidly and markedly in 1975–1976. It is clear that it was not poor profits that impeded investment.[18]

Third, Malkiel (1979) and others have suggested that an increase in the perceived riskiness of investment—caused in part by the severity of the business cycle, in part by the unprecedented burst of inflation, and in part by government regulations of various kinds—damaged investment spending by raising the minimum required rate of return. If true, this factor would bear particularly heavily on long-lived investments such as industrial plants. Is there evidence for this hypothesis? While subjective uncertainties are, almost by definition, unmeasurable, they presumably manifest themselves in financial markets. In this regard, the failure of the stock market to rebound very much from its December 1974 low is interpreted as evidence of increased perceived riskiness. Table 4-7 offers some relevant data. On a monthly basis, the Standard & Poor's Composite Index of 500 stocks peaked in January 1973 and bottomed out in December 1974. From that point until December 1976 its predominant trend was upward, although there were some setbacks. When we correct these figures for changes in the price level, however, the rebound since late 1974 looks much weaker and the level of *real* stock market values in late 1976 is seen to be less than two-thirds of what it was in early 1973.

Because of this behavior, it may be possible to account for the sluggish investment performance during the recovery by the malaise of the stock market.[19] The explanation, to put it bluntly, is that investors were worried. This hypothesis has a certain cogency, since low stock prices imply a high cost of capital. Yet there is something troublesome about explaining one puzzling aspect of economic behavior (the weakness of investment spending) by another aspect of economic behavior that is even more puzzling (the weakness of the stock market). According to the old saying, the pot shouldn't call the kettle black.

Unfortunately, the data do not allow us to discriminate very well among the various hypotheses for why investment performance was so weak. Sales, capacity utilization, corporate cash flow, stock market prices, and other financial variables all deteriorated quickly during the downswing and the improved much more gradually during the recovery.

---

[17] See *Economic Report of the President*, 1978, pp. 68–69, and Malkiel (1979).

[18] This, of course, does not mean that the cause was not poor *expected* profits.

[19] The theory that stock market valuations of industrial assets are the principal determinant of investment has been pioneered by James Tobin and William Brainard. See, for example, Tobin and Brainard (1977).

TABLE 4-7
Stock Market Prices, 1973-1976

Price index	January 1973	December 1974	December 1976
Nominal price index[a]	118.42	67.07	104.66
Real price index[b]	92.73	43.16	60.05

[a]Standard & Poor's Composite Index (1941-1943 = 10).
[b]Standard & Poor's Composite Index divided by Consumer Price Index (1967 = 100).

Investment spending also behaved this way. Consequently, we have more explanations than we know what to do with. Apparently, the normal econometric relationships between investment in *equipment* and the aforementioned determinants held up well during 1975-1976. The situation is a little different, however, in the case of investment in *structures*, where actual spending in 1975 and 1976 remained somewhat below what the equations would have led us to predict.[20]

6. Loose Ends

There is nothing very surprising about the behavior of the other two components of final sales—government purchases and net exports—during the 1973-1976 period.

Government purchases of goods and services followed their typical trends in 1974 and 1975: federal purchases were essentially unchanged while state and local purchases rose about 3.2% per year. Certainly no one would have suspected that there was a major recession going on merely by looking at data on government purchases. Then in 1976 state and local spending came to a virtual halt—the first year of negligible growth in this series in the entire postwar period. Federal purchases were also unchanged. Thus instead of pursuing a countercyclical policy, the government sector (mainly state and local units) placed a small drag on the recovery.

Net exports displayed a very simple pattern. The balance of trade surplus grew steadily from about $2 billion in early 1973 to a whopping $25 billion by 1975:2, as we at first enjoyed the upward sloping portion of the J-curve, and then went into recession ahead of our trading partners.

[20] These conclusions are based on distilling the evidence in Kopcke (1977), von Furstenberg (1977), and some unpublished results of Peter K. Clark. It also agrees with the CEA's assessment (see *Economic Report of the President*, 1978, p. 71).

Consequently, foreign trade was propping up aggregate demand through-out the period. Thereafter, the trade surplus began to narrow (to $13 billion by 1976:4) as Europe's recession coincided with our recovery. Thus foreign trade was another drag on demand during the recovery.

7. The Great Productivity Puzzle

During recessions and recoveries, measured productivity—that is, output per hour of labor—normally displays a procyclical pattern; and the 1973-1976 business cycle was no exception to this rule. As can be seen in Figure 4-6, productivity in the non-farm business sector began to decline in early 1973 (just when growth in output began to stagnate), and continued falling until very near the cyclical trough. It then registered abnormally rapid gains for 2 quarters before resuming something akin to "normal" trend growth.

Two phenomena in the figure cry out for explanation. First, the decline in productivity during 1973 and 1974 was of an extraodinary magnitude—5%. On an annual basis, 1974 exhibits the only sizable decline in productivity levels in the entire postwar period. Second, the trend line that is drawn in Figure 4-6 shows that the losses of productivity were not entirely made up in the recovery.[21] Something like a 3% loss of productivity remained by mid 1975. (Then, from 1975:4 to 1977:4, the productivity growth rate was almost exactly equal to its 1967-1973 average of 1.9% per year.) It seems natural to ask: Why?

Before attempting to give an answer, I should state at the outset that there is today no widely accepted explanation that accounts *quantitatively* for the poor productivity performance. The 1973-1974 productivity drop remains a bit of a puzzle at this stage, and probably will continue to be the object of considerable research for years. Nonetheless, we can gain some *qualitative* understanding of the reasons for the productivity drop by considering the basic causes of fluctuations in productivity.

The most obvious cause of a drop in productivity would be if a given worker, working under unchanged conditions, became less efficient or less hard working. While this anthropomorphic interpretation of the word "productivity" probably best captures the layman's understanding of the word, it has precious little to do with the actual performance of measured productivity.

[21] The "underlying" trend in productivity for this period is quite controversial. The postwar trend since 1947 is about 2.4% per year, but recent years have displayed slower growth. The trend line drawn in the graph extrapolates the observed 1.91% annual growth rate of measured productivity between 1967 and 1973.

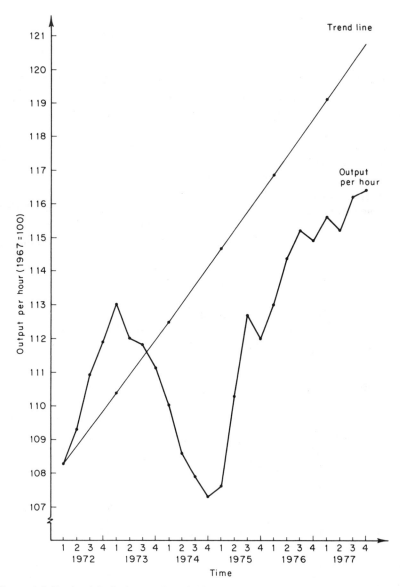

Figure 4-6. Productivity in the non-farm business sector, 1972–1977.

Measured productivity is the ratio of output to *measured* labor input, and the most important reason for cyclical movements in productivity is that official employment data are misleading indicators of actual labor input. Specifically, during cyclical contractions, employers normally are loath to fire workers—preferring instead to shunt labor into maintenance and other less essential tasks rather than the production of goods—until they are convinced that the downturn is not a temporary aberration. As a consequence, *measured* productivity (the ratio of output to *employed* labor) declines. Analogously, once a recovery starts, employers put these underutilized labor resources back on the production line. So output can expand briskly with little need for new hiring, and measured productivity registers dramatic gains.

Even a cursory look at the data makes it quite clear that a great deal of this was going on during the 1973–1975 period. Look at Table 4-8, which shows, in column (1), the productivity data that must be explained and, in the remaining columns, data relevant to the explanation. It is clear that hiring practices did not reflect the weakening economy during the last 3 quarters of 1973, nor even in the first half of 1974. During the last 3 quarters of 1973, employment grew 2.5% despite the fact the output grew only .6%. Then, in the first 2 quarters of 1974, while output was

TABLE 4-8
Percentage Changes in Productivity and Related Data, 1973–1976[a]

Quarter	(1) Output per hour[b]	(2) Output[b]	(3) Hours[b]	(4) Employment[b]	(5) Unemployment rate[c]
1973:1	3.9	11.3	7.1	7.0	5.0
2	− 3.5	0.8	4.4	4.0	4.9
3	− 0.8	1.4	2.2	2.5	4.8
4	− 2.4	0.3	2.7	3.7	4.8
1974:1	− 4.1	− 4.1	0.1	2.4	5.0
2	− 5.0	− 3.4	1.7	2.3	5.1
3	− 2.2	− 4.0	− 1.7	−0.9	5.6
4	− 2.3	− 9.1	− 7.0	−4.8	6.7
1975:1	1.1	−11.0	−11.9	−9.3	8.2
2	10.2	6.5	− 3.4	−3.3	8.9
3	9.1	12.5	3.1	2.5	8.5
4	− 2.4	3.7	6.2	4.0	8.3
1976:1	3.7	11.5	7.5	5.9	7.7
2	5.0	5.7	0.7	3.4	7.5
3	2.7	2.5	− 0.2	1.3	7.7
4	− 0.9	1.2	2.1	2.0	7.8

[a]*Source:* Bureau of Labor Statistics.
[b]Seasonally adjusted annual rate of change, in percentages, for the nonfarm business sector.
[c]In percentage points.

falling by 1.9%, employment *rose* another 1.2%.[22] These data certainly suggest that employers were overstocking labor. As a result, the unemployment rate was almost unchanged from early 1973 to 1974:2.

But then the recession found its way into the labor market. Employment began to decline in 1974:3, slowly at first but then at extraordinarily rapid rates. Consequently, unemployment rose from 5.6% in 1974:3 to 8.2% by 1975:1. Nonetheless, the pace of the layoffs was insufficient to keep pace with the snowballing collapse of production, so measured productivity (output per hour) continued its decline, finally reaching a bottom in 1974:4. Then, once the recovery got underway, employers used their surplus labor to expand production without increasing employment. During 1975:2 and 1975:3, output rose 4.6% while hours of labor were nearly unchanged. The consequence was that measured productivity surged upward at annual rates of 10 and 9% in these 2 quarters.

Another reason for the procyclical behavior of productivity change has to do with shifts in the composition of aggregate output over the business cycle. For example, it is well known that because the demand for durable goods displays great cyclical sensitivity, the share of durable manufacturing in total output declines in contractions and rises in recoveries. Since productivity in durable manufacturing is among the highest of all sectors, this shift in industrial composition makes overall productivity move procyclically even if no individual industry displays a procyclical productivity pattern. In fact, Nordhaus (1972) explained most of the last big productivity mystery by precisely this factor.

Using an equation developed by Peter K. Clark (1978), it is possible to estimate what the "normal" cyclical movement of productivity would have been for a business cycle as severe as we had in 1973–1975. The results are as follows.[23] Owing to the strong upsurge in industrial activity that ended in 1973:1, productivity in that quarter should have been about

---

[22] It will be noted, however, that the growth in *hours* was less than that in *employment*. The work week was shortening.

[23] Clark's equation is

$$h_t = -1.35 + .573y_t + .171y_{t-1} + .128y_{t-2} + .085y_{t-3}$$
$$+ .043y_{t-4} - .00662t + .002T_t + .0138D74 + .016D,$$

where h is the log of hours of work in the private non-farm business sector, y is the log of output, t is a time trend, T is a time trend beginning in 1965:3 (for the break in the productivity trend), $D74$ is a dummy variable equal to 1 in 1974 only, and D is a dummy variable equal to 1 in 1975–1977. A little manipulation translates this into the following equation for the log of productivity:

$$y_t - h_t = 1.35 + .427\Delta y_t + .256\Delta y_{t-1} + .128\Delta y_{t-2} + .043\Delta y_{t-3}$$
$$+ .00662t - .002T - .0138D74 - .016D.$$

The calcuations in the text are made with these equations.

2% above trend (see also Figure 4-6). Over the ensuing 7 quarters until the cyclical trough in 1974:4, output per hour in the non-farm business sector should have declined by about 3.4% *relative to trend*. Since the normal trend increase over this period should have been 3.2%, the net predicted decline in the level of productivity is only .2%. But actual productivity fell 5%; so there is an enormous productivity shortfall that cannot be explained by the severity of the recession. In the 4 quarters from 1974:4 to 1975:4, output grew quite strongly and Clark's equation suggests a cyclical productivity correction of 2.7%. Coupled with the 1.9% normal trend growth, output per hour should have advanced by 4.6%. In fact, it rose 4.4% or roughly as expected. The net outcome of all of this, as can be seen in Figure 4-6, is that the economy wound up something like 3% below its "normal" productivity trend in early 1976— a gap that has not been made up since.

The changing composition of the labor force has also been cited frequently as a cause of productivity slowdown in recent years. Specifically, since it is widely believed that prime age males have higher productivity than teenagers and females, the increasing importance of the latter two groups in the labor force should reduce measured productivity *even if no individual demographic group has declining productivity*. But while this factor can help explain the apparent secular slowdown in productivity growth in the last decade, it evolves too gradually to shed any light on the events of 1973 and 1974.[24]

A final class of explanations for falling productivity centers on the idea that labor will be less productive if it has a less generous supply of cooperating factors to work with. In the context of the mid 1970s, two particular factors suggest themselves. First, the enormous rise in the prices of all energy resources led businesses to economize on the use of energy wherever possible. Second, the weak investment performance beginning in 1973 depressed the capital stock of 1974–1976. Notice that *permanent* changes in the ratio of energy and/or capital to labor ought, in theory, to produce *one-time reductions* in productivity without necessarily affecting the underlying productivity *trend*. Thus the shrinking supplies of energy and capital seem to be natural candidates to explain what appears to have been a "permanent" loss of perhaps 3% in productivity.

Consider first the energy problem. If the elasticity of output with respect to energy inputs is around .1, then a 10% decline in the ratio of energy to labor will produce a 1% decline in the ratio of output to labor. But how much substitution of labor for energy can we reasonably expect? Holding output and other factor prices constant, the elasticity of labor

[24] See Clark (1978, pp. 968–970).

productivity with respect to the price of energy is the negative of the elasticity of labor demand with respect to the price of energy.[25] Berndt and Wood (1975) have estimated the latter parameter to be about .03 for U.S. manufacturing. Since the wholesale price of energy increased 64% from October 1973 to October 1974, this estimate suggests that labor productivity might be expected to fall about 1.9% on this account. This accounts for about two-thirds of the productivity shortfall, but opportunities to substitute labor for energy are quite limited in the short run. Thus, contrary to what is often claimed, it is hard to explain the *immediate* drop in productivity in 1973–1974 by energy prices. However, energy prices can be a factor explaining a widening productivity gap over time as firms adjust their energy/labor ratios downward.

Now consider capital. If the elasticity of output with respect to capital inputs is around .2, then a 5% decline in the capital–labor ratio would produce a 1% drop in labor's productivity. Since this represents less than 1 year's normal gross investment, it seems plausible that the sluggish investment performance might have cost us this much capital. A careful analysis of this effect by Clark (1978) comes close to supporting this back-of-the-envelope calculation. According to his estimates, the actual observed slowdown in the growth rate of the stock of fixed nonresidential capital over the 1973–1976 period can account for a decline in the *growth rate* of productivity of between .16 and .37 percentage points.[26] Compounded over 3 years, this would amount to a decline of between .5 and 1.1% in the *level* of productivity.

Thus it does not seem outlandish to think that the reductions in energy and capital inputs, relative to labor, during 1973–1976 could have reduced the average productivity of labor by something like 3%. However, these explanations will *not* explain how this all could have happened so quickly in 1973–1974. Therein lies the mystery.[27]

---

[25] Let L be labor, P the price of energy, and Y output. Then

$$\frac{\partial \log(Y/L)}{\partial \log P} = -\frac{\partial \log L}{\partial \log P}$$

when Y is held constant.

[26] The total retardation in the productivity growth rate in 1973–1976 (as compared to 1965–1973) was 1.25 percentage points. So it is clear that weak investment performance is very far from a full explanation. However, it should be noted that this hypothesis has more success in explaining the apparent slowdown in the 1965–1973 period (as compared with 1955–1965).

[27] The tremendous realignment of relative factor prices caused by OPEC has been likened to a "destruction of capital" in that it made much of the existing capital stock economically inefficient (i.e., too energy intensive). However, unless this inefficiency was so monumental that it actually paid firms to discard their old plant and equipment, this argument cannot account for the sharp drop in productivity. In the absence of good data on scrappage, we cannot assess the quantitative importance of this idea.

8. Summary

The recession that began in late 1973 and ended in early 1975 was the longest and deepest in our postwar history, while the subsequent recovery period was more hesitant and modest. Three years after the trough, the United States economy had still not regained the levels of unemployment and capacity utilization it had reached in 1973. And it now seems that those buoyant conditions will not be seen again for many years to come. It is as if the economy slipped off a precipice, tumbled rapidly and roughly to the valley floor, and has been struggling its way uphill ever since.

Inventory movements both obscured the timing and exaggerated the severity of the Great Recession. The decline in real final sales lasted longer, but was less than half as large as the decline in real GNP. Yet the fact that inventory accumulation continued in late 1973 and early 1974 despite deteriorating sales does not appear to have been a clear early warning signal of the burgeoning recession, since most industries seem to have entered this period with depleted inventories.

While it is traditional for business cycle analysts to focus on investment, much of the "action" in the 1973–1976 cycle was with the consumer. One major mystery of the period is why consumer spending collapsed so precipitously in the closing months of 1974. Perhaps economists' inability to explain this phenomenon—even after the fact—carries a simple message: people were just plain scared. Then, once we hit bottom, it was the strength of consumer spending that carried the economy out of the abyss. Even the investment component of aggregate demand was dominated by consumer behavior. Both the catastrophe in residential construction in 1973 and 1974, and its rebound in 1975 and 1976, were far more pronounced than the corresponding gyrations in business fixed investment. While business spending was weak throughout the period, there are ample explanations—in fact, too many—for this anemia.

Measured productivity—that is, output per hour of employed labor— took a nose dive in 1973 and 1974 that is unprecedented, and recovered only part way. No one yet has been able to come up with a convincing and complete explanation of this laggard productivity performance, although the low levels of investment and the stunning increases in the prices of energy resources probably both played some role.

In sum, we learned in the mid 1970s that the optimistic reports of the death of the business cycle that had circulated in the halcyon 1960s were vastly exaggerated. Despite all the knowledge of fiscal and monetary policy that had accumulated over a period of 30 years, our economy suffered a recession whose severity many economists would have thought impossible just a few years earlier. The Great Recession shook the confidence of consumers, apparently destroyed the confidence of investors, and left much of the economics profession with what appeared to be egg on its face. Did we have the tools and knowledge to prevent the Great Recession? Did the recession invalidate existing Keynesian theory in the way that the Great Depression invalidated classical monetary theory? Could it all happen again? I argue in subsequent chapters that the answers to these three crucial questions are yes, no, and maybe, respectively.

5

the anatomy of the great inflation

Some circumstantial evidence is very strong,
as when you find a trout in the milk.
—Henry David Thoreau

Though inflation has been a major item on the national agenda in the United States since around 1966, it was the rapid acceleration of prices in 1973 and 1974 that thrust it into the kind of prominence that led President Ford to brand inflation as "public enemy number one." The annual rate of increase of consumer prices averaged 4.6% during the 1969–1972 period—already more than double its historic value.[1] Then inflation rose ominously to 8.8% during 1973, and to the dizzying height of 12.2% during 1974.

This tremendous acceleration in inflation had profound effects on national economic policy. The inflationary events of 1973 quite clearly led to a stiffening of price controls in the summer of 1973 (the so-called "Freeze II"),[2] and may also help to account for the tightening of both monetary and fiscal policy. Furthermore, there is ample documentary evidence—to be presented in Chapters 7 and 8—that it was a preoccupation with inflation in 1974 that prevented any decisive monetary or fiscal policy actions that might have arrested the burgeoning recession.

---

[1] Based on the Consumer Price Index, which rose at an annual rate of 2.2% between 1949 and 1969.

[2] See Kosters (1975, esp. pp. 23–26) and Shultz and Dam (1977, p. 74).

On the contrary, the Federal Reserve gave its already tight monetary policies a further tightening in the second half of the year. And the President of the United States wound up in the absurd position of calling for a tax *increase* in October 1974, just when the recession was assuming epidemic proportions—a recommendation that might have been comical were it not for its grave consequences.

Just what was going on in this country in 1973 and 1974 that led to such attitudes? Why did inflation accelerate so dramatically in 1973 and 1974, and then decelerate just as quickly in 1975? Part of the answer is well known. Food prices and energy prices played major roles in both the 1973-1974 acceleration of inflation and the 1975 deceleration. It is also widely, but not universally, believed that the elimination of wage–price controls in April 1974 was an important factor contributing to the wild gyrations in the inflation rate. Finally, we have the recession itself as a candidate for why the inflation rate dropped so quickly. How important were each of these factors in the U.S. in 1973-1975?

Since this is a long chapter, it will help focus the discussion if I outline the basic argument before delving into the evidence. I begin by showing that first food prices and then energy prices account for most of the 1973-1974 acceleration, but that the spurt of energy inflation was so brief that overall inflation would have decelerated much sooner than it did were it not for a further fillip from non-food non-energy prices in 1974. More specifically, I show that, when the *direct* contributions of food prices and energy prices are removed from the price indexes, what appears to have been a steady mounting of the inflation rate from early 1973 until about the third quarter of 1974 turns into a sharp, but brief, burst of double-digit inflation in the last 3 quarters of 1974. I then argue that this outbreak of additional inflation was the economy's way of adjusting to two major events that required large-scale readjustments of *relative prices*: the rise in energy prices caused by OPEC's actions, and the end of wage–price controls. In a world in which there is considerable (though not complete) price rigidity in the downward direction, such dramatic changes in relative prices can only be accomplished through a rise in the *absolute price level*. Since this rise in the price level does not happen all at once, but takes some time, the *rate of inflation* is *temporarily* increased. Thus the very same factors that made inflation accelerate in early 1974 caused it to decelerate in early 1975. Since empirical research on wage and price inflation points to long lags between changes in aggregate demand and changes in the inflation rate, the alternative view that the recession accounted for most of the decline in inflation by early 1975 seems completely untenable. The recession did play a role, however, in preventing the inflation rate from going still higher and in the further moderation of inflation in late 1975 and throughout 1976.

1. The Inflationary Bulge of 1973–1974

In studying the incredible price performance of the 1973–1974 period, I focus on two measures of consumer price inflation: the Consumer Price Index (CPI) and the deflator for personal consumption expenditures (PCE deflator). The quarter-by-quarter performance of the consumption deflator is depicted by the line labeled PCE in Figure 5-1, and it is clear that we really have *two* distinct accelerations to explain. The first is an increase in the annual inflation rate from an average of about 3.5% during 1972 to an average of about 6.5% during the first 3 quarters of 1973. The second is a further increase to an average annual inflation rate of about 11.5% during the 5 quarters from 1973:4 through 1974:4.

The first acceleration is easy to explain. Food prices, which had increased about 5% during 1972, rose at a 15% annual rate during the first 3 quarters of 1973. With roughly a 20% weight in the overall index, this

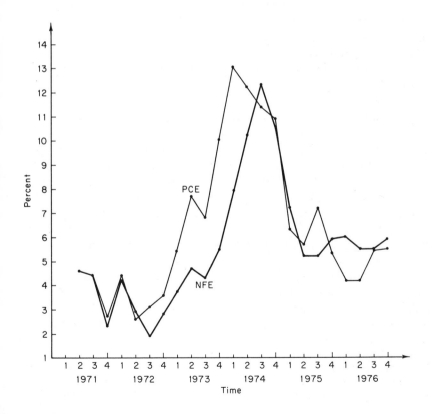

Figure 5-1. Two measures of the inflation rate, quarterly data, 1971–1976.

10-point acceleration in food prices added about 2 points to the inflation rate. Thereafter, while rapidly rising food prices remained a mainspring of *high* inflation throughout 1973 and 1974, food prices ceased being a cause of *accelerating* inflation. Energy was really not yet much of a factor in early 1973, so it was faster increases of non-food non-energy prices that accounted for the remaining 1 percentage point of the acceleration. These increases, in turn, probably reflected the high levels of aggregate demand in 1972 and 1973.

The second acceleration of inflation, from 6.5 to 11.5%, came in two stages. First came the celebrated "energy shock," mainly in 1973:4 and the first half of 1974. During those 3 quarters, retail energy prices rose at an annual rate of 44% (compared with 8% in the previous 3 quarters). Given the weight of energy prices in the overall consumption deflator, this performance was enough to add about 2.5 percentage points to the annual inflation rate—about half the acceleration. The second stage of the acceleration, however, was fueled by non-food and non-energy prices, which really took off starting in 1974:1. (See the line labeled NFE in Figure 5-1, which shows the behavior of a deflator purged of food and energy prices.) A principal goal of this chapter is to explain this acceleration of non-food non-energy prices.

In early 1975, the inflation rate tumbled down to more normal rates (see Figure 5-1 again). But, contrary to what many people believe, this chapter will show that energy prices had almost nothing to do with the deceleration. The return of food inflation to more normal rates (from a 12.5% annual rate in 1974 to a little over 6% in 1975) made a minor contribution—lopping about 1.25 percentage points off the annual inflation rate. But most of the sudden deceleration came from non-food non-energy prices, which rose 10.2% in 1974 but only 5.9% in 1975. This chapter seeks to explain this phenomenon as well.

At this point a closer look at Figure 5-1 may be in order. The consumption deflator (PCE) exhibits a marked acceleration in the inflation rate beginning in about 1973:1 and continuing to mount until 1974:1, with the period of double-digit inflation lasting for the 5 quarters from 1973:4 through 1974:4. However, if we study the specially constructed non-food and non-energy (NFE) deflator,[3] the inflation rate does not really show a sharp acceleration until 1973:4, and the (roughly) double-digit rates lasted only from 1974:2 until 1974:4. The drops in the two series from their 1974 peaks are almost exactly the same.

---

[3] Energy includes gasoline and oil, fuel oil and coal, electricity, and gas. They have a combined weight of about 6.5% in total consumption, while food has about 20%. Since the NFE deflator is an unpublished index, the data are given as an appendix to this chapter (Table 5-A1).

What one reads into graphs like these invariably depends, to an extent, on one's preconceptions. To me, the plot of the consumption deflator (PCE) suggests a persistent building of inflation over a period of roughly 2 years (late 1972 to late 1974), at which point the "bubble" was punctured. By contrast, the graph of inflation in the non-food and non-energy deflator (NFE) shows an economy with a basic inflation rate of, perhaps, 4% suffering a tremendous inflationary shock in the 3 quarters between 1974:1 and 1974:4, before returning to more normal behavior.

Each broad picture, in turn, suggests a story about *why* inflation accelerated and then decelerated. The behavior of the consumption deflator is suggestive of an economy that was pumped up by monetary and fiscal policy during 1971-1972, causing rising inflation in 1972-1974, and which then had the rug pulled out from under it by the recession in late 1974. The inference is that the state of aggregate demand can explain much of the gyrations in the inflation rate during 1973-1975. The movements of the deflator purged of food and energy prices seem to call for a different explanation—one involving a one-shot rise in the *price level* that led to extraordinary inflation rates over 3 quarters, after which the economy settled back to its "baseline" rate of inflation.[4] The massive realignment of relative prices caused by OPEC and the end of formal wage-price controls in 1974 are obvious candidates for this one-time shock.

In this context, it is worth recalling the distinction made in Chapter 2 between steady continuing *inflation* and one-shot adjustments to the *price level*. The former typically is caused by rapid growth of the money supply, and manifests itself as a broad-based increase in the price indexes. The latter may be caused by any of a variety of "special factors" and, because of its special nature, the inflation it engenders is likely to be concentrated in a few specially affected items.

Clearly, detailed analysis is required before we can form an informed judgment on the relative importance of aggregate demand, and such special factors as energy prices and the lifting of controls, in explaining the roller coaster pattern of the inflation rate. The existing empirical evidence on this question will be marshaled in this chapter and the next. But the stunning behavior of food and energy prices in 1973-1974, and the reasons for that behavior, already casts serious doubt on the view that excessive aggregate demand caused the explosion of inflation in 1974.

With a bit more noise due to the monthly observations, the behavior of the Consumer Price Index tells much the same story (see Figure 5-2). If we look at the all-items CPI, the jump to higher rates of inflation seems

---

[4] That the one-time shock to the price level would raise the "baseline" rate for a period of time is an obvious implication of lags in wage setting and in inflationary expectations.

to occur in early 1973. But if we look at a CPI for all items except food and energy, while there is certainly a perceptible quickening of inflation between early 1973 and early 1974, the big jump clearly comes in early to middle 1974.

It seems clear, then, that if we are to understand the anatomy of the Great Inflation it is essential to deal separately with energy prices, food prices, and other prices. Since energy prices have received the most notoriety, I begin the story there.

2. Energy Prices: The High Cost of Heating

It is not in dispute that the decisions of OPEC were the dominating force in the determination of energy prices throughout the 1973-1975 period, although U.S. price controls—which remained on oil long after they were removed from almost everything else—certainly played a supporting role.

The big run-up in the average price of crude oil in the U.S. began with the Arab oil embargo during the 1973 war between Israel and the Arab states. Between October 1973 and February 1974 crude oil rose in price by roughly $1 per barrel per month—from about $4.50 per barrel to about $8.50 per barrel.[5] Retail prices for most energy products reflected this with very little lag. The CPI for gasoline and motor oil, for example, skyrocketed 34% from September 1973 to March 1974. Prices for fuel oil and coal increased 26% in only 3 months and 67% within a year. Rates for electricity and gas displayed a more muted and drawn out pattern, probably because of the many price regulations on natural gas and electrical utilities, but nonetheless increased 23% in 15 months.

While these are all large numbers, it is useful to keep in mind that purchases of energy account for only about 6.5% of total consumer expenditures. So their *direct* weight in the overall price indexes was rather small.

There seem to be two important questions to be asked about the energy shock. First, to what extent did energy prices account for the inflationary bulge of 1973-1974? Second, to what extent did this external inflationary shock account for the Great Recession of 1974-1975?

---

[5] See Perry (1975a Table 2-3; p. 79). The prices cited are the blend price of imported oil, domestic uncontrolled oil, and domestic "old" oil. The rise in import prices was substantially greater.

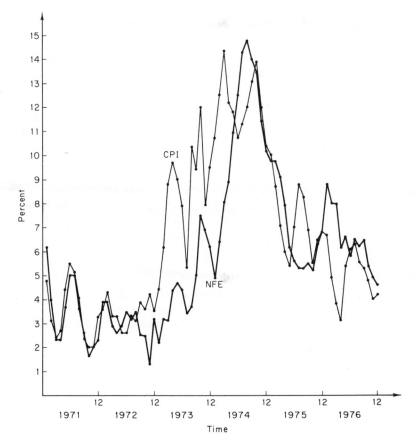

Figure 5-2. Two measures of the inflation rate, monthly data, 1971-1976. (*Note:* Data plotted are seasonally adjusted annual rates of change over the previous 3 months.)

METHODOLOGY

A full answer must proceed in four steps, and even these omit many details. Since these same steps apply to the analysis of food prices later in this chapter, and to price controls in Chapter 6, it is worth spelling them out in detail.

Step 1. What were the direct arithmetical effects of energy prices on the overall price indexes? This just consists of computations based on the definitions of the indexes.

Step 2. What other prices were pushed up *directly* by the shock, though perhaps with a lag? In the case of energy prices, there are two sorts of after-shocks. First, only about half of U.S. energy usage is consumed directly (gasoline, home heating oil, etc.). The rest is used for industrial purposes, and the higher costs of energy can be expected to be passed on to consumers in the form of higher prices for non-energy consumer goods. Second, when OPEC raised the price of imported oil, domestic oil prices were pulled along (though not completely because of price controls). Close substitutes for oil—especially coal and the uncontrolled portion of natural gas—also rose in price.

Steps 1 and 2 measure what may be called the "exogenous shock" in that it cannot be explained by normal macroeconomic relationships, but must be calculated outside of the structure of macromodels. The next two steps involve using macromodels to assess the consequences of these shocks.

Step 3. Any initial shock to the price level will be stretched out and magnified by the usual wage–price spiral. Higher prices lead to higher wage settlements, which, in turn, lead to still higher prices. Conceptually, we may think of any conventional wage-price model as taking the following form:

$$\dot{p} = a + \sum_{j=0}^{n} b_j \dot{w}_{t-j}, \qquad (5.1)$$

$$\dot{w}_t = \alpha + \sum_{i=0}^{m} \beta_i \dot{p}_{t-i}, \qquad (5.2)$$

where $\dot{p}$ is the rate of inflation, $\dot{w}$ is the rate of change of money wages, a includes all the non-wage influences on price inflation, and α includes all the non-price influences on wage inflation. From these two equations, it is easy to derive the final difference equation for the inflation rate and trace out the distributed lag effects of any one-time shock to the *inflation rate* [a change in the constant a in Eq. (5.1) for one period only]. In particular, the solution to (5.1) and (5.2) is

$$\dot{p}_t = A + \sum_{k=1}^{n+m} \gamma_k \dot{p}_{t-k} \qquad (5.3)$$

where

$$A = \frac{a + \alpha \Sigma b}{1 - b_0 \beta_0} \quad \text{and} \quad \gamma_k = \frac{\sum_{i+j=k} b_j \beta_i}{1 - b_0 \beta_0} \ .$$

For purposes of this book, I have estimated the parameters of (5.3) by using the price and wage equations of the 1977 version of the MPS model. (Other empirical models gave very similar results.) The implied γ_k coefficients for selected quarters are given in Table 5-1, which also shows the cumulative effects on the price level. A word of explanation is in order. Like most current wage–price systems, the MPS equations are virtually "accelerationist." Specifically, the sum of the coefficients on wages in the price equation is 1.0 while the sum of the coefficients on prices in the wage equation is .95. Since the product of these is .95, (5.3) turns out to be a difference equation that is just barely stable. Because shocks are estimated to damp down so slowly—Table 5-1 shows that even after 100 quarters convergence is far from complete—it takes an inordinate amount of time to wring an inflationary shock out of the system. In the meanwhile, the cumulative effect on the price level builds to a large multiple of the initial shock.

TABLE 5-1
Effects of 1% Exogenous Shock to the Inflation Rate of Quarter t on Inflation and the Price Level in Quarter $t + j$ [a]

Lag j	Effect on inflation rate [b]	Effect on price level (%)
0	1.00	.25
1	.046	.26
2	.074	.28
3	.092	.30
4	.103	.33
5	.111	.36
6	.116	.39
7	.120	.42
8	.123	.45
9	.126	.48
10	.129	.51
11	.131	.54
12	.134	.58
16	.121	.70
20	.119	.82
24	.116	.94
32	.109	1.16
40	.103	1.38
100	.068	2.68

[a] Calculated as described in text.
[b] All inflation rates are annual rates in percentage points.

Thus, when I use Table 5-1 to simulate the effects of various inflationary shocks over time horizons of a few years, the reader should remember that the model actually implies that these effects keep building for many, many years. This conclusion, which seems vaguely implausible on its face, is an inescapable feature of empirical models that have long lags in wage and price setting and also roughly obey the natural rate hypothesis.[6]

Step 4. It is by now well known that exogenous inflationary shocks can have contractionary effects on output through channels such as those described in Chapters 2 and 3. The Step 3 calculation abstracts from these by holding the constants a and α fixed after the initial shock. Since a normally includes some measure of product–market demand,[7] and α normally includes some measure of labor market tightness,[8] the tacit assumption is that monetary and fiscal policies react to the shock by maintaining the level of real economic activity. An alternative assumption—which seems closer to the events of 1973–1975—is that policymakers do not adjust policy after the shock, but adhere to their previous plans. In this case, real output will fall and the inflation will be mitigated somewhat. Naturally, this complex chain of events can be measured only by simulating a complete macromodel. Fortunately, however, two published studies have done this for the oil price shock of 1973–1974.[9] Their results are summarized below.

RESULTS

The direct arithmetical effects of energy prices are the easiest to calculate, and are displayed in the first few lines of Table 5-2. Three periods of time are distinguished in this and the following tables; they are called the *prepeak period* (1973:2 to 1974:1), the *peak period* (1974:1 to 1974:4), and the *postpeak period* (1974:4 to 1975:3). The selection of these three periods for detailed study was dictated by the behavior of the deflator for non-food non-energy items, which showed a very pronounced acceleration during the peak quarters (see Table 5-7 to follow). Pre- and

[6] One explanation for this is that, in order to maintain real economic activity in the face of ever-increasing prices, more money must continually be injected into the system.

[7] In the MPS price equation, this is the current and lagged ratio of unfilled orders for producers' durables to investment in producers' durables.

[8] In the MPS wage equation, this is the reciprocal and first difference of the overall unemployment rate.

[9] Pierce and Enzler (1974) and Perry (1975a).

TABLE 5-2
Contribution of Energy Price Inflation to Overall Inflation in the Deflator for Personal
Consumption Expenditures (PCE), 1973:2–1975:3[a]

	Prepeak (1973:2– 1974:1)	Peak (1974:1– 1974:4)	Postpeak (1974:4– 1975:3)
(1) 3-quarter inflation rate	24.8	10.4	8.7
(2) Seasonally adjusted annual rate	34.4	14.1	11.7
(3) Direct contribution to PCE inflation[b]	1.7	0.8	0.7
(4) Indirect contribution to PCE inflation[b]	0.3	0.8	1.1
Contribution to acceleration (+) or deceleration (−):			
(5) Direct		− .9	− .1
(6) Indirect		+ .5	+ .3
(7) Total		− .4	+ .2

[a]All figures are in percentage points.
[b]Based on 3-quarter inflation rates.

postpeak periods of 3 quarters duration were chosen for the sake of symmetry. As I noted earlier, direct energy inflation occurred mainly in the last quarter of 1973 and the first 2 quarters of 1974. Thus energy inflation was more virulent during the prepeak period than during the peak period (see lines 1 and 2 in Table 5-2). Given the (variable) weights of energy prices, the *direct* contribution of energy to the overall rise in the consumption deflator was 1.7 percentage points during the 3 prepeak quarters, an additional .8 points during the peak period, and a further .7 points during the postpeak quarters (line 3 of Table 5-2). On this account, then, energy prices served to reduce the acceleration of inflation by almost a full percentage point, and had virtually nothing to do with the deceleration (line 5 of Table 5-2).

But the timing of the indirect effects was quite different, owing to lags in wage and price setting. Using the coefficients of Table 5-1, and treating each quarter's energy inflation as a separate shock, it is possible to compute the indirect effects (through the wage–price spiral) of all the energy inflation from 1970:4 through 1975:3. The results are displayed in line 4 of Table 5-2, and they show that the indirect effects continued to build through the 2-year period. Thus the lagged effects made a moderate contribution to the acceleration of inflation (.5 percentage points), but then reduced the deceleration (by about .3 percentage points).

Putting these two effects together (line 7 of Table 5-2), I conclude that, *holding aggregate demand constant*, energy prices helped to mask both the 1973–1974 acceleration in inflation and the 1974–1975 deceleration. But neither effect was very large.

However, many have argued, and I agree, that aggregate demand should not be held constant in making this assessment. The aftermath of the Arab oil embargo was, after all, one of the major causes of the Great Recession. And it may well be that the inflation it engendered made monetary and fiscal policies *tighter* than they otherwise would have been.

Pierce and Enzler (1974) and Perry (1975a) have used an earlier version of the MIT–Penn–SSRC (MPS) model to simulate the effects of the oil price hikes on the economy under the assumption that monetary and fiscal policies were *unchanged*. By this they mean that the paths of the money supply and the usual fiscal policy instruments are identical in both the control and shock simulations.[10] My examination of the documentary evidence on monetary and fiscal policy in Chapters 7 and 8 suggests that this is a reasonable characterization of policy, at least until the income tax cuts of 1975:2.

Since energy prices are not among the exogenous variables of the MPS model, some ingenuity is required to enter an oil shock into the model, and the methods used by Pierce and Enzler and by Perry differ somewhat. To Pierce and Enzler, the shock consisted of the rise in the cost of imported oil and the sympathetic price hikes for domestic oil and nonoil energy resources. They entered the higher cost of imported oil into the model by raising the deflator for nondurables and services by 2% relative to the private non-farm business deflator. Then, to account for higher *domestic* energy prices, they raised the private non-farm business deflator by 1% relative to labor costs. Thus, in combination, the deflator for consumption of nondurables and services was increased by about 3%. However, since the private non-farm business deflator is the central price index in the MPS model, affecting many other endogenous prices, it is hard to summarize the Pierce–Enzler shock by a single number.

This task is easier for Perry, who operated directly on the consumption deflator.[11] To Perry, the energy shock included the direct effect of higher (imported and domestic) oil prices on consumer items like gasoline and

---

[10] There is a minor difference in the specification of fiscal policy between the two studies. Perry assumes that *nominal* federal purchases are exogenous (so real purchases fall), while Pierce and Enzler assume that *real* purchases are exogenous (so nominal purchases rise). This is one reason to expect slightly stronger effects from Perry's simulation. Perry also ran an analogous simulation using the Michigan model, with broadly similar results.

[11] Consumption in the MPS model differs from consumer expenditures in the national income accounts in that the former excludes purchases of durable goods but includes their imputed service yield.

home heating oil *and* a crude estimate of the cost-push effect of higher energy prices on the prices of other consumer items. He made no attempt to include any sympathetic price hikes for nonoil energy resources, which are small in any case. Taking 1973:3 as the base quarter, Perry entered the oil shock by increasing the consumption deflator by the following percentages:

1973:3 and earlier	1973:4	1974:1	1974:2	1974:3	1974:4 and later
0	.62%	2.37%	3.40%	3.47%	3.55%

This seems to be slightly larger than the shock entered by Pierce and Enzler, which helps account for the slightly stronger effects obtained by Perry.

As a comparison, I have computed the implied *direct* effects of energy prices on the overall *level* of the deflator for personal consumption expenditures from the inflation data that underlie Table 5-2. These are as follows:

1973:4	1974:1	1974:2	1974:3	1974:4
.59%	1.70%	2.22%	2.37%	2.41%

The difference between these two series gives a rough idea of the importance of the effects of oil prices in raising the prices of nonoil consumer goods (what I called Step 2 above).[12]

With this understood, I turn now to the results obtained by Pierce and Enzler and by Perry.[13] Table 5-3 shows the estimated effects on real GNP (in 1972 dollars)[14] and the consumption deflator.[15] The two sets of esti-

---

[12] It gives only a rough idea because of the difference between consumption and consumer expenditures, and because my numbers include all energy sources while Perry's include only oil.

[13] The two studies differ in some other minor respects. Pierce and Enzler made alterations to the money demand and wage equations in the basic MPS model that Perry did not. Perry assumed a direct downward effect of the higher oil prices on automobile sales that averaged $4.9 billion in 1958 dollars (roughly $6.8 billion in 1972 dollars) during the 4 quarters 1973:4–1974:3. Pierce and Enzler did not.

[14] Perry reports his in 1973 dollars, and Pierce and Enzler in 1958 dollars. I converted both of these to 1972 dollars by using the GNP deflator.

[15] For Pierce and Enzler, the effects on the (1972 base) consumption deflator are inferred from their reported effects on the inflation rate. For Perry, who does not report effects on the consumption deflator, a more laborious procedure was necessary. From his reported *absolute* changes in nominal consumption C and real consumption c, the corresponding *percentage* changes were computed. From this the implied percentage changes in the consumption deflator $P = C/c$ were computed by the identity

$$\frac{\Delta P}{P} = \frac{\Delta C}{C} - \frac{\Delta c}{c},$$

where the Δ notation denotes changes *relative to the control solution*. Effects on the price level were computed from these implied effects on the inflation rate.

TABLE 5-3
Estimated Effects of Higher Oil Prices on Economic Activity, Based on MPS Model[a]

| | Real GNP (in billions of 1972 dollars) | | Price deflator for consumption | | | |
| | | | Level (percentage) | | Inflation rate (percentage points) | |
Quarter	Perry	Pierce–Enzler	Perry	Pierce–Enzler	Perry	Pierce–Enzler
1973:4	− 5.1	− 4.4	0.6	1.1	2.4	4.3
1974:1	−15.1	−10.4	2.1	1.9	6.3	3.3
1974:2	−22.8	−17.3	3.0	2.6	3.3	2.7
1974:3	−28.0	−22.3	3.0	2.8	0.4	0.8
1974:4	−33.6	−26.9	3.3	2.9	0.8	0.6
1975:1	−35.0	−31.6	3.2	3.1	−0.2	0.7
1975:2	−35.9	−35.0	3.3	3.3	0.5	0.8
1975:3	−37.1	−37.4	3.6	3.5	0.9	0.8
1976:3	−37.4	−33.3	4.6	4.2	1.0	0.7

[a]*Sources:* Calculated by the author from data in Pierce and Enzler (1974, Table 8, pp. 48–49) and Perry (1975a, Table 2-8, pp. 96–97).

mates agree quite closely, which is hardly surprising. According to the MPS model, the oil shock alone is enough to account for a significant recession. The model suggests that by 1975:1 the energy shock had reduced real GNP by $31–35 billion—almost 3% of its actual value. This decline in output is just over half of the actual drop in real GNP from its 1973:4 cyclical peak to its 1975:1 trough.

These adverse effects on aggregate demand slowed inflation significantly, according to the estimates. By 1975:3, for example, the total effect on the price level in the simulation is just about equal to the original shock. Apparently, the depressing effect of reduced demand on prices just about counteracted what would otherwise have been a rather powerful wage–price spiral. To get a more quantitative estimate of the effect of demand, I have taken the oil shock used by Perry and passed it through the wage–price model that underlies Table 5-1 to produce the effects that the oil shock *would have had* on prices if policy had kept aggregate economic activity unchanged. The results are displayed in lines 2 and 5 of Table 5-4, where they are compared with the Perry and Pierce–Enzler results (lines 1 and 4). Apparently, the restrictive policy stance kept the *level* of consumer prices about 3% lower in 1976:3 than it would otherwise have been. The corresponding effect on the inflation rate was distributed almost equally over the 3 years from 1973:3, reducing inflation by about 1 percentage point each year.

TABLE 5-4
Effects of Higher Oil Prices on the Consumption Deflator

	Price level[c] in:		
	1974:3	1975:3	1976:3
(1) Monetary and fiscal policy fixed[a]	+2.9	+3.6	+4.4
(2) Aggregate demand fixed[b]	+3.9	+5.5	+7.4
(3) Difference (= effect of lower aggregate demand)	−1.0	−1.9	−3.0

	Inflation rate[c] during:		
	1973:3–1974:3	1974:3–1975:3	1975:3–1976:3
(4) Monetary and fiscal policy fixed[a]	+2.9	+0.6	+0.8
(5) Aggregate demand fixed[b]	+3.9	+1.5	+1.8
(6) Difference (= effect of lower aggregate demand)	−1.0	−0.9	−1.0

[a] Average of two simulations reported in Table 5-3.
[b] Based on wage-price model of Table 5-1.
[c] Price level and inflation rate figures are in percentage points.

Otto Eckstein (1978, Chapter 9) obtained very similar results with the Data Resources (DRI) model, which, unlike the MPS model, includes the wholesale price of energy among its exogenous variables. Eckstein defines the ''energy shock'' as the difference between actual energy prices and a hypothetical scenario in which wholesale energy prices rise at a steady 6% annual rate beginning in early 1973. He concludes that overall consumer prices would have been about 4% lower by the end of 1974 without the energy shock, while the recession would have been less than half as severe.[16]

[16] There is some ambiguity here over how to interpret Eckstein's results. The statment in the text is based on his finding that the peak-to-trough decline in real GNP was only 3.6% in his hypothetical scenario without an energy shock, whereas it appeared to be 7.8% in the early GNP data that Eckstein used. However, as noted in Chapter 4, revised data show the peak-to-trough decline in real GNP to have been only 5.7%.

The answers to the questions that begin this section, then, are as follows:

1. If we do the calculation holding monetary and fiscal policy fixed, the higher oil prices increased the price level by about 4.5% over a period of 3 years. About two-thirds of this was felt during the first year, so that the inflation rate for that year was raised by about 3%. Had real demand been maintained instead, prices would have risen about 4% in the first year and 7.5% over 3 years.
2. The oil crisis and its aftermath seem able to account for one-half or more of the 1973–1975 drop in real GNP.

3. Food Prices: The High Cost of Eating

The explosion in world food prices in 1972–1974, and the reasons for it, are probably too well known to merit a detailed account here. Some data on food price inflation are displayed in Table 5-5.

Retail food prices began their rapid ascent at the beginning of 1973, though movements in wholesale prices in the last half of 1972—caused by crop failures in several parts of the world, especially for grains, and by the fabled disappearance of the Peruvian anchovies—clearly presaged this.[17] With carryover stocks of grain very low in 1973, the world food market was beset by another series of adverse developments.[18] The Great Food Inflation persisted from 1973:1 right through to 1974:4, with only a little slackening in the middle 2 quarters of 1974.

Turning first to the direct arithmetical effects, the food price component of the deflator for personal consumption expenditure rose by 8% during the peak period (1974:1–1974:4) as compared to 13% in the prepeak period.[19] Given a weight of about .20 in the overall index, this means that food prices actually *reduced* the acceleration in inflation by about 1 percentage point. Then, since they rose by only 5.2% in the postpeak period, food prices contributed about .6 percentage point to the 1975 deceleration (see Table 5-6, line 5).

Since agricultural products probably are much less important as an industrial input than are, say, energy products, what I have called the Step 2 effects seem small enough to be ignored. In any case, I have no estimate of them.

Indirect effects through the wage–price spiral are calculated from the

---

[17] Bosworth (1973, pp. 268–269).
[18] For a list of these see Schnittker (1973, p. 504).
[19] All inflation rates in this paragraph are 3-quarter rates.

TABLE 5-5
Inflation Rate of Food Prices, 1972-1975[a, b]

	Year			
Quarter	1972	1973	1974	1975
1	7.7	12.3	17.8	4.6
2	2.5	18.3	11.5	5.1
3	5.4	15.4	7.1	11.6
4	6.5	19.2	13.7	3.5

[a]*Source: Survey of Current Business.*
[b]Quarterly percentage change at annual rate of deflator for food consumption, seasonally adjusted.

weights in Table 5-1 in the same way as for oil prices.[20] It turns out that during the 3-quarter prepeak period (1973:2-1974:1), food prices contributed 1.2% to the overall inflation rate, while during the peak period this contribution was 2%. However, the lagged effects of food inflation continued to grow in the postpeak period: its contribution to overall inflation during the first 3 quarters of 1975 was 2.6%. Line 7 of Table 5-6 summarizes both sets of findings. On balance, food prices were a continuing and major source of inflation throughout 1973:2-1975:3, but had little to do with either the acceleration or the deceleration.

Assessing the impacts of the higher food prices on real economic activity is more difficult. By comparison with the oil shock—which, under Perry's assumptions, raised the price level directly by 3.55%—the food shock is clearly larger. For example, if we define the food shock to be the increases in retail food prices that took place between 1972:4 and 1974:4, then it amounts to a *direct* increase in the consumption deflator of 5.73%.[21] But this does not necessarily mean that it should have commensurately larger depressing effects on real GNP, for at least two reasons. First, because the food shock was more gradual and spread out through time, the economy had an easier time adjusting to it. Second, unlike OPEC's actions, the increases in world food prices had favorable effects on the U.S. balance of trade. So the decline in aggregate demand was correspondingly muted.

The only econometric simulation of the real effects of the 1972-1974

[20] For purposes of computing indirect effects, all food inflation from 1970:4 to 1975:3 was included.

[21] This is the compound *direct* effect of the 8 quarters of food price inflation from 1972:4 to 1974:4, each weighted by its respective relative importance.

TABLE 5-6
Contribution of Food Price Inflation to Overall Inflation in the Deflator for Personal
Consumption Expenditures (PCE), 1973:2-1975:3[a]

	Prepeak (1973:2– 1974:1)	Peak (1974:1– 1974:4)	Postpeak (1974:4– 1975:3)
(1) 3-quarter inflation rate	12.9	7.9	5.2
(2) Seasonally adjusted annual rate	17.6	10.7	7.0
(3) Direct contribution to PCE inflation[b]	2.7	1.7	1.1
(4) Indirect contribution to PCE inflation[b]	1.2	2.0	2.6
Contribution to acceleration (+) or deceleration (−):			
(5) Direct		− 1.0	− .6
(6) Indirect		+ .8	+ .6
(7) Total		− .2	0

[a]All figures are in percentage points.
[b]Based on 3-quarter inflation rates.

food shock that I know of is Eckstein's (1978, Chapter 6) experiment
with the DRI model in which he "took out" the food shock by holding
wholesale agricultural prices to a 3% rate of increase after mid 1971.
Compared with actual history, this hypothetical scenario produces a
Consumer Price Index that is almost 4% lower by 1974:4, and an unemployment rate that is 1% lower. Thus Eckstein's estimates of these effects
of the food shock are comparable to his estimates for the energy shock
on the price side, but substantially smaller on the real output side.

4. Conclusion: The Effects of the Oil and Food Shocks

How important, then, were the oil and food price shocks to what
happened in the United States between the end of 1972 and the end of
1975? With a few heroic assumptions I can attempt an answer to this
question. I assume that:

1. We are to measure the effects of the shock on the assumption that
   monetary and fiscal policies were unchanged.
2. Over a horizon of 2 years or so the total effect on the price level is

roughly the same as the direct arithmetical effect, since the multi-plication through the wage-price spiral and the reduction through depressed demand roughly cancel out.

3. The effects of the food shock on real output and employment were smaller than those of the oil shock.

Of these three assumptions, (1) is a matter of defining precisely what we mean by the shock, (2) is suggested by the analyses of the energy shock based on both the MPS model and the DRI model, and (3) is based on Eckstein's simulations of the DRI model.

Under these assumptions, the severe price hikes for food and energy can easily account for two-thirds of the 1973-1975 recession. Also, since together they raised consumer prices by 9.5% over the 3-year period from 1972:3 to 1975:3, they can account *directly* for more than three-quarters of the increase in the inflation rate from its baseline rate in the period prior to price controls.[22]

How would things have differed with a more expansionary stabilization policy? One answer is to go to the opposite end of the spectrum and assume that policy did not allow any recession at all. In this case, a rough estimate is that the oil and food shocks would have raised the 1975:3 price level by 15.6%, rather than 9.5%.[23] That is, the price level would have been about 5.6% higher.[24]

With the advantages of hindsight, then, and with a lot of admittedly rough guesses, the choices open to policymakers in 1973-1974 seem to have been bracketed by the following options.[25]

Option Number 1. Keep policy on a steady-as-you-go path, and allow the surges in food and fuel prices to cause a severe recession while raising the price level of late 1975 by about 9.5%.

---

[22] The calculation is as follows. Price level shocks of 3.55% for oil and 5.73% for food compound to 9.5%. From 1972:3 to 1975:3, the PCE deflator increased 27.1%, for an 8.3% annual inflation rate. Without the food and fuel inflation, the PCE deflator would have risen by only 16.1% (1.271/1.095 = 1.161), for an annual rate of only 5.1%, which is only .7 percentage point above the rate experienced from 1967 to 1971.

[23] The calculation for the food shock takes the food price hikes from 1972:4 to 1974:4, and passes them through the wage-price model of Table 5-1. This yields a total effect (under fixed aggregate demand) of 9.54% on the 1975:3 price level, as compared with a direct effect (assumed to be the effect under fixed policies) of 5.73%. The calculation for the oil shock is as given in Table 5-4.

[24] Computed as 1.156/1.095 = 1.056.

[25] I exclude from consideration the Draconian policy of causing such a deep depression that the shocks to *relative* prices were not permitted to push up the *absolute* price level. Draco did not have to face the voters.

Option Number 2. Accommodate these price level shocks completely so there could be no recession, and permit the shocks to raise the late 1975 price level by about 15.6%.

Since the actual choice was quite close to Option Number 1, it appears that the recession achieved about a 5.6% reduction in the late 1975 price level. Translated into effects on the annual inflation rate, my estimated effects of the recession are as follows:

1972:3 to 1973:3	1973:3 to 1974:3	1974:3 to 1975:3
−.1%	−2.1%	−3.2%

Whether or not such a reduction in inflation was worth the recessionary price tag is a matter of judgment. While my own personal judgment is that we made a bad bargain, it must be remembered that there was a great deal of fear of inflation in late 1973 and 1974. So chopping 2 or 3 points off the annual inflation rate was not an inconsequential achievement.

Furthermore, since the adjustment was not complete by late 1975, the estimated 5.6% figure could be expected to grow somewhat in succeeding years. Indeed, over a run long enough for both velocity and real output to return to their "natural" levels, prices would have to rise in proportion to the amount of money that was created to prevent the recession.

Finally, a word on expectations is in order. The MPS model that is used as a basis for these rough calculations treats the expected rate of inflation as a (fixed) distributed lag on actual realized rates of inflation, precisely the procedure criticized so eloquently by Lucas (1976). Proponents of the policy of nonaccommodation (Option Number 1) have argued that taking a hard line on aggregate demand had beneficial effects on inflationary expectations *over and above* those that are implied by the lower realized inflation rates. Similarly, they argue, accommodation would have had adverse effects beyond those suggested by the model. While this is certainly a possibility, the case is by no means proven empirically. I will have more to say on this issue in the conclusion to the chapter.

5. A Closer Look at Non-Food Non-Energy Prices

Let us now turn our attention away from the spectacular performances of food and energy prices, and focus instead on the rest of consumer prices. When we do this, two rather startling facts show up immediately.

QUARTERLY DATA: THE CONSUMPTION DEFLATOR

The first fact is that the peak rates of inflation during 1974 were nearly as high for non-food non-energy (NFE) prices as they were for overall prices. (This can be seen in both Figures 5-1 and 5-2.) Specifically, using the consumption (PCE) deflator once again, the highest annual inflation rate experienced for a quarter was 13%; with the non-food and non-energy (NFE) deflator, the highest rate was 12.3%. If we look instead for a more protracted period of peak inflation, the 3 quarters of highest inflation in the PCE deflator (from 1973:4 to 1974:3) saw an annual rate of inflation of 12.2%, while the 3-quarter peak in the NFE deflator (which was from 1974:1 to 1974:4) saw an annual rate of inflation of 11%. In a word, if we want to explain the jump to double-digit inflation, we cannot rely entirely on food and energy prices.

The second rather startling fact appears in Table 5-7, which reveals an absolutely amazing degree of symmetry in the 1974 inflationary bulge in non-food non-energy prices—a symmetry that does not appear in overall prices. Comparing the inflation rate during the 3 quarters before the peak (1973:2 to 1974:1) to the inflation rate during the peak period, we see an acceleration of 5.15 percentage points. And this is precisely equal to the deceleration that occurred between the peak and the postpeak (1974:4 to 1975:3) periods.

Nor does the symmetry end there. As Table 5-8 shows, the two most important components accounting for both the acceleration and the deceleration were the same: motor vehicles and parts, and "other nondur-

TABLE 5-7
Acceleration and Deceleration of Inflation, 1973–1975, Based on Non-Food Non-Energy Deflator for Personal Consumption Expenditures[a]

	Prepeak (1973:2– 1974:1)	Peak (1974:1– 1974:4)	Postpeak (1974:4– 1975:3)
Seasonally adjusted annual rate of inflation	5.87	11.02	5.87
Acceleration or deceleration from previous period	–	+5.15	−5.15

[a]All figures are in percentage points.

TABLE 5-8
Major Contributors to Acceleration and Deceleration of Inflation, as Measured by Non-Food Non-Energy Deflator for Personal Consumption Expenditures ("NFE Deflator")

Item	Own rate of inflation (seasonally adjusted annual rate in percentage points)			Contribution to acceleration		Contribution to deceleration	
	Prepeak (73:2–74:1)	Peak (74:1–74:4)	Postpeak (74:4–75:3)	Percentage points[a]	Fraction of total	Percentage points[a]	Fraction of total
Motor vehicles and parts	1.32	17.89	5.35	1.24	.24	−1.00	.19
Other non-durables	5.40	16.92	7.33	1.41	.28	−1.17	.23
Furniture and household equipment	3.44	11.45	4.88	0.71	.14	−0.60	.12
Clothing and shoes	4.80	8.05	1.41	0.35	.07	−0.71	.14
Other services	9.03	12.75	10.52	1.03	.20	−0.51	.10

[a]Contributions are based on 3-quarter inflation rates, and then blown up to annual rates.

able goods.''[26] While accounting for only about 20% of non-food and non-energy personal consumption expenditures, these two components accounted for about 52% of the acceleration and 42% of the deceleration in the inflation rate. Thus, these two items alone accounted for half of the 1974 bulge in the inflation rate.

During the acceleration period, the only other components to make important contributions to the rise in the inflation rate were furniture and household equipment and "other (than energy) services." The former contributed about 14% of the acceleration while accounting for about 9% of the index; nothing terribly notable here. The latter contributed about 20% of the acceleration; but that is less than its approximate weight in the index (25%).

Similarly, during the deceleration, furniture and clothing made contributions that only marginally exceeded their weights in the index (clothing had a weight of roughly 10%), while "other services" contributed substantially less than its weight. Hence the focus on only two culprits.

As is so often the case, wage behavior mirrored price behavior. But in this instance, the movements in the rate of increase of money wages were much smaller than those of prices. Table 5-9, which has the same format as Table 5-7, shows the behavior of compensation per hour in the private non-farm business sector, probably the most comprehensive wage measure available. Both the acceleration from the prepeak period to the peak period, and the deceleration from the peak period to the postpeak period, are about 60% of the corresponding movements in price inflation.

A perennial question about the wage–price spiral, to which no general answer seems possible, is: Which comes first? However, in this particular episode, a strong argument can be made that wages were chasing prices rather than the other way around. First, real wages fell during the acceleration of inflation and rose during the deceleration. Second, during this period exogenous shocks such as controls and drastic adjustments in relative prices were impinging directly on the *price*-setting mechanism rather than on the *wage*-setting mechanism. For example, there is strong evidence (see the next chapter) that wage–price controls *temporarily* "shifted" the price equation, but not much evidence that they shifted the wage equation.

One interesting question that has been raised about wage behavior during this episode is: To what extent did the several one-time shocks to the price level "get into" inflationary expectations? The data in Tables 5-7 and 5-9 suggest that somewhat more than half of the surge in actual inflation was incorporated into inflationary expectations, and thus into

[26] This means nondurables other than food, energy, and clothing and shoes.

TABLE 5-9
Acceleration and Deceleration of Wage Increases, 1973–1975, Based on Compensation per Hour[a]

	Prepeak (1973:2– 1974:1)	Peak (1974:1– 1974:4)	Postpeak (1974:4– 1975:3)
Seasonally adjusted annual rate of increase of money wages	9.60	12.87	9.97
Acceleration or deceleration from previous period	–	+ 3.27	–2.90

[a]All figures are in percentage points.

wages. While this is an admittedly crude way to answer the question, the conclusion is broadly consistent with the Livingston data on observed price expectations.[27] The expected rate of inflation for the coming year rose from 4.21% in June 1973 to 5.36% in December 1973 and to 6.84% in June 1974. The latter date happens to be the midpoint of our "peak inflation" period. If we interpolate the expected inflation rate for the midpoint of our prepeak period, the conclusion is that inflationary expectations rose by 2.5 percentage points. For comparison, the acceleration shown in Table 5-9 is about 3.25 points.

MONTHLY DATA: THE CONSUMER PRICE INDEX

The picture of the inflationary bulge that emerges from the more detailed data available in the Consumer Price Index confirms the findings from the consumption deflator. Based on the CPI excluding food and energy,[28] it appears that the period of peak inflation was the 8 months from February 1974 to October 1974. For the sake of symmetry, the prepeak and postpeak periods were also taken to be 8 months long. The non-food non-energy CPI shows a similar pattern of acceleration and deceleration, though the acceleration is a bit sharper—6.82 percentage points versus 5.15 points for the consumption deflator (see Table 5-10). While the CPI differs from the consumption deflator in weighting,

[27] I should note that these are *economists'* expectations, not *workers'* expectations. Data are from Carlson (1977).

[28] This index is constructed by the BLS by excluding food, gasoline and motor oil, fuel oil and coal, gas, and electricity. Food and fuel have about a 29% weight in the all-items CPI.

TABLE 5-10
Acceleration and Deceleration of Inflation, 1973–1975, Based on Non-Food Non-Energy CPI^a

	Prepeak (June 1973– February 1974)	Peak (February 1974– October 1974)	Postpeak October 1974– June 1975)
Seasonally adjusted annual rate of inflation	5.90	12.72	7.84
Acceleration or deceleration from previous period	–	+ 6.82	–4.88

^{a}All figures are in percentage points.

coverage, and use of base period rather than current period weights, automobiles and other nondurable goods are again singled out in Table 5-11 as the principal contributors to both the acceleration and the deceleration—accounting for about half of each. These numbers are put into perspective by noting that used cars, new cars, and other nondurables[29] have a combined weight of only 16% in the total index.

During the acceleration period, no other component of the CPI was important in the sense of accounting for a disproportionately large share of the acceleration. This includes even mortgage interest (a major component of "household services"), which, while rising fast during the February–October 1974 period, peaked within that period and had inflated even more quickly during the prepeak period.

In the deceleration process, however, both household services (excluding rent and energy costs) and apparel played major roles. In the former case, about half of the contribution came from the falling off of mortgage rates from their peaks (and hence does not show up in the national income accounts). In the latter case, the marked deceleration in clothing prices—from about a 10% annual rate to about 1%—contributed more than 1.1 percentage points to the deceleration of inflation. This behavior is rather remarkable given that real consumer expenditures on clothing and shoes *fell* at an annual rate of 6% during the period of peak inflation, and then *rose* at an annual rate of 12% in the postpeak period. The fact that prices rose quickly as demand fell and were roughly stable as demand spurted casts serious doubt on demand as an explanation of the deceleration, and makes the dismantling of price controls the most

---

[29] In this case, "other nondurables" exclude food, energy, apparel, tobacco products, and alcoholic beverages.

TABLE 5-11
Major Contributors to Acceleration and Deceleration of Inflation, as Measured by Non-Food Non-Energy CPI

Item	Own rate of inflation (seasonally adjusted annual rate in percentage points)			Contribution to acceleration		Contribution to deceleration	
	Prepeak	Peak	Postpeak	Percentage points[a]	Fraction of total	Percentage points[a]	Fraction of total
Used cars	−22.7	79.8	− 4.7	1.75	.26	−1.35	.27
New cars	0	16.9	4.5	0.46	.07	−0.34	.07
Other nondurables	6.3	19.4	10.6	1.14	.17	−0.73	.15
Household services other than rent, gas, and electric	12.6	15.4	8.4	0.60	.09	−1.32	.27
Apparel	4.8	9.9	0.6	0.60	.09	−1.13	.23

[a]Contributions are based on 8-month inflation rates, and then blown up to annual rates.

TABLE 5-12
Acceleration and Deceleration of Wage Increases, 1973–1975, Based on Average Hourly Earnings[a]

	Prepeak (June 1973- February 1974)	Peak (February 1974- October 1974)	Postpeak (October 1974- June 1975)
Seasonally adjusted annual rate	6.96	10.48	8.28
Acceleration or deceleration from previous period	–	+ 3.52	−2.20

[a] In total private nonagricultural sector, adjusted for interindustry shifts and (in manufacturing only) for overtime. All figures are in percentage points.

plausible culprit. Direct confirmation of this conjecture is probably impossible, however, owing to the differing decontrol processes at the manufacturing, wholesale, and retail levels.

Monthly wage data also confirm the impression obtained from the quarterly data. As Table 5-12 shows, the acceleration in average hourly earnings in the private non-farm economy was about half of that in prices. The deceleration was even less than half as large, but most of this was made up in the following 8 months.

6. Prices of Automobiles

One can hardly help noticing the extraordinary performance of used-car prices in Table 5-11. During the June 1973–February 1974 period, the CPI index for used cars fell at an annual rate of 23%; and this rate was even more rapid in the period following the October 1973 oil embargo. Then, during February–October 1974, used-car prices skyrocketed at the annual rate of 80%. Finally, the postpeak period from October 1974 to June 1975 saw used car prices fall once again, though this time only at a 5% rate.

The explanation can hardly be a mystery to anyone who lived through that period. The unavailability of gasoline following the Arab oil embargo led to a precipitous decline in the demand for used cars, especially the large gas-guzzling models. Given the virtually fixed supply of used cars in the short run, the effects on price were calamitous. Then, as the embargo ended, gasoline queues disappeared, and the price rises for gasoline turned out to be rather smaller than had been feared, the used-car market made a strong comeback. The new-car market showed a similar pattern, though less pronounced. Thus new and used cars—though given an expenditure weight of only 6.4% in the non-food non-energy CPI—accounted for about one-third of both the inflationary bulge and the subsequent abatement.

That this agrees reasonably well with the conclusions from the consumption deflator is rather surprising since used cars are not currently produced output. However, value added by sellers of used cars *is* included in GNP, and the finding that used-car inflation was far more important than new-car inflation in the CPI suggests that much of the movement in the deflator for motor vehicles and parts can be attributed to *capital gains* of used-car sellers.[30]

Thus it appears that car prices made a substantial contribution to the inflationary bulge of 1974. While the gasoline crisis seems to be the leading candidate to explain the gyrations of auto prices, price controls may also have had some impact. But used cars were never subject to controls (except during freezes), and probably could not have been. The new-car industry was decontrolled in December 1973, which was hardly a propitious time to raise prices. However, with the revival of the automobile market in the spring of 1974, the auto makers abrogated their nonbinding commitment to limit price increases,[31] and new car prices shot upward in May through September. Given that retail sales of domestic passenger cars in the May–September 1974 period were down about 18% from their levels in the corresponding months of 1973, and that inventories in this period averaged 2.22 months' sales versus 1.88 months' sales in the corresponding period of 1973, the view that demand pulled auto prices up seems completely untenable. The period certainly has all the earmarks of a catch-up following the end of controls. By contrast, weak demand probably played a major role in the slackening of price increases after September 1974. During the 8-month postpeak period, new passenger car sales fell to an annual rate of 6.26 million units. The question here is: How much of the decline in automobile sales can be attributed to the recession per se, and how much to the higher costs of owning and operating an automobile? To answer this question would

[30] Specifically, the implicit price deflator for the "net purchases of used autos" component of personal consumption expenditures (which includes both the margins of used car dealers and the net sales of used cars from the business sector to consumers) rose by about 1.5%, 23.5%, and 5% during prepeak, peak, and postpeak periods, respectively.

[31] This excludes Chrysler, which had never agreed to the limitations, and which increased prices earlier. See U.S. Cost of Living Council (1974, pp. 36–38).

require a detailed econometric model of the supply and demand for autos—a task beyond the scope of this study.

7. Prices of Nondurable Goods

In the CPI, the catchall category "other nondurable goods" consists of the following:

1. Home maintenance and repair commodities (e.g., paint)
2. Textile housefurnishings (e.g., bedding)
3. Housekeeping supplies (e.g., detergents, paper goods)
4. Drugs
5. Personal care toiletries (e.g., toothpaste, soap)
6. Some recreational goods (e.g., film, newspapers)

Of these, only the prices of housekeeping supplies showed an acceleration faster than that of "other nondurables" as a whole between the prepeak and peak periods. The seasonally adjusted annual rate of inflation for laundry soaps and detergents rose from 10% to 36%; for paper napkins, from 7% to 43%; and for toilet tissue, from 12% to 44%.

It is interesting to note that the paper industry—one of the industries most severely constrained by controls—was exempted from controls on March 8, 1974. As the Cost of Living Council observed in its final report, "The paper industry faced problems in early 1974 that went well beyond controls. The most difficult problem was a severe world-wide shortage of raw materials, causing world prices to soar above controlled domestic prices. . . . New capacity was needed as well."[32] In full anticipation of tremendous upward pressure on prices when controls were lifted, the COLC demanded written commitments of restraint in price behavior from the big producers before exempting them. These commitments limited price increases until July and August 1974.[33] Then, from August 1974 to December 1974 prices of toilet tissue rose at an annual rate of 77.4%, while those for paper napkins rose at a 49.2% rate.

In the deceleration period, prices of housekeeping supplies were joined by textiles and newspapers in showing a sharp drop in their inflation rates, though prices of paper goods continued rising at high rates.

To summarize this examination of the non-food non-energy indexes, then, it would appear that a great deal of the inflationary bulge of 1974

[32] U.S. Cost of Living Council (1974, p. 54).
[33] U.S. Cost of Living Council (1974, pp. 54–55, 487–490).

can be attributed to the catch-up after the demise of wage–price controls and to the adjustments in relative prices required by OPEC's actions.

8. Summary and Conclusions

The inflation of the mid 1970s has been called "the new inflation," and the sobriquet appears to be merited. The causes of the inflationary surge, and also of the recession that followed, seem to have been a trio of relative price shocks.

The soaring price of food was the main impetus that pushed the inflation rate up initially from 3–4% in 1972 (a low rate that was obtained with the help of wage–price controls) to 6–7% in early 1973. Food prices, however, had nothing to do with the further acceleration of inflation into the double-digit range in late 1973. This role was left to energy prices, which had their biggest impact in late 1973 and early 1974 and continued to reverberate through the wage–price spiral well into 1975. But it took a stunning surge in the prices of items other than food and energy to sustain the momentum of double-digit inflation through the balance of 1974.

The demise of wage–price controls is the leading candidate to explain this sharp acceleration of non-food and non-energy inflation because of its timing (controls ended in April 1974), because of the absolutely amazing degree of symmetry in the inflationary bulge of 1973–1975, and because of certain fragments of circumstantial evidence mentioned in this chapter. The next chapter is devoted largely to a more serious investigation of this issue.

Readers having some acquaintance with monetarist doctrine will no doubt notice the conspicuous absence of money in my explanations of the 1973–1974 acceleration of inflation and the 1975 deceleration. This omission was *not* an oversight, and merits some comment. As emphasized in Chapter 2, only steady continuing inflation is "always and everywhere a monetary phenomenon"; and I have little doubt that the growth rate of the money supply is the principal factor in explaining why our "baseline" rates of inflation were, perhaps, 4% in 1972 and, perhaps, 6–7% since 1975. But many factors other than money can *and do* account for one-shot inflation, and these factors were pathetically abundant in the 1973–1975 episode. Food prices, energy prices, and decontrol were the unholy trinity.

If the poverty of the monetarist model of inflation is not sufficiently apparent from the analysis in this chapter, Table 5-13 should help drive the final nails into the coffin. The table reports residuals from an equation that predicts inflation on principles that can be considered "monetarist"

TABLE 5-13
Inflation Predictions from a "Monetarist" Equation

Quarter	Actual inflation[a]	Predicted inflation[b]	Error[c]
1973:1	5.4	4.2	+1.2
2	7.7	5.8	+1.9
3	6.8	7.6	−0.7
4	10.0	8.2	+1.8
1974:1	12.9	9.4	+3.5
2	12.3	10.9	+1.4
3	11.4	10.8	+0.6
4	10.9	9.9	+1.0
1975:1	6.3	9.3	−3.0
2	5.6	6.9	−1.3
3	7.2	5.7	+1.5
4	5.3	6.1	−0.8

[a]Quarterly change in the deflator for personal consumption expenditures at annual rates, in percentage points.
[b]Predictions from a regression of inflation on money growth rates and lagged inflation.
[c]Actual minus predicted.

because the growth rate of the money supply is the *only* determinant of inflation.[34] The equation starts off precisely on track in 1972:4, but misses the (mostly food induced) acceleration of inflation in early 1973. It gets back on track by 1973:3 owing to the large coefficients on lagged inflation,[35] but once again misses the effects of the oil shock in 1973:4 and 1974:1. Though the positive residuals for the remaining 3 quarters of 1974 are not large, I would suggest that they may be due to the equation's inability to cope with the postcontrols bout of catch-up inflation.

For the 1973–1974 period as a whole, the inflation forecasts are too low in 7 out of 8 quarters, and cumulate to an underprediction of the 1974:4 price level of almost 3%. The equation also badly misses the sharp deceleration of inflation in early 1975. All in all, this is not a record to be proud of; but it is probably about the best that can be done along "monetarist" lines. The Great Inflation of 1973–1974 was simply not a "monetary phenomenon.".

[34] The equation itself appears in Chapter 7, p. 172, where it is used to generate a proxy for expected inflation.
[35] The coefficient of lagged inflation is .43 and the coefficient of inflation lagged 2 quarters is .22. By contrast, most of the coefficients on lagged money growth are around .03.

In addition to accounting for perhaps three-quarters of the acceleration of inflation during the 1973–1975 period as a whole, the food and energy shocks seem to have been the major causes of the recession. A rough estimate is that these two shocks *alone* might have accounted for a recession two-thirds as severe as the one we actually experienced. In a word, the higher prices of food and energy seem to have constituted a classic example of a serious "supply shock" of the sort considered theoretically in Chapter 2.

When such supply shocks strike, policymakers face an agonizing choice. They can fight inflation by allowing the supply induced recession to run its course, or they can pursue expansionary demand management policies to prevent (or mitigate) the recession at the expense of yet more inflation. I will argue in Chapters 7 and 8 that the former alternative approximately represents what American policymakers did in 1973–1974. Had they adopted the opposite strategy and prevented the recession, my rough estimate is that the price level in late 1975 might have been some 5 to 6% higher than it was. While a 2–3 point reduction in inflation for 2 years is not inconsequential, neither was the price we paid for it. To my mind it was a bad bargain.

Before closing this chapter, it is important to mention that some economists, stressing the role of *expectations,* feel that this estimated trade-off is an incorrect way to tote up the costs and benefits. They argue that by serving notice on the private sector that the government will *not* accommodate supply shocks, policymakers made easier the task of coping with *future* supply shocks. Specifically, they allege, since firms and workers now know that the government will allow a supply shock to cause a deep recession if that is necessary to limit inflation, these firms and workers will be much less reluctant to *slow down* their rates of price and wage increase the next time around. And this enhanced downward flexibility of inflation will make it possible to accomplish the necessary realignment of *relative* prices with much less inflation. With luck, some of this increased price flexibility might even have shown itself during the Great Stagflation.

Without in any way meaning to denigrate the importance of expectations, I must confess that I find the expectationists' arguments none too persuasive. For one thing, their arguments take it as axiomatic that an accommodative monetary policy would raise inflationary expectations *even more* than is implied by econometric models. But why should this be so if the announced policy is a one-time increase in the *stock* of money with no change thereafter in its *growth rate*?

The second problem I find in the expectationist argument is its assumption of a direct and rapid link between government policy actions (or even announcements) and private pricing decisions. It is as if the gigantic, decentralized U.S. economy could be modeled as a two-person game. My guess is that in setting the price of a Chevrolet, the management of General Motors must weigh and evaluate scores (hundreds? thousands?) of factors, among which next quarter's money supply is not terribly important. For the many businesses whose prospects are less well correlated with the state of aggregate demand than is GM's, the link from monetary policy announcements to their own pricing policy must be more tenuous still. I hasten to add that I do not mean to imply by this that money is unimportant for the price level. My point is simply that money may work on prices primarily through markets, rather than directly through expectations.

Third, the behavior of workers and firms that is implied by the expectationist argument strikes me as somewhat implausible. For an anti-accommodative policy to work, firms must voluntarily reduce their margins of selling prices over costs because they fear that otherwise monetary stringency will damage sales. The important aspect of this argument is that firms must *not* wait for the damage to occur, but must act *now* in anticipation of it. Alternatively, it could be workers who take the lead— willingly settling for lower wages out of fear that, if they refuse, widespread unemployment might result. Again what distinguishes this argument from conventional analysis is that slower wage increases *come in anticipation of future unemployment,* whereas standard macromodels imply that wage inflation moderates only *as a result of actual unemployment.* The difference in views is fundamental, and, while the expectationist case is not totally outlandish, I would like to see some evidence in support of it.

Finally, we should not lose sight of the fact the the U.S. monetary authorities did in fact follow non-accommodative policies in 1974. Are prices and wages in the industrial sector now more flexible as a result? Again, I would like to see the evidence.

Until such evidence is presented, the argument that calculations such as presented in this chapter ignore the most important benefit of the policy of non-accommodation remains nothing more than a bold-faced assertion. This, of course, does not imply that it is false, only that it is based on belief, not on evidence.[36]

---

[36] I have dealt with the expectationist argument against accommodation at much greater length in Blinder (1980).

APPENDIX

TABLE 5-A1
The Constructed Deflator for Personal Consumption Expenditures Exclusive of Food and
Energy ("NFE Deflator")[a]

Quarter	Level[b]	Growth rate[c]
1971:1	95.36	5.7
2	96.43	4.6
3	97.48	4.4
4	98.03	2.3
1972:1	99.05	4.2
2	99.75	2.9
3	100.22	1.9
4	100.91	2.8
1973:1	101.83	3.7
2	103.01	4.7
3	104.11	4.3
4	105.52	5.5
1974:1	107.51	7.7
2	110.16	10.2
3	113.40	12.3
4	116.28	10.6
1975:1	118.32	7.2
2	119.82	5.2
3	121.36	5.2
4	123.12	5.9
1976:1	124.93	6.0
2	126.61	5.5
3	128.32	5.5
4	130.17	5.9

[a]*Source:* Constructed by author from data in *Survey of Current Business.*
[b]Index number, 1972 = 100.
[c]Percentage increase from previous quarter at annual rates.

6 wage–price controls and the great stagflation

—According to a Gallup Poll taken earlier this year, a
majority (54%) of the American people believe in angels.

—The same poll showed that a majority (51%) of
Americans believe in extrasensory perception.

—Another Gallup Poll this year showed that a majority
(57%) believe in unidentified flying objects.

—A Harris Poll in November showed that a majority
(58%) believe in wage and price controls.

—*Fortune*, December 1978

When President Nixon announced the beginnings of a program of
mandatory controls over wages and prices in 1971, he pushed national
economic policymaking into an area that previously had been considered
taboo. While the United States had experienced wage–price controls
before, these episodes had been restricted to time of war. Never before
had there been price controls in *peacetime*. With his stunning speech of
August 15th, Nixon changed not only his own game plan, but the very
rules by which the game was played. By this act, America lost part of its
economic innocence. Types of incomes policy that only a few years ago
were unthinkable are nowadays among the standard policy options open
to the President and the Congress.

The subject of this chapter is not price controls in general, but rather
the particular episode that began on August 15, 1971, and ended in an
inflationary shambles on April 30, 1974. The basic argument of the chapter is that the controls program had much more to do with the Great
Stagflation than is commonly realized. Specifically, in the last chapter
circumstantial evidence suggesting that the end of controls was largely
responsible for the inflationary bulge of 1974 was cited. In this chapter,
this suggestion will be buttressed by more conventional econometric

107

evidence. Secondarily, it will be suggested that while controls were far from the major influence on the business cycle, they nonetheless had a noticeable impact on the cycle of boom and bust that took place during 1972–1976.

1. A Capsule History of the 1971–1974 Controls

The controls program began with what must have seemed to the public to be the most natural way to deal with the problem of inflation: wage and price increases simply were made illegal (for a period of 90 days). This freeze, as it was called, was not meant as a constructive incomes policy, but rather had two quite specific objectives. First, it provided the economy with a shock treatment indicating that the government was serious in its intention to battle inflation. Second, and probably much more important, it provided the government with a breathing spell during which a set of rules and procedures with at least some semblance of rationality could be developed.[1] This breathing space was critical because a controls program in a democratic society cannot be negotiated by the usual legislative process since mere discussion of the subject in the Congress will persuade all firms and workers to jack up their prices and wages immediately.

The freeze, which covered virtually all wages and all prices except taxes, mortgage interest rates, and prices of raw agricultural commodities, was spectacular, popular, and apparently quite effective. For example, a special government study of over 120,000 individual prices found that only 7% rose at all between October and November 1971, while 6.6% fell and 86.4% were unchanged.[2]

Phase II of the controls, which turned out in retrospect to be the longest of the several "phases," began in mid November 1971 under the guidance of the newly established Cost of Living Council (COLC).[3] Consistent with the target of lowering inflation to the 2–3% range, the Pay Board posted a general standard for wage increases of not more than 5.5% per year, although exceptions for certain fringe benefits essentially stretched the limit to 6.2%. In addition, provisions were made for wage increases above 6.2% to account for inequities in pay scales. Hourly wages below $2.75 were exempt, as were firms employing 60 workers or less (after May 1972).

---

[1] On this, see Shultz and Dam (1977, pp. 68–69).

[2] *Economic Report of the President*, 1972. Table 21, p. 81.

[3] For an excellent discussion of the history and institutions of the controls program, see Kosters (1975), on which much of the following is based.

The Price Commission's regulations and procedures were also fairly simple. In general, firms were allowed to pass cost increases through to prices on a strict *percentage* basis, so long as these price increases did not raise profit margins above levels that had been attained in the recent past. The regulations were intended to be self-administered by each firm, although large firms were required to prenotify the government of their intention to raise prices, and obtain approval before doing so. The inflation rate during Phase II averaged 3.6%, with prices of non-food items growing even more slowly than this. It thus seemed that the controls were having their desired effect.

Phase III, which began in January 1973, was intended as a first step along the road to decontrol of the economy. Both the Pay Board and the Price Commission were abolished—primarily because the labor members resigned from the Pay Board, and their responsibilities were assumed by the COLC. The general standard for permissible wage increases was maintained, but rigid adherence was de-emphasized and a more flexible case-by-case approach was adopted. This desire for increased flexibility, coupled with the elimination of prenotification requirements and the exemption of all wages below $3.50 per hour, were popularly viewed as a retreat from the stricter standards of Phase II. A similar approach was taken on the price side, only here the government added some explicit easing of the general standard by loosening the profit-margin limitation and by allowing for larger than standard price increases "as necessary for efficient allocation of resources or to maintain adequate levels of supply."[4]

Phase III was an apparent failure: inflation accelerated to a 9.1% annual rate. Far from paving the way toward the end of controls, it led the country back into a second freeze in June 1973. While the public attributed the acceleration of inflation during the first half of 1973 to the loosening of controls, most economists placed the blame on the burst of food price increases (to a 22% annual rate)—an event that neither Phase II nor Phase III controls could have prevented. In any case, it was clearly politics and not economics that installed Freeze II from June to August 1973—a freeze which, remarkably in a capitalist country, covered prices but not wages! As was anticipated, Freeze II disrupted economic activity in a number of ways, particularly in the agricultural and food-processing sectors which were unfrozen after only about a month. By the end of Freeze II, it seemed that both labor and business had soured on controls, and the administration decided to redeem its pledge that controls were to be short lived.

[4] See Kosters (1975, p. 23).

The vehicle for doing this was gradual decontrol on a sector-by-sector basis under Phase IV (August 1973–April 1974). Ironically, gradual decontrol actually meant stiffer controls at first for many industries because cost pass-throughs were limited to a *dollar-for-dollar* basis, rather than a percentage basis. This clearly squeezed profit margins. Apart from this, the standards and regulations of Phase IV were quite similar to those of Phases II and III. On April 30, 1974, the statutory authority to control wages and prices lapsed, and the government was out of the price controlling business.

2. Public Opinion on Controls

In trying to understand the institution of controls in 1971, their evolution through the various phases, and their eventual dismemberment, a useful metaphor is that of a tug-of-war between economic exigencies on the one side and public opinion on the other. While both economic theory and the realities of economic events were pulling inexorably for a weakening or dismantling of the controls, public opinion was resolutely supporting ever more stringent controls.

A look at the public opinion data is sobering, even stunning, to an economist. For it shows that with few exceptions the public always wants controls when controls are not in effect, and wants to make controls stronger when controls do exist.[5]

The Gallup Poll has been asking Americans for their views on wage-price controls sporadically for about 38 years now. The questions began just prior to American entry into World War II. But if we ignore the World War II and Korean War periods on the grounds that appeals to patriotism probably made controls almost irresistible, the interesting period begins in 1958. The evidence from the public opinion polls is fairly easy to summarize.

From 1958 to 1966, public opinion on controls wavered; it seems roughly accurate to characterize the citizenry as evenly divided on the issue. Specifically, of the six surveys conducted during these years, controls won a plurality of support three times and failed to do so the other three times. In no case did the margin of victory for either side exceed 6 percentage points.

A clear pattern begins to emerge in 1968. In five consecutive surveys

---

[5] The public opinion data cited in what follows can be found in Gallup (1972, 1978), and in press releases of the Gallup organization in 1978. The data are summarized in *The Gallup Opinion Index,* Report #159, October 1978.

held between January 1968 and Mr. Nixon's inauguration of controls in August 1971, a plurality of respondents favored controls. It is noteworthy that the policy that they favored was an outright *freeze* on wages and prices for the duration of the Vietnam War—an indefinite period of time that might reasonably have been expected to last several years. This is an extreme policy that virtually all economists would consider totally outlandish. Yet support for it by June 1971 had reached 50% in favor, 39% opposed, and 11% with no opinion.[6]

A few days after Nixon's announcement, the pollsters found that of the 91% of the survey subjects that knew about the program an amazing 68% approved of it while only 11% disapproved (and 12% had no opinion). During the four phases of the Nixon program, the state of public opinion was clear and unwavering. The Gallup organization asked people on six different occasions between November 1971 and April 1973 whether they thought wage-price controls should be made stricter, less strict, or be kept about as they were. In every case an overwhelming plurality (and usually also a majority) supported making the controls stricter. Even more specifically, when people were asked in June 1973 whether or not they favored a return to Phase I (the original freeze) once the 2-month freeze that Nixon had just announced was over, 52% said they would while only 32% were opposed (the rest had no opinion).

Finally, at sporadic intervals since the end of controls (twice in 1974, once in 1976, and four times in 1978), the Gallup Poll has asked people whether they favor a restoration of controls. In every case, this option has won a plurality of support, and usually also a majority. The margins of victory would be considered landslides had they occurred in presidential elections.[7]

To summarize the evidence from the Gallup Poll, the American public consistently clamored for very rigid controls for almost 4 years before President Nixon acted, was steadfastly in favor of making the controls stricter while they were in effect, and has wanted to see them reenacted ever since they lapsed in May 1974. This helps explain why the President ran out of patience and imposed controls in August 1971, why he instituted a second freeze in June 1973, and why Phase IV that followed was rather stricter than Phase II. A desire to mitigate the distortions and inequities caused by controls explains the shift from Phase II to Phase III (which was really a very mild change in policy), the brevity of Freeze II, and the decision to move to phased decontrol in Phase IV.

[6] A special poll in November 1970 asked a less drastic question— "Do you think the government should set wage-price controls?"—and found 65% in favor, 35% opposed.

[7] For example, in July 1978 61% of those who expressed an opinion wanted to bring back controls while only 39% opposed the idea.

3. The Economic Effects of Controls

A Gallup Poll restricted to economists would have come up with far different results. My guess is that the results would have shown an overwhelming majority of economists solidly opposed to controls in the 1960s but that this solidarity might have melted away somewhat by the early 1970s due to the apparent ineffectiveness of the 1969-1970 recession in bringing the rate of inflation down. By 1971, I imagine, a significant minority—though still a minority—of economists were either favorably disposed toward controls or had a sufficiently open mind on the subject that, while retaining skepticism, they were willing to support an experiment with controls. During the years 1971-1974, however, this significant minority all but disappeared; and by April 1974, when controls ended, almost all economists had soured on the idea of controls. This unanimity of opinion, I believe, has survived intact to the present day.

What accounts for this gross disparity in views between the public and professional economists? Why are economists so solidly lined up against controls? Most of the reasons are microeconomic rather than macroeconomic.

MICROECONOMIC EFFECTS OF CONTROLS

Let us ask ourselves: What happens if a government regulation forces the price of some product—say gasoline, to pick a not very hypothetical example—to remain below the free market price? With a lower price, there will likely be more demand for gasoline from consumers, and also from businesses. Similarly, supply is likely to be discouraged by the lower price. Since demand and supply would have been in balance at the free market price (this is precisely what we mean by the free market price), we conclude that a binding ceiling on the price of gasoline will make demand exceed supply.

Price controls thus prevent the price mechanism from performing one of its most significant allocative functions—determining how much gasoline each consumer will get; and some other mechanism must arise to fulfill this role. One possibility is explicit rationing—either organized by the government (as is done on a large scale during wartime shortages) or by suppliers (as was done in 1973-1974). Another possibility is that there will either be overt queueing of consumers for the available supply (as happened with gasoline in 1974 and again in 1979), or sellers will simply satisfy buyers' demands on a first come first served basis (as happened with several grocery items during the 1971-1974 controls). In either case, there will be customers who wish to purchase the good at the official market price, but cannot; and in the queueing case there will also be a hidden element in the "price" of the gasoline—the value of the time spent in the queue.

Actually queueing time illustrates a general phenomenon—there are many ways to raise the true economic price of a commodity to a level sufficiently high that demand and supply are in balance despite the low official price. Some others are covert quality deteriorations, eliminating discounts that were previously standard, requiring the purchase of some other goods as a precondition of getting gasoline, ending collateral services that had previously been supplied free of charge (e.g., washing windows), excessive shopping costs as consumers go from station to station in search of gasoline to buy, high black market prices, and so on. All of these harm the efficiency of the economy's allocation of resources.

Nor are these the only, or even the most important, allocative costs. With prices held below free market levels, oil companies lose some of the incentive to produce gasoline for the market. Perhaps even more significantly, investment in exploration, drilling, and increasing refinery capacity will be discouraged by the reduced prospects for profit.

Now many, and perhaps all, of these formidable allocative inefficiencies and distortions could conceivably be avoided by an ideal wage-price control system. Imagine, for example, that a controls program managed to hold every price and wage in the economy exactly 5% below its free market level. There would be no effect on the profitability of production, since costs would be held down by the same percentage as prices, leaving profit rates unaffected. With profitability unimpaired, there would be no reason for investment to fall. Consumers, for their part, would not increase their demands for any particular items because *relative prices* would not have been affected by controls. There would therefore be no shortages. It would be as if a social compact had renamed the dollar as "95 cents."

But merely to outline this hypothetical scenario is to show how unrealistic it is. It would take an incredible balancing act to reduce both wages and prices in precisely the same proportion. Even if this miracle could somehow be achieved, prices of other inputs—such as interest rates and costs of imported raw materials—would not be so amenable to controls. Furthermore, no one has enough knowledge to devise a set of regulations that would reduce each price in the economy by the same percentage *relative to its free market level*. It might be possible, say, to hold all prices to a zero rate of increase this year. But this will not accomplish the objective of leaving relative prices undistorted because, in a free market, relative prices are constantly changing as patterns of demand and cost shift. So even if we are skillful and lucky enough to devise a program that leaves relative prices undistorted this year, by next year we will surely have introduced distortions into the relative price structure that we never intended. And finally, it is an illusion to think that any real world controls program could leave all relative prices (or relative wages) unaffected even in the short run. As soon as a set of regulations—apparently equal for all firms and all workers—is promulgated, the government will be deluged by a stream of petitioners each of whose case is "special": firms which have suffered "uncontrollable" cost increases, workers who "must" be allowed to restore their traditional wage differentials with other workers, and so on. Many of these pleas for special treatment will be justified; many will not. And the government will find it difficult to tell which claim falls in which category.

In short, the ideal wage-price control program that introduces no distortions is an unattainable dream, and the only relevant question to ask about any real-world program is how grossly it departs from this ideal, and in what direction.

MACROECONOMIC EFFECTS OF CONTROLS

While these are the main reasons for the overwhelming opposition of economists to controls, they seem only remotely related to the question of controls and stagflation. The relation is, however, present; it just takes a little time to ferret it out.

For macroeconomic purposes, our main interest is on the effect of controls on the overall price level: Does the controls program make the price level go up more slowly than it otherwise would have? Unless the program is an exercise in futility, the answer to this question will be: Yes. But the quantitative dimensions of this effect are not so easy to ascertain. Shortly, I will review the rather mixed bag of existing evidence on this question and present the results of my own study.

What we should expect to happen after controls are lifted is a much more controversial matter. One common argument is that prices artificially held down by controls will seek their free market levels once controls are lifted. In a word, there will be a postcontrols catch-up that lifts prices back to where they would have been in the absence of controls. Figure 6-1 offers a stylized representation of this view, which can be "derived" by showing the effects of a temporary (and binding) price ceiling in a simple supply and demand diagram. Proponents of controls, however, counter that the implicit model is fallacious. As noted above, a well-designed controls program could conceivably lower costs in the same proportion as it lowers prices so that, when controls are lifted,

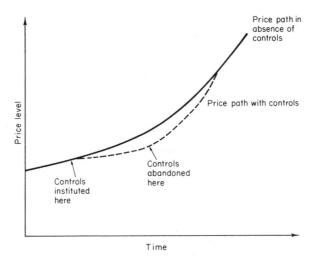

Figure 6-1. Possible effects of controls on the price level.

supply and demand are in balance at the lower prices brought about by controls.

What we know about the 1971–1974 controls, however, suggests that they were more effective on prices than on wages, and hence squeezed profit margins.[8] Thus there is every reason to expect some catch-up on this account in 1974.

Furthermore, it is virtually certain that any real-world controls program will distort relative prices, and it is abundantly clear that the 1971–1974 controls did so. In a world in which prices are rigid downward, equilibrium *relative* prices can only be reestablished through rising *nominal* prices. So this factor, too, points to catch-up inflation.

A third reason to expect a more or less complete catch-up is based on the long-run neutrality of money. If the controls program does not imply a change in the long-run growth path of the money supply, it cannot affect the long-run price level because there are no mechanisms by which temporary controls can *permanently* affect either velocity or the long-run level of real output. Supporters of controls will reply that the money supply path need not be fixed. Specifically, by deflecting the price level path downward for a while, controls allow the economy to get by with less money. If the money supply path is permanently lowered, then the price level path should also be permanently lowered, in contradiction to

[8] See, for example, Schultze (1975) or Gordon (1973). Other observers have reached the same conclusion.

Figure 6-1. However, in the case of the 1971-1974 controls, the institution of controls does not appear to have been accompanied by a deceleration of monetary growth.[9] So, once again, there is reason to expect catch-up behavior.

In the arguments reviewed so far, the nation's productive capacity is assumed to be unaffected by controls. But there are several reasons why it might be affected. For one thing, it is widely suspected (though not, to my knowledge, demonstrated empirically) that controls discouraged business investment. The empirical finding that the 1971-1974 controls program squeezed profit margins by holding down prices more than wages has been used to support this suspicion. If true, we have a reason why the catch-up could conceivably exceed 100%, for in that case controls would have reduced the economy's capital stock.

Finally, the most important intellectual justification for instituting controls in the first place may also provide a reason *not* to expect much catch-up behavior when they are lifted. To the extent that inflation perpetuates itself through self-fulfilling inflationary expectations, *and* to the extent that the shock treatment of controls succeeds in reducing inflationary expectations, even temporary controls can have a permanent effect on the price level. Whether inflationary expectations actually did decline in August 1971, and how durable this decline proved to be, are hard to know. The well-known Livingston data on inflationary expectations did show a drop of almost 1 percentage point between June 1971 and December 1971, and it seems natural to attribute this to the controls.[10] But the effects of dismantling the controls are impossible to untangle from the Livingston data since decontrol was gradual and since so many other shocks were buffeting inflationary expectations in 1973-1974.

On balance, both the a priori theoretical arguements and what we know about how the 1971-1974 controls actually operated seem to point strongly to a postcontrols catch-up period, though the degree of catch-up could be either more or less than the 100% catch-up depicted in Figure 6-1. One important goal of the model of controls presented in this chapter is to estimate the degree of catch up empirically.

4. Previous Research on the 1971-1974 Controls

To measure the effects of controls on the price level, a method is needed to generate two price-level paths: one with controls and the other without. We can then subtract the two paths to estimate the influence of

---

[9] See Chapter 3, pages 32-35.
[10] The series cited was created from Livingston's data by Carlson (1977).

controls. It hardly needs saying that such a calculation is subject to a substantial margin of error given economists' modest ability to predict inflation rates *ex ante*. But this is true of any counterfactual prediction; so it should not dissuade us from making the best guess we can.

Studies of the 1971-1974 episode typically have used *structural models* of the wage price spiral, looking more or less like Eqs. (5.1) and (5.2) of the previous chapter, to measure the effects of controls by one of two methods.

1. *Dummy Variables.* A wage or price equation is estimated through the period of controls, and the coefficients of the dummy variables are the desired measures. This procedure has been criticized by Lipsey and Parkin (1970) and later by Oi (1976) on a variety of grounds. First, the method's validity depends on the coefficients of the model other than the constant being *the same* in the pre- and postcontrols periods even though there may be good reason to suspect that controls might have altered the wage- and price-setting mechanisms. The assumption that the coefficients would be unchanged through a controls period of more than 2 years seems completely untenable.[11] Second, the economy is not like a laboratory; other things are *not* equal. Any unusual event that happens during the controls period, and that is not captured elsewhere in the equation, will be (mistakenly) attributed to the controls.

2. *Postsample Predictions.* In this method, the data generated during the controls period are not used in the estimation; rather the model is estimated only on precontrols data. Then a series of postsample predictions of the price level are generated for the controls period. The differences between these predictions and the actual path are the estimated effects of controls. While this seems to be widely preferred to the dummy variable method, its superiority is not so clear to me. In its favor, the method of postsample predictions does not require that the effect of controls be the same in every period. Nor does it require that controls only shift the intercept. However, just as with the dummy variable method, any random influences during the controls period will be inadvertently attributed to controls. In fact this problem may be even more serious than in the case of dummy variables, for the method is based on the assumption that the equation would have fit *perfectly* during *every* quarter of the period of controls if controls had not existed. Further, there seems to be an obvious inefficiency in appraising the effects of controls by using a model that ignores everything that happened to the economy during the controls period.

---

[11] This is demonstrated at length by Oi (1976).

GORDON'S WORK

A series of papers by Robert J. Gordon probably represents the best-known application of these methods to the 1971–1974 episode, and so merits careful consideration. Using a structural price equation that explains the rate of change of a specially constructed price index for non-food non-energy final sales by trend unit labor costs, the relative prices of both investment goods and spot materials, the effective rate of excise taxation, and a demand variable, Gordon (1975) applied the method of postsample predictions to an equation estimated through 1971:2. He estimated that controls kept the 1973:3 price level about 3.5% below what it otherwise would have been. Then prices started to rise faster than they would have in a world without controls, so that the price level in 1975:1 was actually 1% *above* the no-controls path. Two quarters later, the equation was almost precisely on track.

However, when he reestimated the equation with revised data (Gordon, 1977), several of its important features changed dramatically. Postsample predictions from the revised equation suggested a downward deflection of the price level of about 2.4% by 1972:4—less than his 1975 estimate. Then the equation started underpredicting inflation, and by 1975:1 it was underpredicting the price *level* by about 3.7%. The difference [3.7 − (−2.4) = 6.1%] can hardly be attributed to a postcontrols catch up. When Gordon abandoned the postsample predictions method and used dummy variables instead, his estimate was that controls lowered the price level by 2% from 1971:3 to 1972:4, and the postcontrols catch-up gave this all back between 1974:2 and 1975:1.

MCGUIRE'S STUDY

McGuire (1976) also makes postsample predictions from a structural model, but both his specification and his conclusion differ greatly from Gordon's. First, while the idea behind Gordon's specification is that prices are determined by a markup (which depends on demand) over costs, McGuire adopts the rational expectations approach and models the *deviation* of actual from expected inflation as a function of events that are unknown at the time expectations are formed.

Second, while Gordon uses ordinary least squares to estimate his price equation, McGuire uses a complex systems method that exploits the fact that the expected rate of inflation must enter two other equations as well: a "Phillips curve" for wage increases and a "Fisherian equation" for the nominal interest rate.

Third, McGuire's price equation goes badly off track just before controls start, *under*predicting the price level substantially. Since we look for an effect of controls by looking for *over*predictions starting in 1971:4, this hardly inspires confidence in the results.

Finally, in most of his work, McGuire uses the Consumer Price Index (CPI) without making any adjustments for food and energy prices. His rationale is that when a shock (poor harvests, cartelization) hits some commodity prices, no effect will be felt on a broad-based price index "if the government pursues a non-inflationary monetary policy."[12] But this procedure compares actual U.S. history with a hypothetical scenario in which controls were never invoked *and* an incredibly stringent stabilization policy was followed. In my view, this is a mistake, since combining the two can only obscure the effects of controls. Fortunately, McGuire also provides results using the private non-farm deflator (without an energy adjustment), so we can see what difference the change makes.

Using the CPI to measure inflation, he finds that controls lowered the inflation rate *slightly* in 1971:4 through 1972:4, with the maximum effect on the price *level* (about 1.5%) coming in 1972:2. Thereafter, controls actually *raised* the inflation rate, and by 1974:2 the price level was about 3.5% *higher* than it would have been without controls. These results are surprising, but we can only speculate about the extent to which they are due to the extraordinary behavior of food and fuel prices. When he uses the non-farm GNP deflator, McGuire obtains quantitatively different but qualitatively similar results.

However, as noted, McGuire's equation badly underestimates inflation in 1971:1 through 1971:3. If we add the average prediction error of these 3 quarters to all the forecasts, we conclude that controls lowered inflation in the non-farm GNP deflator in every quarter from 1971:4 through 1973:3, with a cumulative effect on the price level of 2.5%. Thereafter, controls raised inflation so that the 1974:2 price level was only 1.2% below what it would have been without controls. This certainly changes the picture drastically. In fact, the 1973:3 estimate of 2.5% is consistent with Gordon's estimates, and it fails to make any adjustment for energy.

LANZILLOTTI, HAMILTON, AND ROBERTS' STUDY

Lanzillotti, Hamilton, and Roberts (1975) used three conventional wage–price models to estimate the effects of Phase I and II only.[13] All models used the private non-farm deflator to measure inflation. When the models were estimated through 1971:2 and used to generate postsample predictions for 1971:3–1972:4, they yielded estimates of the downward

---

[12] McGuire (1976, p. 118).

[13] The models are those of Gordon (1971,1972), Eckstein and Brinner (1972), and Siebert and Zaidi (1971.)

deflection of the annual inflation rate averaging 3.6, 1.9, and 0.2%. Closer agreement was reached when the models were estimated through 1972:4 and controls appraised by a dummy variable. Estimated downward deflections of the annual inflation rate became 2.0, 1.6, and 1.3%. It is interesting that the two methods give such different results in this case.

In sum, if we agree to focus on the non-farm deflator and adjust McGuire's results for the error in the last few precontrols quarters, the apparently disparate results from the structural models offer a modicum of agreement that controls depressed the 1973:3 price level by 2 to 3%, and then this effect started to dissipate.

In addition to structural models, *reduced form models,* and *ARIMA* (*a*utoregressive *i*ntegrated *m*oving *a*verage) time series models, pioneered by Box and Jenkins (1970), have been used to estimate the effects of controls on prices. The former method seeks to explain prices by their "ultimate" causes—monetary and fiscal policy and other exogenous variables, while the latter method relies solely on the past values of prices themselves in order to produce an equation explaining the behavior of prices.

Although reduced form models are by now well known and, I think, widely discredited in the context of income determination models, Darby (1976) attempts to assess the impact of controls with postsample predictions from a reduced form model in which *only* current and lagged values of the money stock enter the reduced form. He finds that by 1973:3 (the last quarter of his simulation) controls had reduced the deflator for personal consumption expenditures by 4.4% if M_1 is the predictor and 3.6% if M_2 is the predictor. However, his estimates fail to take into account the unusual behavior of food prices, and, if they were removed from the indexes, I presume that his estimated effects of controls would have been even stronger.

Feige and Pearce (1976) use monthly data on the rate of change of the CPI to generate postsample predictions for 16 months after August 1971 from an ARIMA model. They estimate that Phase I cut the annual inflation rate by 1.5%, but that Phase II gave this all back. This result is quite different from those of other studies, but as McGuire (1976) notes, long-term forecasts from ARIMA models have an unimpressive record. They also suffer from the basic problem of having to attribute to controls *any* behavior that is unusual given the past history of inflation. Since the forecast period included the first devaluation of the dollar since 1933, it seems quite likely that any ARIMA model would have *under*estimated inflation in the absence of controls, and that the controls would have helped keep its predictions on track.

5. A New Method and a New Model

In commenting on Gordon's estimate of the effects of controls, Nordhaus (1975, p. 665) despaired that "the methodology that Gordon and others use to test for incomes policies is inadequate. Can't economists be more creative than to use dummy variables? Why can't we *model* price controls and test the model explicitly?" This section reports on an attempt to do precisely this, though the creativity involved is perhaps not very great and the model is not terribly rigorous.

The basic ideas of the approach are two. First, that conventional structural wage–price models determine the rates of inflation in the controlled and uncontrolled sectors; but the parameters of the model may differ between the two sectors. When there are no controls, the uncontrolled sector is the entire economy. Second, that controls are not strictly a *qualitative* phenomenon, being either "on" or "off," but rather have a *quantitative* aspect that has heretofore been ignored. Specifically, the fraction of all prices that are controlled may (and in the U.S. did) vary from month to month and can, in principle, be observed.

THE METHOD

In implementing these ideas, I have adopted a different methodology— the method of *within-sample predictions*. As no other study of controls has adopted this method, it needs both explanation and defense.

To apply the method of within-sample predictions, one estimates the equation right through the controls period, allowing controls to affect all or several of the parameters (intercepts, slopes, etc.), and then uses these equations to generate *two* hypothetical paths:

1. The price path predicted by the equations when the controls are "off"
2. The price predicted by the equations when the controls are "on"

Since the differences between these two paths are the estimated impacts of controls in each period, the method does *not* attribute equation errors to the controls, but lets the model estimate the effects of controls directly. Like the method of postsample predictions, this method does not force the effect of controls to be the same in every period, but can allow it to vary quarter by quarter or month by month. Like the dummy variable approach, however, it does not throw away the valuable data generated by the economy during controls.

There are at least two motives for adopting this apparently novel method in this context. First, in view of the large error variance in a monthly model, I did not want to attribute all equation errors to controls. Hence, I did not want to use the actual history of inflation as my comparison path, but rather have the model generate two paths: one with controls and the other without. The method of postsample predictions cannot do this. It seems worth pointing out that the method of within-sample predictions is not at all novel, but rather quite standard, in a closely analogous context. When large-scale econometric models of the whole economy are used to assess the impact of past monetary and fiscal policies, the standard procedure is to simulate the model twice: once with the actual policy variables, and once with an alternative path for the policy variables. No one would dream of comparing the simulation based on alternative policy variables with the actual history of the economy. Yet this is precisely what is done when the method of postsample predictions is used to appraise controls.

Second, the purpose of the exercise must be recalled: an historical appraisal of a past policy episode. A history of econometric wage–price models of the past 10 years probably would show that they fit well within their periods of estimation, but then did very poorly at forecasting beyond the sample. This fact certainly casts doubts on using postsample predictions to assess controls. However, after the fact modifications of the equations usually enabled these models to rationalize history rather well. And this is, after all, what we seek to do in this case. Thus it seems important not to discard whatever knowledge the years since the New Economic Policy was announced may have given us. By using the data for these years we can run a regression over many years prior to controls, about $2\frac{1}{2}$ years of controls, and several years since the controls ended.

THE MODEL[14]

In order to capture more accurately the timing of the shifts from one phase of controls to the next, and also to give more observations during the period of controls, monthly rather than quarterly data were used. Since the random variation in monthly data is quite large, we must be content with a fairly modest explanatory power for the equation. Also, for this same reason, we must not delude ourselves into thinking that the 32 monthly observations on the controlled economy convey more information that they really do. The number of parameters than can be real-

---

[14] The following is a non-technical explanation of the model that may be annoying to economists, but is probably necessary for more general readers. Technical details of the model (including the equations) can be found in the appendix to this chapter.

istically estimated with these data is severely limited, and this becomes quite apparent when we try to estimate too many.

While I measure inflation by monthly changes in the Consumer Price Index (CPI) for all items, since this is presumably what affects wage demands, I make no attempt to explain the food and fuel components of the CPI. Instead, the variable explained by the equation is the contribution of non-food and non-energy prices to total inflation.[15] As explanatory variables, I use current and lagged values of each of the following:

1. The rate of change of money wages
2. The rate of change of raw materials prices
3. The ratio of inventories to sales, as an indicator of the state of aggregate demand

Beginning in August 1971, two distinct sectors of the economy are considered. In the *uncontrolled sector,* the rate of inflation is determined by the abovementioned factors plus a specially constructed catch-up variable that will be explained presently. In the *controlled sector,* the same factors determine inflation, except that there is no catch-up term.[16] In principle, then, it seems that we have three potentially different wage–price models: one for the entire economy when there are no controls, and two distinct models for the two sectors when controls are in force. In practice, it is impossible to estimate so many different parameters, so assumptions were made to allow estimation to proceed.

First, it was assumed that except for the existence of the special catch-up factor, the *uncontrolled* sector in an economy that has controls behaves like a scaled down replica of the whole economy when there are no controls. Second, it was assumed that wages, raw materials prices, and aggregate demand behaved identically in the controlled and uncontrolled sectors. There are no data that might permit this latter assumption to be tested.

Third, it was also assumed that the effects on inflation of wages, materials prices, and demand were the same in the controlled and uncontrolled sectors. In the case of wages and materials prices, these assumptions accord well with the administrative structure of the controls

---

[15] Symbolically, total inflation π_t can be broken down as follows:

$$\pi_t = r_t^* \pi_t^* + r_t^F \pi_t^F + r_t^E \pi_t^E$$

where the π's indicate inflation rates, the r's indicate relative importances in the overall CPI, and the superscripts F, E, and * refer to food, energy, and non-food non-energy components, respectively. The first term on the right-hand side of this equation is the variable that I seek to explain.

[16] This is definitional. When an industry is decontrolled, it leaves the controlled sector and enters the uncontrolled sector.

program. Except during freezes, there was never any attempt to block the pass through of wages or other costs into product prices. The assumption that the effects of aggregate demand on prices were the same in the two sectors is, on the other hand, a regrettable one forced upon me by the weakness of the data. Controls certainly were *intended* to change the nature of this effect. But in practice the effect of demand on prices is fairly small and hard to measure with much precision in any aggregate price equation, even one that ignores controls. To ask the data to yield estimates of two *different* distributed lag effects of demand on prices was to ask far more than the data could deliver.

Even with all these restrictions, the model still allows controls to have two very different sorts of effects on the inflation rate: controls shift the constant term in the equation for the *controlled* sector, and controls add a catch-up term to the equation for the *uncontrolled* sector. This catch-up term must now be explained.

There is no easy way to devise a theoretically satisfying specification of catch-up inflation. What we expect to happen is something like the following. A particular industry gets decontrolled in a particular month and at this point has a current price that is somewhere below its equilibrium price. The gap between the current price and the free market price is not made up all at once. Instead, we expect supernormal inflation rates for this industry as it "catches up" over the ensuing months.

Now, in fact we cannot really identify with precision which specific industries were decontrolled in which months, nor can we hope to estimate separate disequilibrium gaps and adjustment patterns by industry. It seems that the best we can do is to invoke two heroic assumptions: first, that all industries catch up with the same time pattern; second, that all industries have the same *percentage* disequilibrium gap on the date they are decontrolled. The latter assumption is, in fact, a "theory" of the behavior of the regulators. It asserts that when they decontrol each industry its controlled price is a fixed percentage below its equilibrium price.

Under these assumptions, the catch-up term can be expressed algebraically (as shown in the appendix to this chapter, page 135) and estimated from the data. Before estimating the equation, I expected the time pattern of catch-up inflation for each industry to start low and then to rise to a peak before falling, because the Cost of Living Council often exacted a pledge of restraint as a precondition for decontrolling an industry. However, the estimated coefficients turned out to suggest a steady decline with the largest effect coming in the first month.

Given the measure of extra inflation for "catch-up" reasons, the last step in making the model operational was to devise a time series repre-

TABLE 6-1
Fraction of the CPI Under Price Controls[a,b]

Month	1971	1972	1973	1974
January	0	.818	.477	.426
February	0	.813	.477	.426
March	0	.808	.477	.280
April	0	.802	.477	.121
May	0	.722	.477	0
June	0	.698	.669	0
July	0	.673	.912	0
August	.456	.649	.669	0
September	.912	.624	.426	0
October	.912	.600	.426	0
November	.904	.576	.426	0
December	.845	.551	.426	0

[a]Constructed by author as explained in text.
[b]Controlled relative importance.

senting the fraction of the CPI under control in each month. This series, is, of course, zero except for the months from August 1971 through April 1974. For these months, I constructed it from (sometimes sketchy) information in various publications of the Cost of Living Council (COLC), with missing months filled in by interpolation and some guesswork. Table 6-1 shows the series, and the following paragraphs explain how it was constructed.

According to the Cost of Living Council's first quarterly report,[17] the first freeze covered 91.2% of the CPI. Since it began in August 1971, I entered half of this amount for August, and the full amount for September and October. The same document reports that 81.8% of the CPI was controlled on December 31, 1971. Since most of the 9.4% drop in coverage came right after the freeze ended on November 15, I guessed at the numbers for November and December as shown in the table.

A controlled relative importance of 80.2% on March 31, 1972, was reported in *ESPQR* (January–March 1972), so this was recorded for April 1972, and February and March were simply interpolated. The small firm exemption occurred in May 1972. While the COLC offered no estimate of the fraction of the CPI that was thereby decontrolled, I made a guess

---

[17] U.S. Cost of Living Council, *Economic Stabilization Program Quarterly Report, Covering the Period August 15 through December 31, 1971.* Henceforth these documents are referred to as *ESPQR* with the appropriate dates.

of 8% based on its report that 13% of wages were decontrolled by this action (*ESPQR*, July–September 1972, p. 34). Then, for the period May–December 1972, I simply extrapolated the decontrol rate that had been observed for Phase II between November 1971 and April 1972.

All the remaining observations came from a COLC press release (see *ESPQR*, January–May 1974), which reported the following data:

Date	Fraction of CPI subject to price controls
January 1, 1973	.477
June 1, 1973	.426
September 10, 1973	.426
March 1, 1974	.280
April 1, 1974	.242
April 18, 1974	.122

The remainder of Table 6-1 was filled out from these numbers and from the assumptions that: (*a*) Freeze II, which included half of June 1973 and half of August 1973, controlled the same fraction of the CPI as did Phase I; (*b*) nothing was decontrolled between January 1, 1973, and June 1, 1973.

6. Empirical Results[18]

Preliminary estimates of the effects of the 1971–1974 controls have been obtained from an equation derived in the appendix and estimated on monthly data for the period January 1961 to May 1977. Details of the equation and the estimation technique are provided in the appendix. In general, the equation gave a very good explanation of the data, and reasonable estimates of all the parameters.

Of the many parameters, only the few pertaining directly to controls are of interest here. The coefficient of the specially constructed measure of the fraction of the CPI under control [called a_1 in Eq. (A.8) in the appendix] was estimated to be .0014 (with standard error .0005). This coefficient means that if we had ever had a full controls program, it would have reduced the *monthly* inflation rate by about .14 of a percentage point. Translated to an annual rate of inflation, the implied reduction is about 1.7%. Of course, as can be seen in Table 6-1, we never had complete control and a controlled relative importance closer to 60% was more typical of the actual 1971–1974 program; so its downward pull

---

[18] This section reports on research that is still in progress; hence the results should be regarded as somewhat tentative. See footnote 24.

on the inflation rate was typically about 1 percentage point. Compounded over a period of 32 months, such a program would depress the price level about 2.7%. However, according to the specification used here, some catch-up inflation starts as soon as the first industry is released from controls. In the Nixon controls program, this began already in November 1971 with the end of Phase I. So the 2.7% figure surely does not represent the effect of controls.

The other interesting coefficients are those pertaining to the catch-up term. The estimated disequilibrium gap when the typical industry was decontrolled [g in Eq. (A.8) in the appendix] was 6.6%, and the typical industry apparently took 12 months to rectify this disequilibrium, with the biggest price increases coming in the first months.

Because prices depend on wages and wages depend on prices, it is necessary to append a wage equation to the estimated price equation in order to appraise the effects of controls on the price level. Taking a cue from the many other investigators that failed to turn up any effects of the controls program on wages *given prices,* I simply did not look for any such effect, and estimated instead a conventional "Phillips curve" model: the rate of change of money wages was explained by current and lagged inflation rates and current and lagged unemployment rates, with no special allowance for controls. The equation itself is given in the appendix.

The two equations, when put together, comprise a simultaneous model of wage and price determination.[19] Applying the method of within-sample predictions, I solved this system, first, with the actual controls program in place and, second, with the controls removed. The differences between the two simulations, month by month, are the estimated effects of controls on the inflation rate. These estimated impacts on the *monthly inflation rate* can be cumulated to arrive at the implied effects on the *price level;* and the results are displayed in Table 6-2.

It is interesting to see how these estimates track the changing face of controls. Phase I and the early months of Phase II apparently reduced the annual rate of inflation by about 1.3 percentage points. In total, the price level path was deflected downward by about 1% between July 1971 and April 1972. During the balance of 1972, the effect of controls on the inflation rate, while still negative, was quite small (about −.4% at an annual rate). By the time Phase II ended, therefore, the price level was about 1.2% lower than it would have been without controls.

Under the ill-fated Phase III (January–June 1973), the anti-inflationary

---

[19] There is actually a third equation, given in ftn. 15 on page 123, required by the fact that the price equation explains only non-food non-energy prices while the wage equation requires overall prices as a determinant of wages.

TABLE 6-2
Effects of Controls on the Consumer Price Index, 1971-1977[a]

	Percentage effect on the price level						
Month	1971	1972	1973	1974	1975	1976	1977
January	–	– .66	−1.17	−1.62	+.84	+ .92	+1.00
February	–	– .76	−1.15	−1.66	+.90	+ .92	+1.01
March	–	– .87	−1.14	−1.59	+.93	+ .93	+1.02
April	–	– .96	−1.14	−1.34	+.93	+ .93	+1.04
May	–	−1.02	−1.16	– .95	+.93	+ .94	+1.04
June	–	−1.07	−1.23	– .60	+.92	+ .95	–
July	–	−1.12	−1.36	– .28	+.92	+ .95	–
August	−.10	−1.16	−1.44	0	+.91	+ .96	–
September	−.16	−1.18	−1.46	+ .24	+.91	+ .97	–
October	−.31	−1.20	−1.49	+ .44	+.91	+ .98	–
November	−.38	−1.21	−1.53	+ .61	+.91	+ .99	–
December	−.46	−1.22	−1.57	+ .75	+.91	+1.00	–

[a]Underlines indicate timing of phases as follows: Phase I, August–November 1971; Phase II, November 1971–December 1972; Phase III, January 1973–May 1973; Freeze II, June 1973–August 1973; Phase IV, August 1973–April 1974.

impact of controls in the controlled sector was almost exactly cancelled out by the extra catch-up inflation in the uncontrolled sector; on balance, controls had virtually no effect on the price level during this period. This was followed by Freeze II from mid June to mid August 1973. The estimates show a clear effect of this freeze and its aftermath. From May 1973 until February 1974, when the effects of controls reached their peak (1.66%), the controls program pushed the price level down another .5%.

At this point, according to the estimates, the catch-up began overwhelming the direct effect of controls—a process that accelerated greatly when controls ended at the end of April 1974. By August 1974, the price level had returned to what it would have been in the absence of controls. But then prices continued to rise, leaving the price level ultimately about 1% higher on account of controls. As a result, during the year from February 1974 to February 1975, the controls program added 2.6 percentage points to the inflation rate. After this date, it had almost no effect on inflation.[20]

[20] Recently, Otto Eckstein (1978, Chapter 5) has published estimates of the effects of controls based on the Data Resources econometric model that agree rather closely with my own. Since his method of investigation is so different from mine (he uses quarterly data, a full econometric model simulation with disaggregated price and wage equations, and "models" controls by dummy variables), it is encouraging to see the studies come out with such similar answers.

How can it be that the controls program actually left us with a *higher* price level than we would have had in the absence of controls? There are at least three plausible explanations, but each is highly speculative at this stage.

First, it is frequently asserted that the controls program discouraged investment during 1971–1974, and that this left us with a smaller productive capacity in 1974–1976. If this is true, then any given path of aggregate demand for 1974–1976 would lead to higher prices. However, we lack direct confirmation of this hypothesis through a study of investment spending.

A second—equally speculative—explanation focuses on the distortions in relative prices that the controls introduced. As mentioned earlier, when there is considerable downward rigidity in prices, *relative* prices often come back into equilibrium through an inflationary spiral in which prices of underpriced items outrace those of overpriced items. Chapter 5 outlined some circumstantial evidence that such a sequence of events occurred in 1974, though that "evidence" hardly constituted a proof.

Third, it has been suggested that fears of possible reimposition of controls led businesses to shade prices upward as a kind of insurance against being caught with low prices when controls returned. Again, however, there is only folklore, not evidence, to support this hypothesis.

7. Controls and the Inflationary Bulge

In Chapter 5, I spent some time dissecting the extraordinary bulge in non-food and non-energy prices that took place during the 8-month period from February to October 1974, and several times pointed the finger of circumstantial evidence at the controls program (e.g., in discussing clothing and paper goods). With the preliminary estimates of the effects of controls contained in Table 6-2, I am now in a position to buttress these assertions.

It will be noted that the maximum effect of controls falls in February 1974—precisely the month that begins the period of double-digit inflation. When I compared the peak period (February–October 1974) to the 8 preceding months, I found that the annual inflation rate accelerated by 6.82 percentage points (see Table 5-10 on page 97). The estimated effects of controls in Table 6-2 imply that controls *reduced* the inflation rate by .43% over the 8-month prepeak period (or .65% at an annual rate), and *raised* it by 2.1% (or 3.17% at an annual rate) in the peak period. The difference is 3.82 percentage points on the annual inflation rate. But the estimated effects of controls apply to the entire CPI, whereas our discussion of the inflationary bulge of 1974 pertained only to the non-food non-energy component (roughly two-thirds of the total). When we make the translation, the conclusion is that the controls program contributed 5.70 (=3.82/.67) percentage points to the acceleration in non-food non-energy inflation between the prepeak and peak period. This is 84% of the total acceleration and, along with the unusual behavior of used-car prices (see Table 5-11 on page 98), more than accounts for the acceleration.

The situation is almost as dramatic when we consider the deceleration—a drop of 4.88 percentage points in the annual inflation rate between the peak period (February–October 1974) and the postpeak period (October 1974–June 1975)—again, see Table 5-10. Since our estimates imply that controls added 2.1% to inflation during the peak period, but only .48% during the postpeak period, controls account for a 1.62% deceleration in inflation over 8 months—or 2.44% at an annual rate. This, in turn, translates into a 3.64% (=2.44/.67) deceleration in non-food and non-energy prices, which accounts for 75% of the total deceleration. If we once again add in used-car prices (from Table 5-11) we can account for the entire deceleration in non-food and non-energy consumer prices.

In a word, my preliminary estimates suggest that controls and used-car prices *alone* can account for the entire 1974 bulge in non-food non-energy prices.

8. Controls and Real Economic Activity

There is one respect in which the effects of controls on prices that were just presented may be *overstated*. For reasons outlined in Chapter 2, the introduction of controls should *stimulate* aggregate demand, and this should increase upward pressures on the price level if monetary and fiscal policies are unchanged. Conversely, when controls are lifted, the resulting drain on consumers' purchasing power should ease price pressures somewhat. The importance of these channels can be appraised only through a simulation of a full econometric model of the economy.

Pierce and Enzler (1974) used the MPS model to simulate the real effects of imposing price controls by assuming that *all* of the residuals in the MPS model's price equation from 1971:3 through 1973:3 were caused by the controls. While they did not report the residuals numerically, it appears from a plot of the actual and predicted price levels that the residual grew from nearly zero in 1971:2 to roughly 2.25% in late 1972, and then receded. When Pierce–Enzler fed this shock through the MPS model it was quite clear that:

1. Magnification through the wage–price model dominated the miti-

gating effects of higher aggregate demand. Their estimated full model effect on the consumption deflator got as high as 3.7% in 1973:1, though it dwindled to 2.5% by 1973:4 (the end of the simulation). This is substantially larger than the effect that I detect.

2. The effects of controls on real economic activity were quite substantial. They estimated that the controls added only $8.6 billion (in 1972 dollars) to real GNP and lowered the unemployment rate by .3 percentage points after 1 year. But by the end of the simulation in 1973:4, they estimated that controls had raised real GNP by over $24 billion and reduced the unemployment rate by .9 percentage points.

Roughly speaking, then, the controls seem to have represented a shock about two-thirds as large as the OPEC shock that Pierce–Enzler simulated.[21] If I use my own (lower) estimate of the effects of controls on prices, instead of Pierce–Enzler's, the controls shock appears to have been roughly half as large as the OPEC shock according to the MPS model.

Otto Eckstein's (1978, Chapter 5) estimates with the Data Resources (DRI) model show much smaller real effects from controls. He reports his results only on an annual basis, but they suggest a small .3% increase in real GNP in 1973 because of controls (compared with roughly 1% from the MPS model).[22] This small estimated real effect is puzzling in view of Eckstein's companion estimate that controls held the GNP deflator down by a full 1.3%,[23] because together they imply that controls decreased nominal GNP by 1% *with no change in the money supply*. While not impossible, such behavior would be puzzling indeed.

What to say about the removal of controls is less clear. Pierce and Enzler did their work too early to offer a simulation of this episode. It seems, however, from my estimates that the burst of price increases caused by removing controls happened faster than the retardation of price increases that the controls achieved. If this is so, I would expect the real effects—which this time would *depress* economic activity—to be commensurately stronger. Eckstein's results corroborate this view. Whereas the estimated *positive* effect of controls on real GNP in 1973 was only .3%, the estimated *negative* effect on real GNP in 1975 was .5% (growing to .8% by 1975:4). It does seem, then, that the removal of controls—which became quite rapid in March and April 1974—contrib-

---

[21] Compare Chapter 5, Table 5-3.

[22] The 1% estimate scales down the Pierce–Enzler results in line with my lower estimated direct effects on prices.

[23] As noted in ftn. 20, this price estimate corresponds closely to my own.

uted to causing the recession of 1974-1975. In combination with the real effects of the food and oil price shocks of 1973-1974, the true puzzle about the downswing of 1974-1975 may not be why it was so drastic, but why it was not even worse.

9. Summary

The advisability of instituting mandatory wage and price controls was perhaps debatable in 1971. But with hindsight the program was clearly a mistake—and probably a very serious one. The reasons for this view are not to be found in the usual litany of allocative inefficiencies brought on by controls, though some of these certainly were present. Instead, the worst consequences of the controls program were macroeconomic.

First, by holding down prices (but not holding down monetary growth) just as the economy was entering a pre-election boom period, the controls helped boom the boom to an unhealthy degree. Then the easing of controls during the shift from Phase II to Phase III provided the public with a scapegoat for the acceleration of inflation in 1973, thereby diverting attention from the real culprit: food prices. This misapprehension led directly to a second freeze on prices—a freeze that seemed to cause more serious allocative inefficiencies than had the earlier phases. Finally, the demise of price controls in 1974 turned out to be a masterpiece of ill timing. The government, apparently ignoring inflationary forces coming from the food and energy sectors that were far too obvious to miss, helped fan the inflationary fires by decontrolling the economy at precisely the wrong time. This error not only led directly to the Great Inflation of 1974, but also contributed in at least two ways to the severity of the Great Recession. First, the price level increases arising from decontrol had deleterious effects on aggregate demand somewhat analogous to those of the food and oil shocks that were discussed in the previous chapter. Second, as will be documented in the following two chapters, the stunning inflationary bulge that decontrol helped bring about effectively paralyzed the fiscal and monetary authorities, who stood idly by and watched economic activity collapse.

Thus price controls turned out in retrospect to be the stagflationary shock *par excellence*: their imposition in 1971 and removal in 1974 added an unwanted element of variability to the inflation rate without having much effect on the average inflation rate, and the ill-timed demise of controls helped cause the Great Recession. In sum, and with a degree of discernment that admittedly can be obtained only after the fact, the 1971-1974 controls program constituted a remarkable act of national self-flagellation. More remarkable still is the American public's eagerness to try for a repeat performance at any time.

APPENDIX
The Model of Wage–Price Controls[24]

EQUATIONS OF THE MODEL

As indicated verbally in the text, the basic price equation to be estimated is

$$\pi_t = r_t^F \pi_t^F + r_t^E \pi_t^E + a_0 + \sum_{j=0}^{n} \alpha_j \dot{W}_{t-j}$$
$$+ \sum_{j=0}^{q} \beta_j \dot{R}_{t-j} + \sum_{j=0}^{m} \gamma_j D_{t-j} + C_t + u_t \tag{A.1}$$

where

π_t = The rate of inflation of the Consumer Price Index

π_t^F = The rate of inflation of the CPI food component

π_t^E = The rate of inflation of the CPI energy component

r_t^F = The relative importance of food items in the CPI

r_t^E = The relative importance of energy items in the CPI

$\dot{W}_t$ = The rate of change of money wages

$\dot{R}_t$ = The rate of change of raw materials prices

D_t = An indicator of product-market demand pressures

C_t = A term for postcontrols catch-up inflation, to be derived below

u_t = A stochastic error term

When there are no controls, Eq. (A.1) is assumed to apply to the entire economy. Since I make no attempt here to model the behavior of π^F and

---

[24] This appendix is based on Blinder and Newton (1978).

As noted in the text, the research reported on here was in progress as this book went to press. Several variants of the basic model described herein have been tried to date, with somewhat differing conclusions about the maximum effect of controls and the degree of post-controls "catch up." However, the basic conclusion that decontrol played a dominant role in the acceleration and deceleration of inflation in 1974–1975 has appeared in every version of the model so far.

π^E, $r_t^* \pi_t^* = \pi_t - r_t^F \pi_t^F - r_t^E \pi_t^E$ is the actual left-hand variable. As stated in the text, this variable can be interpreted as the contribution of non-food non-energy inflation to total inflation.

When there are controls, a modified version of (A.1) is assumed to apply to the *uncontrolled* sector:

$$r_{1t}^* \pi_{1t}^* = (r_{1t}^* / r_t^*)$$
$$\times (a_0 + \Sigma \alpha_j \dot{W}_{t-j} + \Sigma \beta_j \dot{R}_{t-j} + \Sigma \gamma_j D_{t-j} + C_t + u_{1t}), \tag{A.2}$$

where r_{1t}^* and π_{1t}^* are, respectively, the relative importance and rate of inflation of non-food and non-energy prices in the uncontrolled sector. The scaling factor r_{1t}^*/r_t^* simply recognizes that the uncontrolled sector is smaller than the whole economy, and hence contributes proportionately less to overall inflation. Dividing both sides of (A.2) by this factor gives

$$r_t^* \pi_{1t}^* = a_0 + \Sigma \alpha_j \dot{W}_{t-j} + \Sigma \beta_j \dot{R}_{t-j} + \Sigma \gamma_j D_{t-j} + C_t + u_{1t}. \tag{A.3}$$

A similar equation applies to the *controlled* sector:

$$r_t^* \pi_{2t}^* = (a_0 + a_1) + \sum_{j=0}^{n} (\alpha_j + \alpha_j') \dot{W}_{t-j} + \sum_{j=0}^{q} (\beta_j + \beta_j') \dot{R}_{t-j}$$
$$+ \sum_{j=0}^{m} (\gamma_j + \gamma_j') D_{t-j} + u_{2t}. \tag{A.4}$$

Here the subscript 2 connotes the controlled sector, and there is no catch-up term.

Notice the identifying assumptions stated in the text: (*a*) the existence of controls does not alter the parameters of the equation for the uncontrolled sector; and (*b*) $\dot{W}_t$, $\dot{R}_t$, and D_t are all the same in the two sectors. While these assumptions can be questioned, it is hard to see what we can do without them. A full wage–price model cannot be estimated from 32 monthly observations.

Since the left-hand variables in (A.3) and (A.4) are unobserved, we need to link the two equations via the following identity:

$$\pi_t = (1 - \lambda_t)\pi_{1t} + \lambda_t \pi_{2t} = \pi_{1t} + \lambda_t(\pi_{2t} - \pi_{1t}) \tag{A.5}$$

where λ_t is the relative importance of the controlled sector—the special variable constructed for this study.[25] Using (A.5), (A.3), and (A.4) can be

---

[25] Data on λ_t are presented in Table 6-1.

combined into a single equation in variables that are actually observed:

$$r_t^* \pi_t^* = a_0 + a_1 \lambda_t + \sum_{j=0}^{n} \alpha_j \dot{W}_{t-j} + \lambda_t \sum_{j=0}^{n} \alpha_j' \dot{W}_{t-j}$$

$$+ \sum_{j=0}^{q} \beta_j \dot{R}_{t-j} + \lambda_t \sum_{j=0}^{q} \beta_j' \dot{R}_{t-j} + \sum_{j=0}^{m} \gamma_j D_{t-j}$$

$$+ \lambda_t \sum_{j=0}^{m} \gamma_j' D_{t-j} + (1 - \lambda_t) C_t + u_t. \qquad \text{(A.6)}$$

CATCH-UP SPECIFICATION

It remains to explain the catch-up variable C_t. As suggested in the text, industry i gets decontrolled in month t_i, and at this point has a price which is g_i percent below its equilibrium price. If a set of distributed lag coefficients v_j^i, where $j = t - t_i$ is the number of months elapsed since decontrol, is used to describe the catch-up process, then the extra inflation attributable to industry i's catch-up would be

$$r_i g_i v_0^i \qquad \text{in month } t_i$$

$$r_i g_i v_1^i \qquad \text{in month } t_i + 1$$

$$\vdots$$

$$r_i g_i v_k^i \qquad \text{in month } t_i + k$$

where r_i is the relative importance of industry i in the CPI, and k denotes the last month of the catch-up process.

As noted in the text, in order to allow estimation to proceed I invoked two strategic assumptions: (a) the lag pattern was the same for all industries, $v_0, v_1, \ldots, v_k$; (b) the percentage disequilibrium gap g was the same in all industries on the date they were decontrolled. Under these assumptions, the catch-up inflation can be written as

$$C_t = g \sum_{j=0}^{k} v_j \delta_{t-j} \qquad \text{(A.7)}$$

where δ_t is the fraction (relative importance) of the CPI that is decontrolled in month t, that is,

$$\delta_t = \begin{cases} \lambda_{t-1} - \lambda_t & \text{if} \quad \lambda_t < \lambda_{t-1} \\ 0 & \text{if} \quad \lambda_t \geq \lambda_{t-1} \end{cases}.$$

Notice that the assumption that the v_i sum to unity can be used to identify the parameter g.

DATA CONSTRUCTION

Prices. The rates of change of the CPI (π_t) and its non-food non-energy component (π_t^*) were computed as *monthly* rates from official BLS data on the *seasonally unadjusted levels* of these series. Seasonal adjustment was accomplished by adding 11 monthly dummies to Eq. (A.6). Relative importances of the non-food and non-energy component of the CPI (r_t^*) were calculated month by month from the fixed weights by the definition that the BLS uses:

$$r_t^* = w^*(P_{t-1}^*/P_{t-1})$$

where w^* is the weight for the non-food non-energy component, P^* is the price index for this component, and P is the all-items CPI. The r_t^* series varied in the .64–.69 range.

Materials Prices. Materials prices were measured by the Wholesale Price Index for crude materials. It should be noted that this index includes prices of energy and agricultural products, and so the equation captures— at least in principle—the *indirect* inflationary effects of these cost increases on non-food and non-energy consumer prices.

Wages. The rate of change of money wages was measured by the BLS's series on average hourly earnings of production or nonsupervisory workers on manufacturing payrolls, seasonally unadjusted and corrected for overtime and interindustry shifts. Monthly changes were used with no attempt to "smooth" the data.

Demand. The demand variable was the ratio of inventories to sales in manufacturing and trade, from the *Survey of Current Business*. Thus it should obtain a negative coefficient. In some preliminary regressions, this measure proved superior to the ratio of unfilled orders to capacity. However, somewhat different results were obtained using the deviations of real personal income from trend.

ESTIMATION PROBLEMS

The distributed lags in Eq. (A.6) were estimated by the Almon (1965) lag technique, after some searching over alternative lag lengths for m, n, q, and k. For wages, materials prices, and demand, a third-degree polynomial with no endpoint constraints was adopted (there was no experimentation with this choice). But, to conserve on parameters, the lag coefficients in the catch-up term were assumed to follow a quadratic and constrained to zero at the far end. On estimation, this quadratic turned out to be almost exactly linear, so a linear form was substituted. Even so, the equation contained 27 parameters: 13 for the precontrols economy, and 14 for the controlled and postcontrols economy. While the former posed no unusual problems, the latter proved to be far more than the data could handle. It was necessary to drop most of the terms involving λ_t, owing to the extreme multicollinearity among all these terms. Thus the equation actually estimated was

$$r_t^* \pi_t^* = a_0 + a_1 \lambda_t + \sum_{j=0}^{34} \alpha_j \dot{W}_{t-j} + \sum_{j=0}^{24} \beta_j \dot{R}_{t-j}$$

$$+ \sum_{j=0}^{41} \gamma_j D_{t-j} + (1 - \lambda_t) \sum_{j=0}^{11} g v_j \delta_{t-j} + u_t. \qquad (A.8)$$

This is obtained from (A.6) by substituting in (A.7) and imposing these constraints:

1. $\alpha_j' = 0$ for all j—controls did not alter the pass through of wages into prices.
2. $\beta_j' = 0$ for all j—controls did not alter the pass through of materials costs into prices.
3. $\gamma_j' = 0$ for all j—controls did not alter the effect of aggregate demand on prices.

As noted in the text, (1) and (2) are not terribly objectionable,[26] but (3) is an assumption I would have preferred to dispense with if only the data allowed—if only!

ESTIMATION RESULTS

Equation (A.8) was estimated by ordinary least squares using monthly data from January 1961 to May 1977. As the contemporaneous feedback of prices on wages within a single month is quite trivial, there did not seem to be any needed for a simultaneous equations technique. Furthermore, and somewhat remarkably for an aggregate price equation, there

---

[26] If the coefficient of λ_t is set equal to zero, it is possible to estimate the α_j''s. Their sum turns out to be negative; but controls are estimated to have an implausibly large impact on the pattern of wage effects on prices. This is why I prefer the equation with $\alpha_j' = 0$. Nonetheless, the equation with non-zero α_j''s tracked history nearly as well and, when simulated, implied almost the same effects of controls as those that are presented below.

was no evidence of autocorrelation. The results were as follows:[27]

$$r_t^* \pi_t^* = .0064 - .0014\lambda_t + .421\dot{W} + .103\dot{R} - .0041D + .066\delta$$
$$\quad\quad (.0043) \quad (.0005) \quad (.087) \quad (.031) \quad (.0029) \quad (.015),$$

$$R^2 = .74, \quad\quad D.W. = 1.85, \quad\quad S.E. = .0010,$$

$$n = 197 \text{ months}, \quad\quad \text{mean of LHV} = .0023.$$

The fit of this equation is remarkably good since the left-hand variable is the *monthly* inflation rate—an extremely noisy series. As a standard of comparison, consider a similar equation estimated by Gordon (1977) using the much smoother *quarterly* data for the period 1954:2 through 1976:4. With the rate of change of the non-food non-energy deflator for private business product as the dependent variable, and several more explanatory variables, Gordon obtained a standard error (expressed in comparable units) of .0026. My standard error, when converted to quarterly rates, is .0030. Since the Durbin–Watson statistic did not indicate autocorrelated residuals and inspection of the residuals did not suggest heteroskedasticity, it did not seem necessary to use more sophisticated estimation methods.

The coefficients of λ_t and the catch-up variable were discussed and interpreted in the text. Turning to the other coefficients, we note that the estimated equation is not quite accelerationist. If we add up the sums of the coefficients on wages and materials prices, we obtain .524. Under the usual interpretation of the accelerationist hypothesis, this sum should be equal to r^*, the relative importance of non-food non-energy prices, which averages around .67.

The estimated effects of aggregate demand on prices are interesting. While the sum is rather small, and insignificantly different from zero, individual coefficients are sometimes sizeable and very significant. According to the estimates, higher demand (as proxied by lower inventory-to-sales ratios) actually *slows down* inflation for about the first 10 months. After this, higher demand does raise inflation, and its effects become quite large at very long lags. The finding that demand stimulation lowers prices in the very short run is a common one that is familiar from simulating large-scale econometric models. In the short run, higher sales and production enable the firm to utilize its labor and capital resources more thoroughly, and thus hold down unit costs by increasing productivity. The effect is a transitory one, however.

---

[27] Numbers in parentheses are standard errors. Apart from the coefficient of λ_t, coefficient estimates shown are those for the *sum* of the distributed lag weights. Eleven seasonal dummies were also included in the regression.

SIMULATION RESULTS

To estimate the effects of controls on the price level, Eq. (A.8) must be coupled with a wage equation. My choice was the following conventional "Phillips curve":

$$\dot{W}_t = A + \sum_{j=0}^{n} B_j \pi_{t-j} + \sum_{j=0}^{m} C_j \log U_{t-j} + \epsilon_t, \qquad (A.9)$$

where U_t is the unemployment rate. The results turned out to be accelerationist, with a sum of the inflation coefficients equal to 1.04, and to show remarkably little sensitivity of wage inflation to unemployment.

To close the model, it was necessary to add the following identity relating π_t^* to π_t:

$$\pi_t = r_t^* \pi_t^* + r_t^F \pi_t^F + r_t^E \pi_t^E. \qquad (A.10)$$

As noted earlier, π_t^F and π_t^E were taken as given.

Table 6-2 in the text shows the results obtained with this three-equation system in a 69-month *dynamic* simulation of the effects of controls. Actual wage and price data were used up to July 1971, and predicted values were used thereafter. (For all other variables, actual values were used throughout.) The entries in the table are the implied effects of the controls program on the *level* of the all-items Consumer Price Index.

7

fiscal policy
and the great
stagflation

Where you stand depends on where you sit.
—popular adage

It would be hard to imagine a period of time that provided more am-
munition for the opponents of discretionary fiscal policy than did the
years from 1972 to 1975, when, it seems, fiscal policy did almost everything wrong. With the advantages of hindsight, at least, it is clear that
the government pumped up aggregate demand to an unhealthy degree
before the 1972 election. Not only did this undermine the controls program, and make the efficiency losses worse, but it also added to the
stockpile of suppressed inflation that was awaiting us when controls were
lifted. While a shift in policy clearly was imperative in 1973, the turn
toward restriction was much too abrupt. In conjunction with the sky-
rocketing prices of food, this cut the growth of aggregate demand from
exuberant rates to nearly zero in a very short time. Then, as real economic activity deteriorated during late 1973 and 1974, the government
allowed inflation to increase the real tax burdens of both businesses and
consumers, placing an enormous "fiscal drag" on the economy. Only as
the recession hit bottom were antirecessionary tax cuts enacted. And
then the authorities weakened the effects by making them temporary.
Finally, as the recovery of 1975–1976 muddled along, the government
refused to take any further actions to support demand, and even proposed
some restrictive (and also inflationary) actions.

141

This is not a record to be proud of. Since being deliberately perverse was presumably not the government's intent, why did it do what it did? In an effort to answer this question, this chapter provides a somewhat interpretive history of the fiscal policy of the period. For each episode, I investigate what the policymakers did, why they made these decisions, and the economic effects that these policies had. In the case of the 1975–1976 tax cuts, this last question is a matter of some controversy among economists, and so I single it out for special attention. A detailed study of consumer behavior, reported in this chapter and its appendix, suggests that the effectiveness of the tax cuts was undermined significantly by making them explicitly temporary.

1. The Pre-Election Stimulation of the Economy

In his January 1972 State of the Union address, President Nixon placed the major emphasis on the unemployment problem, suggesting that inflation was on the downturn.

> The rate of inflation is down. We can look with confidence to 1972 as the year when the back of inflation will be broken.
> Now, this is a good record, but it is not good enough—not when we still have an unemployment rate of six percent. . . .
> Our goal in this country is full employment in peacetime. We intend to meet that goal, and we can.[1]

These were not just idle words, for by any measure 1971 and 1972 were years of tremendously expansionary fiscal policies. The politicians and bureaucrats that opened the watergates of federal spending were far more effective than the burglars who were caught in Democratic National Headquarters. The high employment budget, which was nearly balanced in 1970, swung into a $10 billion deficit in 1971 and a $12 billion deficit in 1972. I have already cited the Blinder–Goldfeld (1976) series on fiscal influence, which show a tremendous peak in 1971 and 1972 (see page 33). During 1971, social security benefits were raised significantly, the investment tax credit was restored, excise taxes were reduced a bit, and personal income tax exemptions were increased. As a result, real personal taxes net of transfers fell by $8.5 billion.[2] In 1972, increases in

---

[1] U.S. President, *Weekly Compilation of Presidential Documents*, Vol. 8, No. 4, p. 69. Henceforth, this publication will be referred to as *Documents*.

personal transfers (mostly a 20% increase in social security benefits just prior to the election) and in grants-in-aid were the main vehicles of fiscal stimulus, while inflation pushed personal income taxes higher.

In Chapter 3, I mentioned the widely held suspicion that the 1971-1972 stimulation of the economy was politically motivated. Edward Tufte, who has studied this episode with great care, notes with evident disapproval that

> Transfers in the 1972 campaign were administered with high political spirit, and part of the flow of federal money came under the heavy-handed influence of the White House "Responsiveness Program." The aims and methods of that sleazy program have been captured in some 1,200 pages of memoranda put into the exhibits of the Senate Watergate (Ervin) Committee.[3]

While motivation is hard to prove, the timing was certainly ideal from the standpoint of the political business cycle; and it is clear that members of the administration—from the President on down—believed that the state of the economy affects the vote.[4] Nor does what we know about the incumbent President make the notion of political manipulation of the economy implausible on its face.

Mr. Nixon, in fact, had been victimized before by the influence of the economy on the polity. He recalled in his *Six Crises* that as Vice President in 1954 and 1958 he had witnessed Republican losses in the midterm congressional elections, which he attributed to lackluster economic performance. Specifically:

> The power of the "pocket-book" issue was shown more clearly perhaps in 1958 than in any off-year election in history. On the international front, the Administration had had one of its best years . . . . Yet, the economic dip in October was obviously uppermost in people's minds when they went to the polls.

As a presidential candidate in 1960, Mr. Nixon remembered this episode well. So when Arthur Burns, then a private citizen but formerly head of President Eisenhower's Council of Economic Advisers, warned him in March 1960 of an upcoming slump in the fall, and urged stimulative policies, the Vice President was receptive to the message. He carried

---

[2] The calculation is based on the sum of personal tax and nontax payments *plus* contributions for social insurance *minus* transfers to persons, all deflated by the PCE deflator.

[3] Tufte (1978, p. 52n).

[4] See Nixon (1962, pp. 309-310) where the following quotations can be found, or Tufte (1978, pp. 6, 46-48) where the entire episode is recounted.

Burns' plea—unsuccessfully, as it turned out—to President Eisenhower's cabinet, noting ruefully that

> In supporting Burns' point of view, I must admit that I was more sensitive politically than some of the others around the cabinet table.

The outcome was unfortunate for candidate Nixon, who lost a very narrow election to John F. Kennedy. As Nixon recalled

> Unfortunately, Arthur Burns turned out to be a good prophet. The bottom of the 1960 dip did come in October and the economy started to move up in November—after it was too late to affect the election returns. . . . All the speeches, television broadcasts, and precinct work in the world could not counteract that one hard fact.

Despite all this circumstantial evidence, it must be pointed out that many Democrats, who certainly had no interest in Nixon's reelection, were strong supporters of stimulative policies in 1971 and even in 1972. After all, 1970 had been a recession year and the unemployment rate remained relatively high at the start of 1972. In retrospect, it seems clear that economists overestimated potential GNP in 1972. Furthermore, many people naively believed that wage-price controls had "taken care of" inflation, so that fiscal stimulus could be pursued safely. That they were wrong did not make this opinion any less influential.

While the motives are perhaps not entirely clear cut, there is widespread agreement on the effect of the policy actions that were taken—the economy was given a strong push forward. But how much did fiscal policy contribute to the boom of 1971-1972 (which actually ended in 1973:1)? To answer this, I need something different from the Blinder-Goldfeld measures of fiscal influence, for these indicate the effect of current (or current and past) policies on the growth in real output between the current quarter and some horizon quarter. However, from these measures it is possible to construct an indicator of the *total* effect of all fiscal policies on the real GNP of quarter t, denoted $F(t)$.[5] Table 7-1 shows the resulting series through 1974:2, though I wish to focus on the period 1971:1-1973:1 right now.

The first two columns document the tremendous expansion in fiscal stimulus. Fiscal policy subtracted $21 billion from the GNP of 1971:1,

---

[5] In particular, since $F_y^j(t)$ is defined as the effect of quarter t's actions on the real GNP of quarter $t + j$, the desired indicator is

$$F(t) = F_y^0(t) + F_y^1(t - 1) + F_y^2(t - 2) + \cdots,$$

where one of the truncation procedures will permit the computation of this infinite sum. I have used truncation procedure B, which forces fiscal effects on real GNP to be zero by the end of 3 years.

TABLE 7-1
Portion of Real GNP Attributable to Fiscal Policy[a]

Quarter	$F(t)$ in 1958 \$[b]	$F(t)$ in 1972 \$[c]	Real GNP	Real GNP less $F(t)$
1971:1	−13.9	−21.0	1095.3	1116.3
2	− 3.2	− 4.9	1103.3	1108.2
3	+ 5.9	+ 8.9	1111.0	1102.1
4	+16.7	+25.2	1120.5	1095.3
1972:1	+23.5	+35.5	1141.2	1105.7
2	+30.5	+46.2	1163.0	1116.8
3	+30.9	+46.8	1178.0	1131.2
4	+36.9	+55.9	1202.2	1146.3
1973:1	+42.0	+63.6	1229.8	1166.2
2	+41.7	+63.1	1231.1	1168.0
3	+34.7	+52.5	1236.3	1183.8
4	+26.7	+40.4	1242.6	1202.2
1974:1	+18.4	+27.9	1230.2	1202.3
2	+10.0	+15.1	1224.5	1209.4

[a] In billions of dollars.
[b] *Source:* Computed as described in text from measures in Blinder and Goldfeld (1976).
[c] Converted by GNP deflator.

and *added* \$63.6 billion to the GNP of 1973:1. This \$84.6 billion swing is a very large fraction of the total growth in real GNP over the period (\$134.5 billion). If we subtract $F(t)$ from GNP (see Table 7-1) we conclude that the annual growth rate of real GNP over the 2 years would have been only 2.2% (versus an observed 6.0%) in the absence of fiscal stimulus.[6] If we focus on the 4 quarters prior to the election—which Kramer (1971), Fair (1978), and others have found is what matters most to voters—fiscal policy raised the growth rate from 4.7 to 7.3%. In other words, fiscal stimulus transformed 1972 from a year of healthy growth into an unsustainable and inflationary boom.

2. The Post-Election Switch to Restrictive Policy

The switch to restrictive fiscal policy, which came rather abruptly after the election, had been presaged by President Nixon's speeches as early

---

[6] By the nature of these measures, the thought experiment asks what would have happened if none of the changes in fiscal policy between 1968:3 (the earliest quarter that still has effects on real GNP in 1971:1) and 1973:1 had occurred.

as July 1972, when he complained that the Congress was spending more than his budget proposals had requested and threatened to veto bills "calling for excessive spending."[7] (Who, after all, could be in favor of "excessive spending"?) The turnabout was complete by his January 1973 budget message, which followed the inauguration of Phase III of price controls. There he clearly labeled inflation as the nation's biggest economic problem, and advocated fighting it by reduced federal spending.

> During the past 2 years, . . . the Federal budget provided fiscal stimulus that moved the economy toward full employment. . . . However, instead of operating primarily as a stimulus, the budget must now guard against inflation.
> *The surest way to avoid inflation or higher taxes or both is for Congress to join me in a concerted effort to control Federal spending.*[8]

This continued to be the major theme of President Nixon's fiscal policy pronouncements right up to the time he was forced from office.

The words were translated into actions. In 1973:1 grants-in-aid were cut and higher social security taxes went into effect. Purchases of goods and services dropped sharply in 1973:2. The precipitous decline in the Blinder–Goldfeld series on fiscal influence during 1973 was recorded in Chapter 3 (see especially Figure 3-2). The new indicator of the fiscal contribution to GNP (see Table 7-1) falls from $63.6 billion in 1973:1 to $27.9 billion in 1974:1. These calculations indicate that without any fiscal policy the economy would have achieved a moderate 3.1% real growth rate between 1973:1 and 1974:1. With fiscal policy, there was no growth at all, and the recession was on its way.

3. Inflation and Fiscal Drag in 1974

The Blinder–Goldfeld series on the effects of discretionary fiscal actions end in 1974:2, but not much is lost because the important aspects of fiscal policy in late 1973 and throughout 1974 were *automatic* rather than discretionary. The high employment *deficit*, which had declined slightly from $12 billion in 1972 to $8 billion in 1973 because of the shift in discretionary policy, turned into a high employment *surplus* of $3 billion with no important discretionary actions.[9] Rather, this $11 billion swing was entirely attributable to the fact that inflation raises real tax burdens in our unindexed tax system.

---

[7] *Documents*, Vol. 8, No. 31, p. 1177.
[8] *Documents*, Vol. 9, No. 5, p. 87. Italics in original.
[9] The data referred to are the CEA's estimates.

Since the federal personal income tax has a progressive rate structure that is fixed in nominal terms, higher prices push taxpayers into higher tax brackets even if real income does not change. Between 1973:4 and 1974:4, the implicit deflator for national income rose by 11.9% while personal income less transfers (an approximation to the tax base) rose only 7.2%. Thus "real taxable income" fell. Yet, because of the progressive rate structure, federal personal tax and nontax receipts rose faster than the rate of inflation. So real tax receipts increased. The "tax rate" computed by dividing federal personal tax and nontax payments by personal income less transfers rose from 12.4 to 13.1% over these 4 quarters, with no discretionary tax hikes. Had the 12.4% rate been maintained, federal personal taxes would have been $8.4 billion lower. Thus, instead of acting as an automatic stabilizer, the federal tax system actually made real disposable income fall faster than real personal income.

Corporations also pay higher taxes during rapid inflations because of inventory profits, only some of which are avoided by LIFO accounting, and because of the reduced real value of depreciation allowances.[10] Between 1973:4 and 1974:4, corporate profits after the inventory valuation adjustment[11] fell from $99.3 billion to $77.6 billion in current dollars, but corporate profits tax accruals rose slightly. As a result, the "tax rate" rose from 48.9 to 64.9%.[12] The comparison is even more dramatic if we look at 1974:3, when the tax rate computed in this way hit 71.4%. Had the average tax rate remained at 48.9%, federal corporate profits taxes in 1974:3 and 1974:4 would have been lower by $18 billion and $12.5 billion (at annual rates) respectively.

A long stalemate between two Republican Presidents and a heavily Democratic Congress resulted in essentially no discretionary actions between, say, 1973:3 and 1975:1, as the outgoing Nixon administration was preoccupied by Watergate and the new Ford administration was preoccupied with various *contractionary* measures.

It was one of the cruel ironies of recent history that the summer and fall of 1974—just the period when inflation hit its peak and the storm

[10] Offsetting this are untaxed capital gains on their outstanding bonds and other financial liabilities. According to Shoven and Bulow (1976) and von Furstenburg and Malkiel (1977), these gains *exceeded* profits in 1974. However, such gains do not appear in the government budget, and hence do not affect calculations of "fiscal drag." They do, of course, affect the corporations and therefore the economy.

[11] This can be thought of as a rough deduction for inventory profits. The figures cited also include the capital consumption adjustment, but this is minor.

[12] When inventory profits are included in the denominator (i.e., the inventory valuation adjustment and the capital consumption adjustment are *not* made), the tax rate declines from 41.5 to 40.7%. This certainly suggests that the taxation of inventory profits is the reason for the higher tax burden.

clouds of a deep recession were forming—found America embroiled in a serious constitutional crisis. The resolution of the Watergate crisis left America with the spectacle of a former President, whom many thought guilty of a variety of crimes, escaping prosecution in favor of what was in effect banishment to his southern California estate, while his hand-picked successor took over at the White House. The economic problems facing the new President were perhaps the most severe ones for this country since the Great Depression. And the devilish combination of inflation and recession probably put any President, no matter who he was, in a "no win" situation. In these dire circumstances Gerald Ford, a veteran Congressman who had never sought national office, was thrust into the White House. It may be that not even the wisdom of Lincoln could have unearthed a successful economic policy in these times; and the new President himself confessed that he was a Ford, not a Lincoln.

Mr. Ford made his first major economic address on August 12, 1974, just a few days after assuming office. At the time inflation was roaring along at double-digit rates and the economy had experienced 2 consecutive quarters of negative real growth in GNP—thus satisfying the popular definition of a recession.[13] As was probably inevitable given the political climate, the new President decided to take his chances on inflation fighting, stating flatly that, "My first priority is to work with you to bring inflation under control. Inflation is domestic enemy number one."[14] He further pledged to fight inflation through reduced federal spending, and 1 month later backed this up with the first of several messages to Congress recommending deferrals or recisions of various expenditure measures.[15]

The period surrounding the much ballyhooed White House "Summit Conference" on inflation in September gave the new President many well-publicized opportunities to express his sincere intention to battle the inflationary dragon—opportunities he did not squander. It also provided the nation with a little comic relief, though few people were finding any humor in inflation at the time. He closed the conference, in dead seriousness I suppose, by asking all Americans to

> Make a list of some 10 ways you can save energy and you can fight inflation. Little things that become habits . . . habits that you can abandon if we are all faced with this

[13] In fact, with the data on hand at the time, the decline in real GNP during the first half of 1974 (4% at an annual rate) looked more severe than it does now with the final revised data (under 3%). See *Survey of Current Business,* August 1974.

[14] *Documents,* Vol. 10, No. 33, p. 1032.

[15] *Documents,* Vol. 10, No. 38, pp. 1173–1174.

emergency. I suggest that each person exchange your family's list with your neighbors, and I urge you to send me a copy.[16]

This plea resulted in some suggestions that would have done the Marx brothers proud.[17]

In an address to a joint session of Congress in early October, President Ford presented his own shopping list of 10 items—a list that was less lighthearted, I presume, than many of the suggestions the White House had received. This list included requests that Congress place a tight ceiling on federal spending and enact a 5% temporary income tax surcharge on corporations and upper-income families. Thus the President of the United States was recommending a contractionary fiscal-policy package just as the slide into recession was assuming epidemic proportions. In the same speech, he coined the famous slogan "Whip Inflation Now," which was subsequently to grace thousands of WIN buttons and provide grist for many of the nation's comedians. He closed with the following bit of hyperbole:

> I say to you with all sincerity, that our inflation, our public enemy number one, will, unless whipped destroy our country, our homes, our liberties, our property, and finally our national pride, as surely as any well-armed wartime enemy.[18]

Jimmy Carter did not invent the moral equivalent of war.

It is perhaps worth pausing to consider the hindsight-versus-foresight issue once again. In October 1974 President Ford did not know that real GNP would plummet so spectacularly during 1974:4 and 1975:1, making the 1973–1975 downswing the greatest recession since the 1930s. Few, in fact, were forecasting such an extreme decline. He did, however, know that real GNP had declined for 3 consecutive quarters and that the fourth was more than likely in progress. In fact, the real GNP estimates of October 1974 showed a decline over the previous 3 quarters amounting to 2.8%, whereas the final revised data make it only 1.8%.[19] Thus it does not take the notorious wisdom of hindsight to brand the proposed tax hike of October 1974 as badly out of touch with reality, as many contemporary observers so branded it.

---

[16] *Documents,* Vol. 10, No. 40, pp. 1208–1209.

[17] I can remember two such ideas: taking a bath in a half-tub of water, and holding the door open for at most 10 seconds while the family cat decided whether or not to go outdoors.

[18] *Documents,* Vol. 10, No. 41, p. 1247.

[19] See *Survey of Current Business,* October 1974.

4. Concern with Recession and the 1975 Tax Cut

As late as Thanksgiving the President held to this hard line against inflation despite a badly deteriorating economy. While he reiterated his advocacy of an increase in unemployment benefits, he still requested budget cuts and listed inflation as his number one concern.[20] But 2 weeks later, in a speech to the Business Council in Washington, this attitude began to soften. Mr. Ford admitted that recession was a serious problem, though he denied that the country was in an "economic crisis." And he added these words of warning to the business leaders:

> If there are any among you who want me to take a 180 degree turn from inflation fighting to recessionary pump priming, they will be disappointed.[21]

By January 13, 1975, the economic slide had worsened dramatically, and President Ford's attitudes had changed accordingly. In a televised address to the nation, he conceded that it was time to "shift our emphasis from inflation to recession," though he added that "in doing so, we must not lose sight of the very real and deadly dangers of rising prices."[22] Instead of the income tax increase he had requested just 3 months earlier, Mr. Ford now called upon Congress to enact a $16 billion tax reduction— including a $12 billion reduction for consumers (mostly through a rebate of 1974 taxes) and a $4 billion cut for businesses (mostly in the form of an increase in the investment tax credit). However, at the same time he called for a moratorium on further federal spending, threatening to veto any new spending proposals that the Congress sent him.

The tax cut proposal was changed in fairly predictable ways by the Congress—made bigger (to about $23 billion) and tilted somewhat more toward lower-income households. But it emerged at the end of March in broadly the form that the President had proposed. After expressing some hesitancy about the distribution of the tax cuts and a number of "extraneous" provisions in the bill, the President dramatically signed the tax cuts into law on March 29, 1975. Even more dramatically, he vowed that any further fiscal stimulus would be intolerable, given the inflation, and drew the line (literally, with pen and ink, as the nation watched on television!) at a $60 billion federal deficit.[23]

The Tax Reduction Act of 1975, the centerpiece of fiscal policy during

---

[20] *Documents,* Vol. 10, No. 48, pp. 1500–1501.
[21] *Documents,* Vol. 10, No. 50, p. 1554.
[22] *Documents,* Vol. 11, No. 3, p. 42.
[23] *Documents,* Vol. 11, No. 14, p. 322.

TABLE 7-2
Effects on Disposable Income of 1975–1976 Tax Cuts and Transfers[a,b]

| Quarter | Taxes | | Transfers | | |
	Rebate	Other tax cuts	Social security	Earned income	Total
1975:2	+31.2	+ 8.5	+6.7	0	46.4
1975:3	0	+12.3	0	0	12.3
1975:4	0	+11.9	0	0	11.9
1976:1	0	+14.2	0	+1.9	16.1
1976:2	0	+14.0	0	+1.6	15.6

[a]Sources: For taxes, Survey of Current Business, February 1976 and March 1977; for transfers, kindly supplied to the author by Joseph Wakefield of the Bureau of Economic Analysis in conversation.
[b]In billions of current dollars, at annual rates.

the recession, included the following major elements:

1. A *one-time* rebate of 1974 taxes, amounting to just under $8 billion
2. A reduction in personal income taxes for *1 year* of about $12 billion, accomplished mostly through reduced withholding and subsequently extended
3. A *one-time* payment of $50 to each recipient of social security benefits, amounting to about $1.7 billion
4. A so-called "earned income credit" (a type of negative income tax) of about $1 billion, also for 1 year, and also subsequently extended

Table 7-2 details the effects on personal disposable income (in current dollars) of the various provisions of the 1975 tax cut and its extension into the first half of 1976.

In addition, there were small temporary cuts in corporate income taxes and large temporary increases in the investment tax credit. In total, the fiscal package moved the high employment budget from approximate balance in 1975:1 to a deficit of $29 billion in 1975:3.[24]

At that time, and since then, many economists were disappointed by the explicitly temporary nature of the consumption oriented aspects of the fiscal package. They argued that such changes have little effect on a family's permanent income, and hence would have little effect on its consumption. Pointing to the apparent failure of the 1968 tax surcharge

[24] I omit 1975:2, which was distorted by the huge rebate.

to curb consumer spending as evidence, they asserted that only permanent changes could be expected to exert a strong influence over consumer
behavior.

But not all economists—and certainly not all politicians—were persuaded by the logic of the argument. They viewed the "permanent income
school" as arguing from *a priori* theoretical notions without firm empirical support. Why, they asked, need consumers behave in the way pre-
scribed by economic theory? And they cited Okun's (1971) well-known
paper, which claimed that the 1968 tax hike really had worked, to buttress
their position.

After completing the historical narrative, I take a fresh—and hopefully
objective—look at the debate in Section 6 of this chapter. Do consumers
react to temporary tax and transfer changes in a special way, as asserted
by the theory? Or do they treat them more or less like any other income
change, and, in particular, just like a permanent tax change?

5. Fiscal Policy in the Early Recovery Period

In retrospect the recession appears to have bottomed out just about as
the Congress was passing the 1975 tax cuts, so fiscal policy did nothing
to stem the slide into recession but did provide some support for the
recovery. After the tax cuts, the rhetoric of the Ford administration
reverted to its former restrictive posture, though this attitude was, for
the most part, not translated into action. The high employment budget
remained in substantial deficit (generally between $20 and $30 billion) for
the remainder of 1975 and throughout 1976.

The President made two major pronouncements in late May 1975.
First, in a televised speech on the energy problem, he began to carry
through on a proposal first made in January to impose special import
duties on oil,[25] and advocated a rapid decontrol of domestic oil prices.
Second, he vetoed the Emergency Employment Appropriations Bill on
the grounds that it exceeded permissible budget levels—one of many
vetoes of spending bills in 1975.[26]

By coincidence, the critical budget cycle that started in the spring of
1975 was the first tryout for the new budget procedures embodied in the
Congressional Budget and Impoundment Control Act of 1974.[27] The Act

---

[25] *Documents,* Vol. 11, No. 22, p. 565. He imposed the first $1 of what was planned to
be a $3 per barrel fee. These fees were later ruled unconstitutional, and removed.

[26] *Documents,* Vol. 11, No. 22, p. 568.

[27] While often described as a "dry run" to test out the procedures, Congress did make
the budget *totals* (though not the allocation by budget function) legally binding. So from
the macroeconomic viewpoint the budget reform was fully effective.

established Budget Committees in both the House and the Senate charged with responsibility for the overall size of the budget. Under the new procedures, these committees are to agree on a ceiling on spending and a floor on revenues and present these in a First Concurrent Resolution on the Budget to the entire Congress for approval in May. Then there is an opportunity to modify the budget in a Second Concurrent Resolution in September, after which the ceiling becomes legally binding for the fiscal year beginning in October.[28] The spending ceiling for fiscal 1976 that Congress set in May 1975, and modified only slightly in September 1975, was $367 billion. This was much higher than what the Ford administration had requested in its February 1975 budget proposal ($349 billion) and moderately above what the President was requesting at the time ($359 billion).[29] But most observers thought it was lower than what the Congress would have spent in the absence of the new budget procedures.

However, the most controversial fiscal policy issue of 1975 was not the budget, but energy policy, a topic which dominated the economic news for much of the year. Beginning in January, the President made a series of proposals to free domestic oil prices of controls. His first proposal was for complete and immediate decontrol, but subsequent suggestions asked for phased decontrol over several years. Each proposal was accompanied by requests for excise taxes on domestic oil to capture what would otherwise have been windfall gains for the oil companies, and for reductions in personal income taxes designed to compensate consumers for their higher oil bills.[30] And each proposal was greeted with a marked lack of enthusiasm by the heavily Democratic Congress.

There were several reasons for Congress's attitude, including a clear lack of respect for the workings of a free market. But perhaps foremost among these reasons was a concern that rapid decontrol might injure, and perhaps even abort, the nascent recovery. The argument, quite simply, was that rapid decontrol would constitute a supply shock not unlike the devastating shocks of 1973 and 1974 that had caused the Great Stagflation. For example, in June 1975, the Congressional Budget Office (CBO) estimated that phased decontrol of domestic oil prices over a 2-year period, coupled with the special import duties and an anticipated price hike by OPEC in October, would raise the GNP deflator nearly

[28] Technically, the floor on revenues is also binding, though it is hard to see what this could possibly mean.

[29] Congressional Budget Office (1975a), pp. 44–45.

[30] One specific example is described in *Economic Report of the President,* 1975, pp. 20–24.

2.5% by late 1976 and add more than .5 percentage point to the unemployment rate.[31] The administration claimed that the CBO exaggerated the dangers, but other sources on Capitol Hill claimed even larger effects. In any case, political support for the rapid decontrol plan was nil.

Other, more gradual, decontrol plans were proposed by the White House during the summer of 1975, but rejected by the Congress; and legal authority to control oil prices actually lapsed without an agreement at the end of August. In September 1975, with oil prices released from control *de jure* though not *de facto*,[32] the CBO estimated that immediate (*de facto*) decontrol would raise the late 1976 price level by 1.5%, and add .5 percentage point to the unemployment rate.[33] While the administration did not dispute these estimates, the executive–legislative battle raged into the winter. It was December before a reluctant President reached an accord with Congress under which a very gradual process of decontrol was started after an initial price rollback.

In his January 1976 economic messages, President Ford advocated an additional tax cut of approximately $10 billion which, coupled with extension of the 1975 cuts (estimated at roughly an $18 billion annual rate) would have meant that taxes were down some $28 billion relative to what they would have been under a continuation of 1974 law. However, he linked this proposal to a $28 billion cut in federal spending. While the administration advertised the policy as a matched reduction in both taxes and spending,[34] skeptics in Congress and elsewhere saw it as a $10 billion tax cut coupled with a $28 billion drop in spending, and worried about serious contractionary effects. On closer examination, however, there was probably less to the $28 billion in spending cuts than met the eye, for the cuts were from a hypothetical baseline budget for fiscal year 1977 that was well above spending levels for fiscal 1976. In any case, the President's budgetary proposals probably never had a serious chance of passing the Congress, despite the fact that Congressional spending habits were much less profligate in 1975 than they had been in previous years because of the new budgetary procedures.

---

[31] Congressional Budget Office (1975a, Table 12, p. 76). These estimates did not take account of the tax aspects of the President's energy program, which would have mitigated the effect on unemployment and output but exacerbated the effect on prices.

[32] The oil companies, expecting subsequent legislation, did not raise prices. The legislation finally came in December.

[33] Congressional Budget Office (1975b, Table 9, p. 55). The lower estimated price effects are attributable to the removal of the special import duties and a reduction in the price hike expected from OPEC (from $2.25 per barrel to $1.50 per barrel; in fact, it wound up just over $1 per barrel).

[34] Since the spending cuts were mainly on transfer payments, the balanced budget multiplier did not apply.

6. The Effectiveness of the 1975-1976 Tax Reductions

I come now to the important question of whether the effectiveness of the tax cuts of 1975 and 1976 was undermined by their explicitly temporary nature and, if so, to what extent. The discussion is divided into three sections. The first section reviews reasons why the implications of the pure permanent income (or life-cycle) theory must be modified, reasons that make the issue an empirical one, not to be decided on *a priori* grounds. Accordingly, the section also includes a brief review of previous empirical work on the question. The second section presents the basic ideas of the model to be estimated in as nontechnical a form as possible. (Details and equations are reserved for the appendix to this chapter, pages 167-177.) The empirical results are presented and analyzed in the third section.

THEORETICAL ISSUES AND EMPIRICAL PRECURSORS

Eisner (1969) seems to be the first to have brought the debate over the effectiveness of temporary income tax changes into print. Basing his argument on the permanent income theory of consumption, he claimed that we might expect a marginal propensity to consume (MPC) from the surtax as low as .04. But calculations I have made (Blinder, 1978) with a simple life-cycle model indicate that .09 is a better first guess as to the implications of the pure permanent income hypothesis. While these are crude estimates, not to be taken seriously, they do suggest that Okun's (1971) "zero effect" hypothesis goes well beyond the permanent income hypothesis. Moreover, there are a number of reasons to believe that the pure permanent income theory systematically *understates* spending from a temporary tax.

A first reason for why surtaxes may affect spending more strongly than indicated by pure theory is that the concept of *consumption* to which the theory applies differs from the *consumer spending* that is relevant to aggregate demand.[35] The theory may be correct in predicting little effect of a temporary tax on *consumption,* yet there could be a strong effect on aggregate demand if consumers "save" their tax rebates by purchasing durable goods. The extent to which consumers do this is, of course, an empirical question.[36]

A second reason is that some households may have their spending constrained by limitations on borrowing that are usually ignored by the

---

[35] The former is obtained from the latter by subtracting purchases of consumer durables and adding back the imputed service flow from the existing stock of durables.

[36] See, for example, Darby (1972).

permanent income theory. Such constrained households may react strongly to even temporary income changes.[37] Thus the aggregate MPC for a temporary tax is a weighted average of the low MPC's of unconstrained households and the high MPC's of constrained ones. Again, the importance of this phenomenon is an empirical question.

Third, as Okun (1971) pointed out, consumer behavior depends on what people *believe* rather than on what the government *announces*. If consumers disbelieve the government when it tells them that a tax hike is only temporary, then the spending response will be greater than that predicted by pure theory.[38] It is the *perceived* duration of the surtax, not the *declared* duration, that is relevant from the standpoint of the permanent income theory. This, too, is an empirical issue.

Finally, we must recognize the possibility that households may be more shortsighted than the rational long-term planners envisioned by the theory, or, what amounts to the same thing, may have very high discount rates. If they are very shortsighted, then temporary fluctuations in disposable income may have substantial effects on spending.

Notice that all four of these caveats point in the same direction: toward a greater MPC from temporary tax changes than would be predicted from the pure life-cycle theory. Thus Okun was surely right when he claimed that *a priori* reasoning like Eisner's could not settle the issue. Empirical tests are necessary.

Using the (somewhat disaggregated) consumption functions of four econometric models, Okun (1971) generated predictions of spending after the 1968 surcharge under two alternative hypotheses:

Full Effect. That consumers treated the income lost to the surtax just as they treat any income loss

Zero Effect. That consumers ignored the surtax entirely, and consumed just as they would have in its absence

He concluded that the "full effect" hypothesis fit the data better, but this conclusion has not gone unchallenged.

First of all, as was pointed out already in Okun's (1971) paper,[39] these two hypotheses are only two points on a continuum. Other intermediate hypotheses may be better than either extreme. In fact, when Solow and I (Blinder and Solow, 1974, pp. 107–109) used Okun's data on total consumer spending to consider an intermediate "50% effect" hypothesis,

---

[37] See Blinder (1976), Dolde (1979), and many of the references cited in these sources.

[38] The point has rather less cogency for tax cuts, but here too consumers may believe them to be more permanent than the government says.

[39] See especially page 190 and the appendix of Okun's paper.

we found that this hypothesis outperformed both of the possibilities considered by Okun.

Next, when Springer (1975) studied the same episode with an alternative consumption function, he reached the opposite conclusion from Okun: that "zero effect" always predicted better than "full effect." Furthermore, Springer argued, these disparate conclusions were not caused by using different models, but rather were attributable to several technical errors made by Okun. Springer found that while no single one of these errors of procedure would have been sufficient to reverse the conclusion that the "zero effect" hypothesis dominated, the combination of all three was indeed enough to do precisely this.[40] And Springer did not note that the "zero effect" hypothesis goes well beyond what the permanent income theory really claims; nor did he test the suggestion that a "50% effect" model would be better yet.[41]

Using a series of savings equations based on the Houthakker–Taylor (1966) model, Juster (1977) concluded that "consumers do not differentiate between tax changes advertised as permanent and those advertised as temporary." His conclusion was based on two findings: first, that the coefficient of taxes did not change much when the estimation period was extended from 1974:4 to 1976:4 (it did change some, however, and in the expected direction); second, that dummy variables for 1975:2 were insignificant (i.e., that his equations track that quarter's savings performance very well without dummies).

Finally, Modigliani and Steindel (1977) used a modified version of the life-cycle estimating equation to assess the effectiveness of the *rebate* portion of the 1975 tax cuts, assuming that the nonrebate portions were perceived as *permanent* right from the start and treating the 1968 surtax by dummy variables. They estimated their equation through 1975:1, and then used postsample residuals to estimate the effect of the rebate on spending. Their estimates implied a negligible impact of the rebate over a horizon of 1 or 2 quarters, but a virtually "full effect" view over a horizon of 6 quarters.

A MODEL OF A TEMPORARY TAX CHANGE

The theoretical and empirical review of the previous section leads to three conclusions that influenced the design of my own research. First,

---

[40] Okun (1977) and Springer (1977) have recently debated these points, especially whether Okun's alleged "errors" really were errors after all.

[41] But see Springer (1975, ftn. 18, p. 657). In his unpublished thesis, Springer (1974) offers a more general quantitative estimate of the impact of the surcharge. Unfortunately, his estimates for the distributed lag effects of windfalls on consumption are implausible.

the "zero effect" hypothesis of Okun is really outside the reasonable range; even the purest form of the permanent income hypothesis suggests that a temporary tax change will have *some* short-run effect. Second, if we consider a long enough period (e.g., a period equal to the planning horizon of the consumer), then *every* tax will be fully effective, regardless of how temporary or permanent it is. This conclusion follows simply because consumers *eventually* will spend almost all of any income change. Thus, if we want to inquire into the "effectiveness" of a temporary tax, it is crucial to specify the time horizon over which this "effectiveness" is to be judged. Third, and finally, both theory and evidence suggest that it is inappropriate to run a contest between two polar cases such as "zero effect" and "full effect," however these two extremes may be formulated. There is every reason to believe that the truth, as so often happens, lies between the two extremes.

One aspect of more recent economic theory was also relevant to the research design. Modern macroeconomic theory has riveted attention on the many ways in which people's *expectations* about the future affect their present economic behavior, and has suggested that a useful way to model these expectations is to assume that they are "rational," that is, that individuals and firms make the optimal use of whatever information they have in generating forecasts.[42] The relevance of this idea to the consumption function lies in the fact that the permanent income hypothesis assigns a critical role to expectations of *future* incomes as a determinant of *current* consumption. Thus, if we want to predict how consumers will react to a tax change, we must infer how this tax change affects their expectations of future incomes.

Two extreme examples will drive home the essential point. Suppose first that the government cuts taxes today, and announces that this will be a one-shot affair. (Suppose also that people believe this announcement.) Since no future income is affected, we would anticipate rather small spending responses by consumers whose "permanent incomes" are barely affected. As the other extreme, consider a tax cut announced (and believed) to be literally permanent.[43] Since every consumer would find his permanent income raised by the full amount of the tax cut, the response of spending should be rapid and complete.

These simple intuitive ideas can be generalized and given mathematical expression. They apply to tax changes whose degree of "permanentness"

---

[42] Though the literature on rational expectations is by now voluminous, the fundamental reference on both these points is Lucas (1976). For recent applications to the consumption function, see Hall (1978) and Sargent (1978).

[43] Dolde (1979) argues that, in view of the frequency with which the federal individual income tax is changed, this is an elusive concept in the real world.

is not so clear, and also to income changes for other reasons. The general principle is that *income changes believed to be relatively "permanent" will elicit stronger and quicker spending responses than income changes believed to be relatively "temporary."* This principle forms the basis for my model of consumer behavior, and provides an *a priori* presumption that temporary taxes should be less effective than permanent ones.

To implement this view and test its validity, three models were formulated which segregated sources of income according to their degree of "permanentness" or "temporariness."

In *Model 1*, I distinguish between only two sources of income: income (positive or negative) attributable to explicitly temporary income tax changes; and income from all other sources. Notice that other income is not "permanent" income, but rather represents a normal blend of permanent and transitory components. The basic idea of the model is that income gains or losses from temporary taxes are less permanent than ordinary income fluctuations, and we should be able to measure the corresponding differences in their effects on consumer spending.

In *Model 2*, the assumption that permanent taxes and other income have equal and opposite effects on spending is dropped, and three sources of income are distinguished: special income from temporary tax measures; income (or rather income losses) from permanent taxes; and income from all remaining sources. This separation was motivated by Dolde (1976) and Modigliani and Steindel (1977), who suggested that permanent income tax changes are probably more enduring than most other types of income changes experienced by consumers.

Finally, in *Model 3* income from transfer payments is separated from factor income and thus four income sources are distinguished: temporary taxes; permanent taxes; transfer payments; and factor income.

A tiny bit of algebra will explain the way in which the degree of "permanentness" of a temporary tax was assessed. Suppose that a consumer, on receiving a $1 increase in income from a permanent tax reduction in quarter t, spends according to the following distributed lag pattern:

w_0 in quarter t
w_1 in quarter $t + 1$
w_2 in quarter $t + 2$
$\vdots$
w_n in quarter $t + n$

where n is the spending horizon of the consumer.[44] The long-run MPC

---

[44] In pure theory, n is sometimes taken to be infinite. In my empirical work, I estimated n to be 7 (i.e., a 2-year spending horizon).

is $\Sigma_{j=0}^{n} w_j$, which I will hereafter just call "MPC," and is known to be around .9.

Suppose next that if the consumer received a *pure windfall gain* of $1 in quarter t (i.e., a receipt that had absolutely no impact on any future expected income), he would spend it in the following way:

β_0 in quarter t
β_1 in quarter $t + 1$
$\vdots$
β_n in quarter $t + n$

Theory implies that $\Sigma_{j=0}^{n} \beta_j$ is equal to the MPC; but the time pattern of the β's may be very different from that of the w's. Specifically, since "permanent" taxes are presumably more permanent than windfalls, we suspect that the "early" w's will be greater than the corresponding β's, while the "late" w's will necessarily be smaller.

I model consumer reactions to a temporary income tax change in the following way. While the temporary tax law remains in effect, I assume that consumers treat any income gains or losses from it as a weighted average of permanent taxes and pure windfalls. The weights are to be determined empirically. Thus spending in quarter $t + j$ is taken to be

$$\lambda w_j + (1 - \lambda)\beta_j, \qquad 0 \le \lambda \le 1.$$

The parameter λ is the central parameter to be estimated, as it indicates how "permanent" consumers consider a temporary tax to be. If $\lambda = 1$, there is no difference between tax changes announced to be temporary and those announced to be permanent. If $\lambda = 0$, temporary tax changes are treated like pure windfall gains or losses.

On the other hand, once the temporary tax measure has lapsed, I assume that consumers look back on the income gain or loss from that tax change as if it were a pure windfall, and thus use the spending weights β_j.

Other details of the model, including the precise derivation of the equations, are explained in the appendix. For now I content myself with listing the variables used to explain consumer expenditures in the model.[45] They are

1. Income gains (in the case of the 1975–1976 tax cut) or losses (in the case of the 1968 tax increase) from temporary taxes
2. Income from other sources, which is just one variable in Model 1, two variables (permanent taxes and everything else) in Model 2,

---

[45] Note that the variable to be explained is *consumer expenditures,* as defined in the national income accounts, not the economist's concept of *consumption.*

and three variables (permanent taxes, transfer payments, and factor incomes) in Model 3

3. The value of consumer wealth, which is subdivided into two components: wealth held in the stock market, and all other wealth
4. The real after-tax rate of interest[46]

Finally, there is a methodological issue that must be settled. Just as in the case of measuring the effects of wage–price controls in Chapter 6, one could appraise the effectiveness of the 1975–1976 temporary income tax cuts by using dummy variables, by the method of postsample predictions, or by the method of within-sample predictions. In fact, dummy variables were used (in one of his equations) by Juster (1977) and also by Modigliani and Steindel (1977) in dealing with the 1968 surcharge, while postsample predictions were used by Modigliani and Steindel (1977) to deal with the rebate. The issues in choosing among these three techniques are much the same as they were in the case of wage–price controls and, for much the same reasons, I have again chosen to adopt the method of within-sample predictions. My estimated equations cover the period from 1953:1 through 1977:4, and are used to generate predictions of consumer spending with and without the 1975–1976 tax cuts.

ESTIMATION RESULTS AND THEIR IMPLICATIONS

The actual estimating equations are quite complex and have many coefficients; rather than present and try to interpret them, Table 7-3 summarizes the most important findings.[47] The table is organized into three parts, corresponding to the three models that were estimated. In each part, columns (1)–(3) show, respectively, the cumulative marginal propensities to consume over various horizons from a permanent tax cut, a temporary tax that remains on the books for 2 years, and a rebate (i.e., a temporary tax that is on the books for only 1 quarter). Columns (4) and (5) indicate the relative effectiveness of the two types of temporary taxes by comparing the cumulative MPC's of 2-year taxes and rebates with those of a permanent tax. Thus, columns (4) and (5) display the principal results of the study.

Consider first Model 1, which, it will be recalled, assumes that spending patterns for permanent tax changes are equal and opposite to those for other sources of income. The estimate of λ for this model was .26, with standard error .40. While this is a wide standard error, it is probably about as good as could be hoped for given the paucity of data on tem-

---

[46] This is a complex variable to "measure." Its construction is described in the appendix.
[47] For the full results, see the appendix to this chapter.

TABLE 7-3
Relative Effectiveness of Temporary Taxes

	Model 1				
	(1)	(2)	(3)	(4)	(5)
		Cumulative spending propensities		Ratios	
Quarter	Permanent	Two-year	Rebate	(2)/(1)	(3)/(1)
0	.59	.15	.15	.25	.25
1	.79	.14	.08	.18	.10
2	.77	.10	.04	.12	.05
3	.69	.10	.07	.15	.10
4	.63	.21	.20	.32˙	.31
5	.65	.40	.40	.61	.63
6	.72	.63	.64	.87	.88
7	.81	.81	.81	1.00	1.00

	Model 2				
	(1)	(2)	(3)	(4)	(5)
		Cumulative spending propensities		Ratios	
j	Permanent	Two-year	Rebate	(2)/(1)	(3)/(1)
0	.28	.18	.18	.66	.66
1	.36	.22	.16	.59	.45
2	.37	.20	.14	.55	.37
3	.38	.23	.17	.60	.44
4	.43	.31	.28	.73	.64
5	.55	.47	.45	.87	.83
6	.69	.66	.66	.96	.95
7	.81	.81	.81	1.00	1.00

	Model 3				
	(1)	(2)	(3)	(4)	(5)
		Cumulative spending properties		Ratios	
j	Permanent	Two-year	Rebate	(2)/(1)	(3)/(1)
0	.34	.19	.19	.55	.55
1	.46	.25	.20	.54	.42
2	.49	.28	.22	.57	.45
3	.49	.32	.29	.65	.58
4	.53	.41	.40	.78	.76
5	.62	.55	.56	.90	.90
6	.73	.71	.72	.97	.98
7	.83	.83	.83	1.00	1.00

porary taxes (just two episodes). As explained in the appendix, the estimate enables us to reject the extreme hypothesis that $\lambda = 1$ (i.e., that temporary taxes are treated the same as permanent taxes), but does not allow us to reject the alternative extreme hypothesis that $\lambda = 0$ (i.e., that temporary taxes are regarded as pure windfalls). The numbers in Table 7-3 indicate that, according to Model 1, temporary taxes are far less effective than permanent ones over horizons of 1 to 5 quarters. For example, over a 1-year period (a relevant horizon for stabilization policy), a tax rebate would lead to only about 10% as much spending as would a permanent cut of the same magnitude. Notice also that, as must be the case, the two types of tax cut are equally effective over the entire horizon, which is estimated to be 2 years. This means that *because* rebates have so much less impact on spending in the first year, they *must* have correspondingly greater impacts on spending in the second year. Thus the estimated 2-year horizon will assume some importance in drawing conclusions about the 1975-1976 episode.

Models 2 and 3, which separate permanent taxes from other sources of income, lead to very similar conclusions; for convenience I will discuss only the estimates from Model 2. The estimated value of the weighting parameter λ in Model 2 was .52, with standard error .62. This large standard error makes it impossible to reject either $\lambda = 1$ or $\lambda = 0$, though the estimates are tantalizingly close to the ''50% effect'' hypothesis suggested by Solow and myself (Blinder and Solow, 1974, pp. 107-109). The ''relative effectiveness'' ratios in columns (4) and (5) are quite different from those of Model 1, and suggest a much greater (relative) impact from a temporary tax. Specifically, a rebate is about 66% as potent as a permanent tax in the initial quarter, and about 44% as strong over a year. (The corresponding figures from Model 1 are only 25 and 10%.) A glance at columns (1)-(3) reveals that the discrepancy arises not from the estimated effects of *temporary* taxes on consumer spending [columns (2) and (3)]—these are broadly similar in all three models. Instead, the differences arise because Models 2 and 3 are far more pessimistic than Model 1 about the short-run impact of a *permanent* tax [see column (1)].

These findings carry two important messages to fiscal policy planners. First, and most obvious, is that temporary taxes are less powerful devices for short-run stabilization purposes than are permanent ones. Second, and perhaps almost as important, the short-run relative ineffectiveness of such taxes implies (given the estimated 2-year spending horizon) that the impact of these measures in the second year is quite large. If the need is for a truly *short-run* stimulus to aggregate demand, this affect may also be unwanted.

I can illustrate both of these points by examining what the equations

TABLE 7-4
Average Propensity to Consume, 1975–1977[a]

Quarter	1975	1976	1977
1	.913	.914	.935
2	.881	.918	.926
3	.903	.922	.922
4	.907	.926	.925

[a]Source: Survey of Current Business.

have to say about the 1975–1976 episode. First, it is useful to display the observed average propensities to consume (APC) for this period (see Table 7-4). There are two obvious phenomena crying out for explanation in these data. First, why did the APC drop so sharply in 1975:2—the quarter of the rebate? Second, why did it thereafter begin a steady climb to what is a truly extraordinary level by 1977:1? (The corresponding personal saving rate was only 4.2%—the lowest figure recorded since the Korean War.)

According to my estimated equations, the temporary tax cuts of 1975–1976 caused both phenomena. Using the coefficients from each model, Table 7-5 shows the estimated *direct* (excluding multiplier) effects on consumer spending of the tax cuts listed in Table 7-2.[48] While the models differ in details, they all agree that (*a*) very little of the rebate was spent in 1975:2, (*b*) rather little of the disposable income attributable to the

TABLE 7-5
Estimated Effects of the 1975–1976 Temporary Tax Cuts on Consumer Expenditures[a]

Quarter	Model 1	Model 2	Model 3
1975:2	5.6	6.8	6.9
1975:3	− 0.7	1.3	2.6
1975:4	− 0.4	1.2	3.3
1976:1	2.4	3.5	5.5
1976:2	5.9	6.5	7.8
1976:3	7.9	7.7	8.0
1976:4	11.0	9.9	8.9
1977:1	11.9	10.4	8.8

[a]In billions of 1972 dollars.

[48] Only the 5 quarters from 1975:2 through 1976:2 are considered temporary cuts.

temporary tax cut package was spent during the first 4 quarters, (c) most of the spending was actually done in the next 4 quarters, (d) the peak effects on spending came in 1976:4 and 1977:1—precisely the quarters in which the saving rates were puzzlingly low. The equations track both the low APC of 1975:2 and the high APC's of 1976:4 and 1977:1 very well.

Finally, there is one more question. If instead of the 1975:2–1976:2 package of temporary measures, the government had cut taxes *permanently* by *T* in 1975:2 and then raised them *permanently* by *T* starting in 1976:3, how large a tax cut would have had the same average effect on aggregate demand?[49]

Table 7-6 provides answers to this question for the three different models and for three different horizons for measuring the average effect on aggregate demand. (For comparison, the average real value of the 1975–1976 tax cuts was $16 billion over the 5 quarters and $17.1 billion over the first 4 quarters.) The 4-quarter horizon from 1975:2 until 1976:1 seems the most relevant for this stabilization policy. In this case, Models 2 and 3 agree that about 45% of the tax cut was squandered because of its temporary nature. Model 1, on the other hand, implies that almost all of it was squandered. If we adopt a 6-quarter planning horizon instead, Models 2 and 3 agree that about 20% of the total revenue loss was wasted, while Model 1 makes this loss over 60%.

7. Summary

While not all of the misjudgments were as obvious with foresight as they are now with hindsight,[50] it is hard to find much good to say about

TABLE 7-6
Equivalent Permanent Tax[a,b]

Horizon	Model 1	Model 2	Model 3
4 quarters	2.4	9.2	10.2
6 quarters	5.9	13.0	13.1
8 quarters	12.2	16.6	16.1

[a]See text for definition.
[b]In billions of 1972 dollars.

[49] Note that for this calculation I assume that consumers were successfully fooled into thinking the tax cut of *T* would be permanent.

[50] Lest this sound too charitable, quite a few of the errors of policy were quite obvious even without the need for foresight!

fiscal policy during the period of the Great Stagflation. More often than not, policy was pushing in the wrong direction. And when the direction was right, the dosage was either too strong (as in 1973) or too weak (as in 1975).

In 1972, fiscal policy was pretty clearly too stimulative. Many economists held this view at the time, and virtually all hold it now. As a result of this policy error, what might have been a normal and healthy recovery from the 1970 recession turned into a runaway boom that, among other ill effects, undermined the existing program of price controls. There seem to be more-than-good reasons to believe that it was President Nixon's desire to defeat George McGovern, not the gap between actual and potential GNP, that motivated the fiscal policies of 1972, though an overestimate of potential may also have contributed.

A reversal in policy was clearly indicated in 1973, as pressures on industrial capacity and in labor markets became rather intense. But the turn we got was stunningly abrupt. Coupled with the stagflationary shocks from higher food prices (which started in early 1972 and were easy to see coming) and higher energy prices (which started in late 1973 and were far less easy to foresee), and with the simultaneous reversal in monetary policy (see the next chapter), these actions sent the economy into a tailspin.

The fiscal policy of 1974 was largely one of neglect. Whether this is to be interpreted as "benign neglect" or "malign neglect" depends on your attitudes toward inflation and unemployment for, as the old adage says, where you stand depends on where you sit. But among policymakers it is quite clear that the desire to combat inflation through tight budgetary policy was the dominating consideration. Perhaps fortunately, the country was too busy with Watergate related matters to pay too much attention to fiscal policy, so the damage was done mainly by "fiscal drag"— by automatic stabilizers that backfired in this instance and acted like automatic destabilizers.

Only at the start of 1975, after the worst of the recession was over, did the President turn from inflation fighting to recession fighting with a recommendation (quickly acted upon by Congress) for a tax cut. Many economists at the time viewed this as too little (part of it merely counteracted the inflationary "fiscal drag" of 1974) and much, much too late. Even beyond this, there are both solid theoretical and empirical reasons to believe that the tax medicine in this instance was much less effective than it could have been because the tax cuts were explicitly temporary. Ironically, the tax package was subsequently extended several times and eventually made a permanent feature of the tax code, so this loss of effectiveness was, in retrospect, pure waste.

During the recovery period in the second half of 1975 and throughout 1976, fiscal policy could be characterized as permissive, but no very important fiscal policy actions were taken. In part, this inaction resulted from a political stalemate between a Republican President, who wanted to restrain the economy with a tight budgetary policy and apply yet another supply shock by rapidly decontrolling old oil prices, and a Congress that would have none of either. In part, it was due to the new Congressional budgeting procedures that gave the Congress tighter control over the budget than it ever had before. In part, it was because the economy seemed to be recovering very nicely on its own, thank you. But in no small part it was due to the enormous budget deficits of the time, which scared even liberal legislators away from any policies that threatened to widen the deficit any further.

One striking feature of the 1972–1976 period is that, while a number of disparate economic and political influences guided fiscal policy actions, there were precious few times when the balance between aggregate demand and productive capacity appears to have been of much relevance to the conduct of national economic policy. So much for what we academic economists teach students about stabilization policy!

A second striking feature is how little awareness there seems to have been, in the public discussions, of the nature of the 1973–1974 inflation. Policy seems to have proceeded exactly as if the economy were experiencing a continuing inflation fueled by excessive aggregate demand—the sort of inflation that can be combatted successfully by contractionary fiscal (and monetary) policy. While this assessment was probably accurate in 1972 and early 1973, it was painfully inappropriate after late 1973, when the economy was mainly adjusting to several large one-time shocks to the price level coming from the supply side. In my view, the economy paid a high price for this misjudgment. Worse yet, the lesson of 1973–1974 has apparently not been learned.

APPENDIX
A Model of Temporary Tax Changes[51]

DERIVATION OF THE EQUATIONS

Starting with Model 1, let me introduce the notation S_t for special income (positive or negative) from temporary tax measures, and the notation R_t ("regular income") for income from all other sources. Since

---

[51] This appendix is based on Blinder (1978). A revised version will appear in the *Journal of Political Economy*.

three different temporary tax measures are considered in this analysis, the accounting identities are

$$Y_t = R_t + S_t, \tag{A.1}$$

$$S_t = S_t^1 + S_t^2 + S_t^3, \tag{A.2}$$

where S_t^i is the income attributable to the ith special tax measure. As indicated in the text, I suppose that consumption responds to R_t with the following fixed distributed lag pattern:

$$\frac{\partial C_t}{\partial R_{t-j}} = w_j, \qquad j = 0, 1, \ldots, n,$$

and that the distributed lag response of C_t to S_{t-j}^i is given by

$$\gamma_j = \lambda w_j + (1 - \lambda)\beta_j \tag{A.3}$$

while the tax remains on the books, and by β_j after the legislation lapses.

One further complication must be dealt with here, and can be explained best by an example. Suppose a special tax is on the books from period k to period $k + \tau$ (i.e., for $\tau + 1$ periods) and consider how S_k affects spending. During the $\tau + 1$ periods in which the tax is in effect, the model assumes that consumers apply the following marginal propensities to consume (MPC's):

$$\gamma_0 + \gamma_1 + \cdots + \gamma_\tau = \sum_{j=0}^{\tau} \beta_j + \lambda \sum_{j=0}^{\tau} (w_j - \beta_j)$$

by Eq. (A.3). If they then started treating S_k as a windfall loss, a naive application of the model would state that consumers cut spending by an additional

$$\beta_{\tau+1} + \beta_{t+2} + \cdots + \beta_n$$

in the remaining quarters. In that case, however, the total MPC out of S_k would be

$$\sum_{j=0}^{n} \beta_j + \lambda \sum_{j=0}^{\tau} (w_j - \beta_j) \neq \sum_{j=0}^{n} \beta_j.$$

Since this inequality is unreasonable in theory, it is necessary to adjust the $\beta_{\tau+1}, \ldots, \beta_n$ downward to make the sum correct. Thus, once a special tax is *off* the books, I assume that the distributed lag spending weights attached to it are

$$\gamma_j^i = \alpha_i \beta_j, \tag{A.4}$$

where α_i is a ratio that scales down the β's according to how long the ith special tax was on the books. The α_i depend on the estimated w's and β's, since they are defined to make

$$\sum_{j=0}^{\tau} \beta_j + \lambda \sum_{j=0}^{\tau} (w_j - \beta_j) + \alpha_i \sum_{j=\tau+1}^{n} \beta_j = \sum_{j=0}^{n} \beta_j. \qquad (A.5)$$

By introducing a dummy variable defined as

$$D_t^i = \begin{cases} 1 & \text{if the } i\text{th temporary tax remains on the books in quarter } t \\ 0 & \text{otherwise,} \end{cases}$$

it is possible to combine (A.3) and (A.4) into a single expression:

$$\gamma_j^i(t) = D_t^i[\lambda w_j + (1 - \lambda)\beta_j] + (1 - D_t^i)\alpha_i\beta_j, \qquad (A.6)$$

where the notation now indicates that the γ weights depend both on calendar time (because of the dummy variable) and on the specific tax under consideration (because of the α_i factor).

With these definitions and assumptions, I can explain the estimating equation. First, suppose there were no special taxes to worry about; then the basic empirical model of consumer behavior described in the text would be as follows:

$$C_t = k_0 + k_1 r_t Y_t + \sum_{j=0}^{n} w_j Y_{t-j} + k_2(W_t - A_t) + \sum_{j=0}^{q} k_{3+j} A_{t-j} + u_t,$$

where r_t is the real after tax rate of interest, W_t is real consumer net worth at the *beginning* of period t, A_t is the real market value of stock market wealth at the beginning of period t, and u_t is a stochastic error. The specific way in which assets are entered into the consumption function is suggested by the MPS model, and is also consistent with the theoretical analysis since stock market gains and losses are very transitory in nature. However, the long-run effects should be identical, so the constraint

$$k_3 + k_4 + \cdots + k_{3+q} = k_2$$

is imposed in estimation.

Now using (A.1) and (A.2) the model can be expanded to

$$C_t = k_0 + k_1 r_t Y_t + k_2(W_t - A_t) + \sum_{j=0}^{q} k_{3+j} A_{t-j}$$

$$+ \sum_{j=0}^{n} w_j R_{t-j} + \sum_{j=0}^{n} \gamma_j^1(t) S_{t-j}^1 + \cdots + \sum_{j=0}^{n} \gamma_j^3(t) S_{t-j}^3 + u_t. \qquad (A.7)$$

Substituting (A.1) and (A.6) into (A.7), and rearranging terms, gives

$$C_t = k_0 + k_1 r_t Y_t + k_2(W_t - A_t) + \sum_{j=0}^{q} k_{3+j} A_{t-j}$$

$$+ \sum_{j=0}^{n} w_j(Y_{t-j} + \lambda X_t^j - S_{t-j}) \tag{A.8}$$

$$+ \sum_{j=0}^{n} \beta_j \left[(1 - \lambda)X_t^j + \sum_{i=1}^{3} \alpha_i(1 - D_t^i)S_{t-j}^i \right] + u_t,$$

where

$$X_t^j \equiv D_t^1 S_{t-j}^1 + \cdots + D_t^3 S_{t-j}^3, \qquad j = 0, \ldots, n.$$

This is not the actual estimating equation because the α_i factors are defined by (A.5) to be functions of the w's and β's, because the distributed lag coefficients are constrained in several ways, and because corrections are made for both heteroskedasticity and serial correlation in the error term.[52] Nonetheless, (A.8) is the most useful form for interpreting the estimated parameters.

One obvious generalization of the model is to disaggregate disposable income Y_t into its two main components—personal income and personal taxes:

$$Y_t = P_t - T_t.[53]$$

Personal income is assumed to be spent according to the lag weights w_j, while "regular taxes" are assumed to be subject to a different set of lag weights $- v_j$. However, the constraint $\Sigma_{j=0}^{n} w_j = \Sigma_{j=0}^{n} v_j$ is imposed to insure equal long-runs MPCs. Special taxes are treated as previously explained, except that the v's replace the w's in Eqs. (A.3), (A.5), and (A.6). Thus the basic consumption function is[54]

$$C_t = k_0 + k_1 r_t Y_t + k_2(W_t - A_t) + \sum_{j=0}^{q} k_{3+j} A_{t-j}$$

$$+ \sum_{j=0}^{n} w_j P_{t-j} - \sum_{j=0}^{n} v_j(T_{t-j} - \lambda X_t^j + S_{t-j}) \tag{A.9}$$

$$+ \sum_{j=0}^{n} \beta_j \left[(1 - \lambda)X_t^j + \sum_{i=1}^{3} \alpha_i(1 - D_t^i)S_{t-j}^i \right] + u_t.$$

This equation represents Model 2.

[52] Details can be found in the appendix to Blinder (1978).

[53] In making this separation, I departed a bit from national income accounting conventions by including the employer's share of social insurance contributions in both P and T.

[54] Regular taxes are defined as $T + S$ because temporary tax increases are treated as negative values of S (losses of disposable income), while all tax increases are treated as positive values of T.

The final generalization is to disaggregate personal income into its two main components—factor income and transfer payments:[55]

$$P = F + V.$$

Thus the estimating equation is

$$C_t = k_0 + k_1 r_t Y_t + k_2 (W_t - A_t) + \sum_{j=0}^{q} k_{3+j} A_{t-j}$$

$$+ \sum_{j=0}^{n} w_j F_{t-j} + \sum_{j=0}^{n} \phi_j V_{t-j} - \sum_{j=0}^{n} v_j (T_{t-j} - \lambda X_t^j + S_{t-j}) \quad \text{(A.10)}$$

$$+ \sum_{j=0}^{n} \beta_j \left[(1 - \lambda) X_t^j + \sum_{i=1}^{3} \alpha (1 - D_t^i) S_{t-j}^i \right] + u_t,$$

which represents Model 3. Notice that Model 2 is nested in Model 3, and Model 1 is nested in Model 2.

DATA

As mentioned in the text, I use *consumer expenditures*, rather than pure *consumption*, as C_t. This seems most appropriate where the focus is on the evaluation of stabilization policy (as it is here) rather than on testing the permanent income or life-cycle models of consumption.

Official national accounts data are used for C_t, Y_t, P_t, T_t, and V_t, except for the minor modification mentioned in footnotes 53 and 55. All data are in billions of 1972 dollars, at annual rates.

Data for the 1968 surcharge are taken from Okun (1971) and converted to 1972 dollars by the deflator for personal consumption expenditures. These constitute the series S_t^1. The data for the various 1975–1976 tax cuts, shown in Table 7-2, are similarly deflated and segregated into two time series. S_t^2 is defined as the explicitly one-shot measures: the tax rebates and the social security bonuses. The rest comprise S_t^3. Since the 1975 cuts were extended several times and are now a permanent feature of the tax code, an arbitrary decision had to be made as to when they became "permanent." I decided to cut off S_t^3 after 1976:2, because by then the cuts had already been extended once in the Revenue Adjustment Act of 1975 and a second time in the Tax Reform Act of 1976.

Data on consumer net worth W_t, and its breakdown into stock market and nonstock market components, A_t and $W_t - A_t$, respectively, are taken from the data bank of the MPS model and converted to 1972

---

[55] For this purpose, both employer contributions and business transfers are considered to be factor income, and the aspects of the 1975–1976 tax cuts that are classified as transfer payments in the national income accounts are grouped with temporary taxes.

dollars. They are based on a number of primary sources, the most important of which is the flow of funds.

Because of the recent findings of Boskin (1978), I thought it important to use a *real after tax* interest rate in the consumption function. Thus

$$r_t = i_t(1 - \tau_t) - \pi_t,$$

where i_t is the nominal rate on Treasury bills, τ_t is the *marginal* tax rate, and π_t is the *expected* rate of inflation. The latter two series require some explanation.

The tax rate τ_t was obtained by dividing the sum of federal and state-local personal tax and nontax payments by personal income excluding transfers (an approximation to the tax base), and then applying a correction factor to convert this *average* tax rate into a *marginal* tax rate.[56]

Inflationary expectations were generated by a model in which I assume that consumers base their expectations of the inflation rate $\dot{P}_t$ on its own past history and on the history of the growth rate of the money supply $\dot{M}_t$. To make this idea operational, I estimated an equation of the form

$$\dot{P}_t = a_0 + \sum_{j=1}^{J} a_i \dot{P}_{t-j} + \sum_{i=0}^{I} b_i \dot{M}_{t-i} + e_t$$

on actual U.S. quarterly data, using the deflator for personal consumption expenditures for P_t and M_2 for M_t, and assumed that consumers used this equation to generate expectations. In estimation, I used the Almon (1965) lag technique with third-degree polynomials, no endpoint constraints, and various choices for J and I. The best results were obtained with $J = 11$ and $I = 17$, viz.,[57]

$$\dot{P}_t = \underset{(.38)}{-.60} + \sum_{1}^{11} a_j \dot{P}_{t-j} + \sum_{0}^{17} b_i \dot{M}_{t-1}, \qquad R^2 = .73, \qquad DW = 1.98,$$

$$\sum a_j = \underset{(.10)}{.67}, \qquad \sum b_i = \underset{(.09)}{.27},$$

standard error = 1.42, mean of dependent variable = 3.35.

It will be noted that the long-run elasticity of $\dot{P}$ with respect to $\dot{M}$ is almost unity.

---

[56] For details, see Blinder (1978, pp. 23–25).

[57] Standard errors are in parentheses. DW is the Durbin–Watson statistic. The period of estimation was 1951:3 through 1977:4, the longest period possible given the need for 17 lagged values of M.

EMPIRICAL RESULTS

Model 1. In the first model, disposable income is separated into only two components: regular income (with expenditure weights w_j) and temporary taxes. As the equation is highly nonlinear, estimation was done by the numerical optimization package developed by S. M. Goldfeld and R. E. Quandt. The results from estimating Eq. (A.8) on quarterly data covering 1953:1 through 1977:4 are presented in Table 7-7. The number in parentheses next to each estimated coefficient is its asymptotic standard error (or rather a numerical estimate thereof).

In interpreting the standard error of the regression, it should be mentioned that in order to avoid heteroskedasticity, the equation was transformed so that the left-hand variable was the *average propensity to consume,* C_t/Y_t, rather than consumer spending. Thus, the standard error of .0046 is relative to a typical value for the APC of about .90. This

TABLE 7-7
Parameter Estimates for Model 1^a

k_0 = constant = 9.2 (3.9)
k_1 = coefficient of interest rate = $-.0005$ (.0008)
k_2 = coefficient of non-stock-market wealth = .021 (.008)
λ = weight on regular income = .26 (.40)
ρ = autocorrelation coefficient = .80 (.07)
sum of squared residuals = .00208
standard error = .00456
standard error of unadjusted errors^b = .00763
number of observations = 100

j	w_j	β_j	k_{3+j}	γ_j	Rebate
		Distributed Lag Coefficients^c			
0	.59 (.05)	$-.01$ (.35)	.008 (.003)	.15	.15
1	.19 (.02)	$-.08$ (.16)	.006 (.002)	$-.01$	$-.07$
2	$-.02$ (.03)	$-.05$ (.08)	.004 (.002)	$-.04$	$-.04$
3	$-.08$ (.03)	.04 (.10)	.002 (.001)	.01	.03
4	$-.06$ (.02)	.16 (.13)		.10	.13
5	.01 (.02)	.26 (.14)		.19	.21
6	.08 (.02)	.29 (.13)		.23	.23
7	.09 (.02)	.22 (.09)		.18	.18
Sum	.81	.81	.021 (.008)	.81	.81

^{a}Asymptotic standard errors are in parentheses.
^{b}Without a correction for autocorrelation.
^{c}Components may not add to totals due to rounding.

represents a fairly good fit.[58] Of course, obtaining a good fit with a consumption function is hardly a notable achievement, and the equation—like most consumption functions—suffers from severe autocorrelation.

The most critical parameter for purposes of this study is λ, the weight attached to regular income in Eq. (A.3). The point estimate of .26 suggests that temporary taxes that are still on the books are treated much more like windfalls than like regular income. However, the standard error is regrettably large; there are, after all, pitifully few observations that can be used to estimate λ. The null hypotheses $\lambda = 0$ or $\lambda = 1$ can nonetheless be tested by the following likelihood ratio test, which is analogous to a standard F test.[59] Let l denote the likelihood ratio. Then, under the assumption of normal errors, the statistic

$$-2 \log l = T \log \left(\frac{\text{SSR}_r}{\text{SSR}} \right)$$

is distributed as χ^2 with r degrees of freedom where

T = number of observations (=100 in this case)
SSR = minimized value of the sum of squared residuals in the unconstrained regression
SSR_r = minimized value of the sum of squared residuals in the constrained regression
r = number of constraints (=1 in this case)

When these tests were run with Eq. (A.8) as the unconstrained regression, the results were as follows:

Null hypothesis	Test statistic
$\lambda = 0$	0.37
$\lambda = 1$	18.13

Since the critical 1% point of the χ_1^2 distribution is 6.63, $\lambda = 0$ (temporary taxes are regarded as pure windfalls) cannot be rejected, but $\lambda = 1$ (temporary taxes are regarded as regular income) can be decisively rejected at any reasonable level of significance.

Notice that the β_j's reported in Table 7-7 are in some sense out of sample extrapolations since there are no "pure windfalls" recorded in the data.[60] Their only use is to form the weighted average $\lambda w_j + (1 -$

---

[58] The standard errors of a comparable equation in Modigliani and Steindel (1977) are .0056 with an autocorrelation correction and .0065 without.

[59] See Goldfeld and Quandt (1972, p. 74).

[60] I made an attempt, in some early regressions, to treat the National Service Life Insurance Dividends of 1950 in this way. But I was not successful.

$\lambda)\beta_j$, which is reported in the column marked γ_j. These are the expenditure coefficients for income from a temporary tax *if* that tax remains on the books for the entire 2-year horizon. To illustrate the opposite extreme, the column titled "Rebate" shows the spending coefficients for a temporary tax that lasts only 1 quarter. These two columns differ in details, but are broadly similar. There is a moderate spending response in the initial quarter, followed by very little spending over the next 3 or 4 quarters. Apparently, most of the spending out of a temporary tax cut comes 5, 6, and 7 quarters later.

Model 2. In the second model, spending coefficients for taxes are allowed to differ from those for permanent income, and the interpretation of λ is changed accordingly. Thus γ_j when a temporary tax is on the books is now defined as

$$\gamma_j = \lambda v_j + (1 - \lambda)\beta_j,$$

where the v_j's are the spending coefficients for "regular" taxes. The estimates obtained with Eq. (A.9) are displayed in Table 7-8.

TABLE 7-8
Parameter Estimates for Model 2[a]

k_0 = constant = 9.3 (0.2)
k_1 = coefficient of interest rate = $-.0006$ (.0008)
k_2 = coefficient of non-stock-market wealth = .021 (.008)
λ = weight on regular taxes = .52 (.62)
ρ = autocorrelation coefficient = .85 (.07)
sum of squared residuals = .00183
standard error = .00428
standard error of unadjusted errors[b] = .00802
number of observations = 100

			Distributed Lag Coefficients[c]			
j	w_j	v_j	β_j	k_{3+j}	γ_j	Rebate
0	.58 (.05)	.28 (.10)	.08 (.26)	.008 (.003)	.18	.18
1	.17 (.02)	.08 (.05)	$-.03$ (.13)	.006 (.002)	.03	$-.02$
2	$-.03$ (.03)	.01 (.05)	$-.03$ (.10)	.004 (.002)	$-.01$	$-.02$
3	$-.09$ (.02)	.01 (.04)	.03 (.09)	.002 (.001)	.02	.03
4	$-.05$ (.02)	.06 (.03)	.13 (.09)		.09	.11
5	.03 (.02)	.11 (.04)	.21 (.11)		.16	.18
6	.10 (.02)	.15 (.05)	.24 (.12)		.19	.20
7	.11 (.02)	.12 (.04)	.18 (.09)		.15	.16
Sum	.81	.81	.81	.021 (.008)	.81	.81

[a]Asymptotic standard errors are in parentheses.
[b]Without a correction for autocorrelation.
[c]Components may not add to totals due to rounding.

TABLE 7-9
Parameter Estimates for Model 3^a

k_0 = constant = 9.2
k_1 = coefficient of interest rate = $-.0005$
k_2 = coefficient of non-stock-market wealth = .018
λ = weight on regular taxes = .46
γ = autocorrelation coefficient = .78
sum of squared residuals = .00174
standard error = .00417
standard error of unadjusted errors^b = .00670
number of observations = 100

			Distributed Lag Coefficients^c				
j	w_j	ϕ_j	v_j	β_j	k_{3+j}	γ_j	Rebate
0	.61	.40	.34	.05	.007	.19	.19
1	.17	$-.04$	.12	.01	.005	.06	.01
2	$-.05$	$-.19$	.02	.03	.004	.03	.02
3	$-.11$	$-.14$	.01	.09	.002	.05	.07
4	$-.06$	.01	.04	.14		.09	.12
5	.04	.20	.08	.18		.14	.15
6	.12	.31	.12	.19		.16	.16
7	.12	.28	.10	.14		.12	.12
Sum	.83	.83	.83	.83	.018	.83	.83

^{a}Due to technical problems with the numerical optimization routines, standard errors of parameter estimates were not obtained.
^{b}Without a correction for autocorrelation.
^{c}Components may not add to totals due to rounding.

In terms of fit, it is an open question whether Model 2 is superior to Model 1. The standard error of the regression falls by about 6%; but the autocorrelation becomes a bit worse, so that the standard error of the uncorrected residuals actually is higher than in Model 1. However, the null hypothesis that the v's are equal to the w's (which, if true, would reduce Model 2 to Model 1) is resoundingly rejected by the data with a likelihood ratio test statistic of 12.78, which is significant at the .5% level and beyond.

Apart from the new v_j coefficients, the only major change in the estimates is in λ—which rises from .26 to .52. However, the huge standard error of λ suggests that we really have very little ability to pin this parameter down. More precisely, likelihood ratio tests fail to reject either $\lambda = 0$ or $\lambda = 1$.[61] The γ_j column sheds some further light on this. While

[61] The test statistics are .37 and .57, respectively.

the values of the γ's look a little better than in Table 7-7, since the negative coefficients are virtually gone, the main observation is that the γ's change very little as we move from Model 1 to Model 2. In order to keep the γ's relatively constant across models, the regression must give a much greater weight to the v_j's in Model 2 than it did to the w_j's in Model 1.

Model 3. The final model allows the two major components of personal income—factor payments and transfer payments—to have different spending coefficients. In this case, the coefficients w_j refer to factor income while a new set of coefficients ϕ_j refers to transfers. Table 7-9 shows the estimation results.

Both the fit of this equation and the degree of first-order serial correlation are a bit better than in the previous model. Model 3 reduces to Model 2 in the case that $\phi_j = w_j$; and it is easy to test this equality constraint by a likelihood ratio test. The resulting test statistic—which is distributed as χ_2^2 under the null hypothesis—is 4.97, which is significant at the 10% level but not at the 5% level.

In general, the parameter estimates are quite similar to those of the previous two models. Note that the distributed lag coefficients for windfalls and both varieties of temporary taxes no longer have any negative entries. But, on the other hand, factor and transfer income have some negative coefficients that are surprisingly large.[62]

On balance, then, it is not clear which is the better model—which is why I have reported the results from all three.

---

[62] The SSR function for Model 3 appeared to be somewhat less well behaved than that for the other two models, and so it took more effort to find a minimum. It is these computational problems that account for the absence of standard errors in Table 7-9, and also make me wonder about the superiority of Model 3.

8 monetary policy and the great stagflation

Lack of money is the root of all evil.
—George Bernard Shaw

Monetary policy during the 1972-1976 period has been indicted along much the same lines as fiscal policy; this chapter sets forth and examines the particulars of that indictment.

There is by now wide agreement that the Federal Reserve System pumped up the economy to an unhealthy degree in 1972, though its motives are still highly controversial. While a movement toward tighter money was probably imperative in 1973, many believe that the Fed switched gears much too abruptly. It would be an understatement to say that monetary policy did little to stem the slide into recession in 1974, or even to soften the landing; and by the beginning of 1975 there was an almost universal chorus of condemnation of the Fed for its tight money policies. Then, during the early stages of the recovery in 1975 and 1976, the System was again criticized by Keynesians for giving insufficient support to aggregate demand, though monetarists generally dissented from this view.

It is, however, difficult to make the case against the Fed airtight because of the erratic behavior of the demand for money during the 1974-1976 period.[1] Federal Reserve actions operate on the real economy by affecting the balance of supply and demand in the markets for money and

[1] The view that the demand for money behaved in strange ways in these years is widespread. See, for example, Goldfeld (1976). But for a dissenting view see Hamburger (1977).

179

credit. In normal times, with the *demand* for money and credit behaving in predictable ways, analysts can appraise the Fed's actions by looking at the money *supply*. But when the demand for money shifts in unpredictable ways, the analyst, just like the policymaker, finds himself at sea without a rudder. As a result, in trying to write an objective appraisal of monetary policy during the 1973–1975 downswing and the 1975–1976 upswing, I get the same uneasy feeling I always get when I buy a pair of new shoes: it always seems that one shoe is too loose while the other is too tight.

1. Loosening the Monetary Reins in 1972

In early 1972 the Federal Reserve System, like the administration, was more concerned with bringing down the unemployment rate than with fighting inflation. Its policy directives during the first quarter basically continued the policy of late 1971 of ''fostering financial conditions consistent with the aims of the new government program.''[2] As is so often the case, the ''aims'' that the Federal Open Market Committee enumerated were broad enough to rationalize *any* policy: ''sustainable real economic growth and increased employment, abatement of inflationary pressures, and attainment of reasonable equilibrium in the country's balance of payments.'' One wonders why they excluded apple pie, motherhood, and the American way.

Slightly more specifically, the FOMC sought ''greater growth in the monetary aggregates over the months ahead'' in its January meeting and ''moderate growth'' in its February and March meetings. Chairman Arthur Burns told the Joint Economic Committee in February that ''the Federal Reserve does not intend to let the present recovery falter for want of money or credit,'' but added, ''just as firmly, that the Federal Reserve will not release the forces of a renewed inflationary spiral.''[3] Dissents from the Committee's expansionary policy during these months came from members Alfred Hayes and Monroe Kimbrel who worried that the Fed's policies might push short-term interest rates down too far.

The Committee hesitated a bit in April and May, calling for some slowdown in the rapid rates of money growth that had been achieved during 1972:1,[4] but resumed its call for ''moderate growth in the monetary

---

[2] Jordan (1973, p. 14). This is also the source of other information about FOMC decisions in 1972 cited below.

[3] *Federal Reserve Bulletin*, February 1972, p. 125, as quoted by Jordan (1973).

[4] This rate is 8.2% in the latest data, but appeared much larger then.

aggregates'' in the summer months. Philip Coldwell of the Dallas Fed, in a July dissent, was the only voice arguing that the policy stance was too expansive. But by September the majority of the Committee was convinced that slower money growth was necessary, and this attitude prevailed through the end of the year and into 1973.

The money growth rates that the Fed actually achieved are depicted in Figure 8-1. Growth in the aggregates, which had accelerated tremendously in the first half of 1971 and decelerated even more in the second half, generally increased throughout 1972. (The story is less clear with M_2 than with M_1.) In total, the annual growth rates over the 2-year period 1970:4 to 1972:4 were 7.5% for M_1 and 11.3% for M_2. Both were extraordinarily exuberant rates by historical standards.

The Blinder–Goldfeld series on monetary influence on real GNP (see Chapter 3, especially Figure 3-3) records an enormous move toward expansion beginning in mid 1970 and culminating in mid 1972. This seems roughly consistent with what the Fed was saying it wanted to do. But if we seek a measure of the effect of monetary policy on each quarter's real GNP, we need something analogous to the $F(t)$ measure that I constructed for Chapter 7's evaluation of fiscal policy. For this purpose, I have constructed a monetary indicator, called $M(t)$, which measures

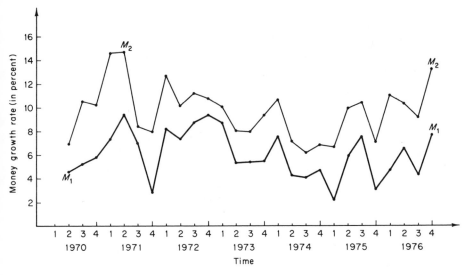

Figure 8-1. Monetary growth rates, 1970–1976 (seasonally adjusted annual rates). (*Source:* Federal Reserve.)

TABLE 8-1
Portion of Real GNP Attributable to Monetary Policy (in Billions of Dollars)

Quarter	$M(t)$ in 1958 \$ (1)	Deviation from trend in 1958 \$ (2)	Deviation from trend in 1972 \$ (3)	Actual real GNP (4)	Real GNP less $M(t)$ deviation (5)
1971:1	72.4	0	0	1095.3	1095.3
2	77.2	− 1.3	− 2.0	1103.3	1105.3
3	78.4	− 6.7	− 10.1	1111.0	1121.1
4	89.9	− 2.2	− 3.3	1120.5	1123.8
1972:1	101.8	+ 2.1	+ 3.2	1141.2	1138.0
2	124.1	+16.0	+ 24.2	1163.0	1138.8
3	149.6	+32.5	+ 49.2	1178.0	1128.8
4	170.8	+43.9	+ 66.5	1202.2	1135.7
1973:1	192.5	+55.0	+ 83.3	1229.8	1146.5
2	216.2	+67.2	+101.7	1231.1	1129.4
3	226.2	+64.8	+ 98.1	1236.3	1138.2
4	225.4	+50.5	+ 76.5	1242.6	1166.1
1974:1	210.4	+21.0	+ 31.8	1230.2	1198.4
2	205.3	0	0	1224.5	1224.5

the total effect of *all* monetary policies on real GNP in quarter t.[5] The series is shown in the first column of Table 8-1, and it is clear that its growth between, say, 1971:3 and 1973:3 is enormous.

A problem with this series, as with all of the Blinder–Goldfeld series on monetary influence, is that it compares actual history with what would have occurred with *no changes* in the monetary policy instruments. In particular, the comparison path holds the nominal monetary base fixed. Since any path that claims to represent a "neutral" monetary policy would include some growth in the nominal base, substantial positive values for $M(t)$ are normal. But how large? There seems to be no natural baseline analogous to the baseline that constant real government purchases and constant tax rates provides for fiscal policy, so some arbitrary choice must be made. In the second column of Table 8-1, I have de-trended $M(t)$ by fitting an exponential trend from 1971:1 to 1974:2. This

---

[5] $M(t)$ is defined by

$$M(t) = M_y^0(t) + M_y^1(t - 1) + M_y^2(t - 2) + \cdots,$$

where once again some truncation procedure makes this sum computable.

In this case I have used procedure D, which forces monetary effects on real GNP to be zero after 4 years. Recall that each $M_y^j(t - j)$ measures the effect of quarter $t - j$'s monetary actions on real GNP in quarter t; so the combined $M(t)$ measure gives the total effect of monetary policy.

"trend" policy gives the economy the same real growth from monetary sources over the entire 3.5-year period as did the actual policies, but distributes it smoothly through time. Since there is no suggestion that monetary policy was "right" for either 1971:1 or 1974:2, I want to stress that the deviations shown in column (2) are meant to be purely descriptive, not normative. They are but a crude measure of the "bulge" in monetary stimulus.

The deviations are converted to 1972 dollars in column (3), and subtracted from actual GNP [column (4)] to give an indication of how real GNP would have behaved under a steady monetary policy in column (5).[6] The hypothetical series in column (5) behaves quite differently from the actual GNP. For example, the 2-year growth in GNP (at annual rates) from 1971:1 until the end of the boom in 1973:1 was 6%, but would have been only 2.3% if $M(t)$ grew on trend. More dramatically, during the 1 year before the election (1971:4–1972:4), actual GNP rose by 7.3%, but the hypothetical GNP of column (5) increased only 1.1%.

My personal view is that the MPS model, if anything, overstates the potency of monetary policy during this period, so the *quantitative* dimensions of Table 8-1 may be exaggerated. But the qualitative aspects are too clear to be missed. It appears that the boom during the 2-year period ending in 1973:1, and especially the spurt before the 1972 election, was largely a consequence of monetary policy. Without tremendous support from the Federal Reserve, the 1971–1972 economy would have been much weaker.

That Federal Reserve policy was a powerful expansionary engine in 1972 seems beyond dispute. Knowing *why* is less easy. The simplest explanation is that the Chairman of the Fed was assisting the President of the United States in orchestrating the most successful political business cycle in our history. The notion that Federal Reserve decisions are objective and "nonpolitical" has long been recognized to be a myth.[7] Furthermore, we know that Arthur Burns was Richard Nixon's appointee and long-time associate, and we may surmise that neither of them had forgotten the close election of 1960 (see pages 143–144). Given the slender margin by which Nixon was defeated by Kennedy, statistical studies of voting behavior buttress the notion that a little economic stimulation in 1960, as Burns had suggested, would have turned the election in Mr.

---

[6] Two caveats here. This is certainly *not* a policy of steady monetary growth, but rather of steadily growing influence on real GNP. Second, it seems certain that the trend observed in $M(t)$ over this period is much more vigorous than what would be found along a steady growth path. For example, $M(t)$ grew by 184% while real GNP grew by only 11.8%. So, if anything, monetary policy is "too expansive" when it is on trend.

[7] See, for example, Maisel (1973).

Nixon's favor. This is a lesson that neither Nixon nor Burns would have been likely to have forgotten by 1972.

Still, a conspiratorial explanation may be too facile. The Federal Reserve is not nearly as independent in practice as it appears to be on paper; as Mr. Dooley said of the Supreme Court, it watches the election returns. The folklore has it that Mr. Nixon's political operatives, and possibly Mr. Nixon himself, put tremendous political pressure on the Fed to support the expansionary fiscal program.[8] So it may be that Burns and the Fed were coerced into joining the fun against their better judgment. Or it may be that vestiges of the old policy of stabilizing interest rates induced the Fed to supply enough money to keep interest rate increases in bounds despite the soaring demands for money and credit. Indeed, as William Poole (1979) suggests, Mr. Burns' position as Chairman of the Committee on Interest and Dividends under the price controls program would have placed him in an awkward public-relations position had interest rates been allowed to rise.

Thus, even with the advantages of hindsight, I can do no more than speculate on the motives. But one does not need to understand motivation to recognize a mistake. The Fed erred in 1972—and in a big way.

2. The Turn toward Restraint in 1973

As already noted, the Fed was backing away from its extremely expansive stance in late 1972. In its December 1972 directive, for example, it called for "slower growth in monetary aggregates over the months ahead than appears indicated for the second half" of 1972.[9] This attitude continued right through the first 8 months of 1973, with every policy directive calling for slower growth in the coming months than had been achieved over the near term past.

As documented by the Federal Reserve Bank of St. Louis,[10] these wishes were translated into actions despite the System Account Manager's continuing difficulty with meeting the monthly target for growth of bank reserves. Monetary growth slowed significantly in 1973 (see also Figure 8-1). While this was happening, not surprisingly, short-term interest rates were rising. The 3-month Treasury bill rate, for example, rose

[8] See, for example, Pierce (1979), Maisel (1973, pp. 267–268), and a number of journalistic accounts cited by Tufte (1978, pp. 49n–50n).

[9] With the revised data, these growth rates turned out to be about 9% for M_1 and 11% for M_2.

[10] Balbach and Jordan (1974, p. 5). This article is the source of all characterizations of the quotations from the 1973 minutes of the FOMC that follow.

from 5.3% in January to 8.7% in August. However, inflation was on the upswing, so we should not be too quick to label this a consequence of monetary restraint.

Then attitudes in the FOMC began to change. With the staff in September and October predicting slower real economic growth than it had predicted earlier, the Committee agreed that the economic situation required "moderate growth" in the aggregates. This continued to be the policy directive in November, though the staff was projecting sluggish economic growth in the first half of 1974, even in the absence of an oil crisis. Frank Morris of the Boston Fed dissented in November that more stimulus was appropriate, given the deterioration in the economic outlook. And by the December meeting the majority of the FOMC[11] was persuaded that a "modest easing of monetary policy" was required "provided that the monetary aggregates do not appear to be growing excessively." Growth in M_2, but not in M_1, increased a bit in 1973:4, and interest rates fell.

The Blinder–Goldfeld series on the thrust of *current* monetary policy again accords reasonably well with what the FOMC was saying during 1973. It shows a tremendous reduction in monetary stimulus from 1972:4 to the first half of 1973, a very tight monetary policy in 1973:3, and a large move toward stimulus in 1973:4. The corresponding series on the impact of current and past policies, however, falls steadily through the year, implying successively less stimulus. But monetary policy works with long lags, so the $M(t)$ series computed for Table 8-1 rises in 1973:1–1973:3, and is virtually steady in 1973:4. When considered as a deviation from trend, the peak effect of monetary policy on real GNP comes in the second and third quarters, and there is a notable slackening already by 1973:4 (see Table 8-1). On balance, real growth during 1973 (3.4%) was only slightly larger than it would have been if monetary policy had adhered to trend (2.7%).[12]

3. Monetary Policy during the Downswing, 1974:1-1975:1

The year 1974 was a critical one for the U.S. economy, but, unfortunately, our ability to appraise monetary policy started to fail us in the second half of the year, for it was then that the demand for money (M_1) began to shift rapidly. When Stephen Goldfeld (1976) estimated a con-

---

[11] Alfred Hayes of New York, in dissent, argued against easing policy while inflation was so rapid.

[12] Compare columns (4) and (5) in Table 8-1.

ventional demand function for M_1 through 1973:4, and used it to predict the money stock in 1974:1–1976:2, he found the residuals shown in Table 8-2 from a dynamic simulation. The equation, which did so well through 1973, consistently overpredicted the demand for M_1 balances, and by increasingly large amounts, over the 1974–1976 period.

However, because of the long lags, we can be reasonably confident that monetary policy was a drag on the economy in early 1974. The $M(t)$ series of Table 8-1 declines from \$225 billion to \$205 billion (in 1958 dollars) during the first half of 1974—a drop of roughly \$30 billion when converted to 1972 prices. The lagged effects of the restrictive monetary policies of 1973 clearly helped bring on the 1974–1975 recession. But what are we to say about policy during the downswing of 1974 and early 1975?

Perhaps a good place to start is with the FOMC minutes, as an indication of what the Fed was *trying* to do. There can be no doubt that up until December 1974 that Committee's chief worry was inflation, and that it desired to keep monetary conditions quite tight.

Each month between February 1974 and May 1974, the Committee lowered its ranges of tolerance for money growth and raised the range for the Federal funds rate. And, for the most part, it was able to hit these targets. In its May and June operating instructions to the Trading Desk, the FOMC declared its desire "to maintain about the prevailing restrictive money market conditions."[13] The only dissent in either meeting came from George Clay of the Kansas City Fed who worried in June that such high money growth rates would aggravate the inflation problem. In September and October, while the ranges of tolerance were still below those of June,[14] the operating instructions were calling for "conditions consis-

TABLE 8-2
Residuals from a Money Demand Equation[a,b]

Quarter	1974	1975	1976
1	−1.2	−14.7	−22.3
2	−3.0	−14.0	−22.3
3	−5.8	−15.1	−
4	−9.5	−19.4	−

[a] *Source:* Goldfeld (1976, Table 2, p. 687).
[b] Actual minus predicted in billions of 1972 dollars.

[13] This statement and what follows are taken from Roesch (1975).
[14] Growth of M_1 badly missed the target ranges (on the low side) in both July and August. M_2 growth missed (also low) in August.

tent with moderate growth in monetary aggregates." Alfred Hayes, dissenting in September, observed that inflation continued unabated while a severe recession was unlikely! Only in mid December 1974 did the FOMC take the view that "somewhat more rapid growth in monetary aggregates" should be achieved, with Governors Henry Wallich and George Mitchell dissenting that this easing of monetary policy was too timid.

The minutes of the FOMC clearly indicate that the Fed *wanted* to speed up growth in the monetary aggregates moderately in early 1975, but it did not succeed in this goal. Instead, as Table 8-3 shows, growth in M_2 was roughly constant while that of M_1 decelerated sharply. However, the shocking behavior of M_1 from 1974:4 to 1975:1 presumably had a lot to do with the downward shift in the demand function for M_1. And these downward shifts in demand, in turn, were not independent of the Fed's regulatory actions. Goldfeld's residual increased by \$5.2 billion in real terms in the first quarter of 1975 alone—an annual rate of decline of 9.3%; and it is clear that financial innovations permitted or encouraged by the Fed explain part of this decline. How well the Fed could have anticipated the *quantitative* results of its regulatory changes is another question entirely, however. Retrospective studies of the demand for money suggest that it would have taken an extraordinary amount of prescience to have estimated the quantitative dimensions at all well.[15]

Looking at the downswing as a whole, the money growth rates in Table 8-3 reveal a general pattern of deceleration as the economy slid into recession, which hardly suggests an appropriate policy stance. Furthermore, the FOMC minutes suggest that this was just about what the Fed wanted to accomplish from 1974:1 to 1974:4. The fact that M_1 and M_2 marched in lock step during these 4 quarters buttresses the notion that

TABLE 8-3
Money Growth Rates during the Recession[a,b]

Money definition	1973:4	1974:1	1974:2	1974:3	1974:4	1975:1
M_1	5.4	7.6	4.2	4.0	4.7	2.0
M_2	9.3	10.8	7.1	6.2	6.7	6.6

[a]*Source:* Federal Reserve.
[b]Change from average of preceding quarter at annual rates, based on seasonally adjusted data.

[15] See, for example, Goldfeld (1976), or Enzler *et al.* (1976).

things were going just about as the Fed intended them to go. This may mean that the downward shifts in the demand function for M_1 helped the Fed rather than hindered it.

The behavior of interest rates during 1974 (see Table 8-4) probably adds further evidence to the brief against the Fed, but also shows the reasons for the money-demand muddle. From 1973:4 to 1974:4, the price level (GNP deflator) rose by about 12% while real GNP fell by 4%. Given the observed elasticities of the demand for M_1 balances,[16] this behavior would be expected eventually to raise the demand for money by about 9%. Since the supply of money rose only about 5% during this period, substantial upward pressures on interest rates would be expected.[17] Table 8-4, however, shows that this did not happen. While interest rates rose during 1974, by 1974:4 they were back down to their 1973:4 levels.

The behavior of money and interest rates from 1974:4 to 1975:1 raises still more puzzles. Growth rates in M_1 and M_2 diverged sharply in that quarter, with the former dropping by 2.6 percentage points while the latter hardly dropped at all. This had not happened in earlier quarters. Yet interest rates fell. As noted above, the queer behavior of M_1 is "explained" by the large "shift" in the demand function for M_1. But Goldfeld's analysis shows that the demand function for M_2 was quite stable throughout this period. This means that *if the Fed wanted to control M_2, it could have done so* with reasonable accuracy. In such a

TABLE 8-4
Nominal Interest Rates during the Recession[a]

Interest rate	1973:4	1974:1	1974:2	1974:3	1974:4	1975:1
Three-month Treasury bills	7.46	7.60	8.27	8.29	7.34	5.87
Prime commercial paper (4 to 6 months)	8.98	8.30	10.46	11.53	9.05	6.56

[a]*Source:* Quarterly averages computed by the author from monthly averages in *Economic Report of the President,* 1977.

[16] A unitary elasticity for nominal balances with respect to the price level, and an income elasticity of demand for real balances of .63, which is taken from Goldfeld's (1976) "conventional" money demand function.

[17] The story is much different with respect to M_2, however. With a price elasticity of nominal balances of unity, and an income elasticity of real balances of 1.8 (from Goldfeld, 1976), the projected rise in M_2 demand is only 4.5%—considerably less than the rise in the supply of M_2.

case, we could use the observed behavior of M_2 as a basis for saying that policy was fairly steady from 1974:4 to 1975:1. But I, for one, hesitate to stake everything on the notion that the Fed ignored M_1 and interest rates in an effort to control M_2!

By the early months of 1975, observers with views as far apart as Paul Samuelson and Milton Friedman were criticizing the Fed sharply—which is hardly unusual. What is unusual is that both men agreed on the direction in which the Fed had erred. In Congressional testimony in late February 1975, Friedman noted the anemic money growth rates between June 1974 and January 1975 and claimed that they "surely contributed to the recent deepening of the recession." Writing in *Newsweek* one week later, Samuelson charged that "if we do go into a depression, the Fed will justly bear much of the blame."[18] The Fed seemed to have few friends.

Yet, in retrospect, the brief against the Fed is not quite as airtight as was thought at the time. While interest rates rose in mid 1974, we must remember that inflation was very high and rising. The actual rate of increase of the personal consumption deflator (at annual rates) was 10.0% in 1973:4 and 10.9% in 1974:4, which, on the surface, could account for a 1% rise in the interest rate. But it is *expected inflation* that is really relevant if we want to know what was happening to *real interest rates*. Given the sharp acceleration in the inflation rate in 1973–1974, it seems likely that expected inflation was catching up to actual inflation during this period, so I would guess that the expected rate of inflation rose by much more than 1 percentage point during the year. But how much?

The series on expected inflation that I constructed for use in the consumption functions of Chapter 7 is one way to provide a quantitative answer. Line 1 of Table 8-5 shows this series for the recession quarters, and compares it with the actual rate of inflation in line 2. Then lines 3 and 4 use the expected rate of inflation to convert the nominal interest rates of Table 8-4 into real interest rates. The results are quite dramatic. Apparently, real rates of interest dropped by about 1.8 percentage points from 1973:4 to 1974:4 and plummeted further to astonishingly large negative values in early 1975.

This basic picture is confirmed by other estimates of inflationary expectations. Using methods similar to those employed here, Elliott (1977) estimated that the short-term real interest rate fell by 1.34 percentage points from 1973:4 to 1974:4.[19] The Livingston data on directly observed

---

[18] Both quotations are cited by Jianakoplos (1976, p. 8).

[19] Elliott actually generates five series on the real short rate, but prefers the one cited in the text because of its superior ability to predict the *ex post* real rate.

TABLE 8-5
Expected Inflation and Real Interest Rates during the Recession

Item	1973:4	1974:1	1974:2	1974:3	1974:4	1975:1
(1) Expected inflation[a]	8.22	9.41	10.86	10.75	9.95	9.33
(2) Actual inflation[b]	10.0	13.0	12.2	11.4	10.9	6.3
(3) Real Treasury bill rate[c]	− 0.76	− 1.81	− 2.59	− 2.46	− 2.61	−3.46
(4) Real commercial paper rate[d]	0.76	− 1.11	− 0.40	0.78	− 0.90	−2.77

[a]Computed from regression equation relating inflation to past inflation and growth rates of M_2. Expectation is the forecast made in the quarter indicated based on inflation rates of past quarters and money growth rates of current and past quarters.

[b]Annual rate of change of deflator for personal consumption expenditures.

[c]Line 1 of Table 8-4 less line 1 of Table 8-5.

[d]Line 2 of Table 8-4 less line 1 of Table 8-5.

price expectations for the coming 6 months, as developed by Carlson (1977), show the real rate on 6-month Treasury bills falling 2.76 percentage points from December 1973 to December 1974. This last piece of evidence is particularly significant because predictions of inflation from past money growth rates make no allowance for the special one-shot nature of much of the 1973–1974 inflation. Livingston's panel of economists, we may hope, did make some such adjustment.

It seems clear, then, that real interest rates fell substantially during the downswing. If we calibrate monetary policy by real interest rates, therefore, it would appear that money was very easy indeed. This gives the Fed more credit than it deserves, however, for we know that the bottom fell out of the economy during these quarters, and with it the demand for money and credit. However hard it is to define a ''neutral'' monetary policy, it seems clear that under such dire circumstances real interest rates would have fallen under such a policy.

Furthermore, it is presumably *long*-term interest rates rather than *short*-term interest rates that have the greatest effect on aggregate demand.[20] While there are no time series on the long-term rate of expected inflation, we may surmise that it rose by less than did the short-term

[20] Short rates, however, are not irrelevant. For example, they have great bearing on the flow of funds to thrift institutions, which in turn is quite important for residential construction activity. See the following paragraph.

rate. If so, the rise in *nominal* long-term interest rates from late 1973 to late 1974 might have corresponded to constant, or even rising, *real* long rates. I can do no more than speculate on this matter, however.

Finally, it should be noted that, given our institutional arrangements, *nominal* interest rates do matter for aggregate demand. The most prominent example is in housing finance, where Regulation Q and usury ceilings make it almost impossible for prospective home buyers to obtain mortgages when interest rates get very high. Specifically, with the interest rates that thrift institutions may pay limited by legal ceilings, savings accounts and certificates of deposit look less and less attractive to investors as open market interest rates rise.[21] As investors withdraw their deposits to invest in the money market (the process called "disintermediation"), thrift institutions lose the wherewithal to make mortgage loans. When this disintermediation is coupled with binding usury ceilings on the rates that banks can charge on mortgages, as was the case in 1974, the effect on housing finance can be devastating. It was devastating in 1974. Indeed, during a period in which shifts in the demand for money are disturbing the normal relationship between money and interest rates, it may be that the best way to appraise monetary policy is to look at what is happening in those sectors of the real economy that are most sensitive to financial conditions (especially housing). From this perspective, monetary policy during the recession looks devilishly restrictive.

One final indicator of the stance of monetary policy may be worth mentioning—the *real* supply of money, defined here as the money stock divided by the GNP deflator. During the year from the cyclical peak in 1973:4 until 1974:4, real M_1 balances declined 5.3% while real M_2 balances declined 3%. The drop during the last quarter of the recession was more precipitous—a 7.8% annual rate for M_1 and a 3.7% rate for M_2.[22] What happened, in a word, is that the Fed simply refused to accommodate the 1974 inflation and chose instead to let real balances decline. One does not have to be an advocate of fixed growth in real balances to read a rather contractionary message into these data.

On balance, then, there seem to be several dimensions in the appraisal of monetary policy during the recession. According to the real interest rates presented in Table 8-5, which are subject to all the usual uncertainties about estimating inflationary expectations, monetary *conditions* loosened considerably, though this does not necessarily imply that monetary

---

[21] A 1978 reform that allows banks to issue certificates tied to the Treasury bill rate may have made this obsolete. But it was certainly operative in 1973–1974.

[22] It is interesting to note that, as of this writing, real M_1 balances (but not M_2 balances) are still well below their 1973:4 peak levels and are, in fact, close to their recession low.

policy eased. But, according to the growth rates of M_2—which Goldfeld's results show are more reliable guideposts than those of M_1—monetary policy tightened during the recession, and was quite restrictive during the worst quarters (the last half of 1974 and 1975:1). During these 3 quarters, M_2 growth averaged 6.5% per annum—almost identical to its historic average from December 1959 to December 1969 (6.4%), and far below its average from December 1969 to December 1973 (9.9%). Nominal interest rates suggest a very restrictive monetary stance until 1974:3, but an easing of policy thereafter. The performance of the housing industry and its related financial institutions clearly indicate that money was quite tight. And the steady decline of real balances points to unrelenting financial stringency.

While this mixed bag of evidence is open to a variety of interpretations, a temperate point of view might be that monetary policy was restrictive in the first 3 quarters of 1974 and roughly maintained this posture for the balance of the recession. Given what happened to real economic activity, such a policy stance nonetheless allowed real interest rates to drop. Whether such a policy was one of benign or malign neglect depends upon your point of view. For myself, I am happy to throw in with Friedman and Samuelson. There was, after all, an economic catastrophe in progress in late 1974 and early 1975, and no reading of the data will lead to the conclusion that the Fed took a vigorous antirecessionary stand. Furthermore, there can be no doubt that a preoccupation with inflation was the reason for this.

What could the Fed have done differently? Many economists have advanced the view that an appropriate policy response to the oil shock would have been a step increase in the *money stock* large enough to finance the higher oil prices. Some, in fact, were even suggesting this at the time. Since the shock was roughly 3.5% on the overall price level, and since it happened in 1973:4 and 1974:1, such a policy would have increased the annual money *growth rate* by about 7 points in each of these quarters, that is, to roughly 12% for 1973:4 and 14% for 1974:1 (the figures apply to M_1). Of course this would not have counteracted the current and lagged effects of the rising food prices, and so would not have stopped the economic retardation entirely. Furthermore, the economy had another large shock in 1974:2—the end of wage-price controls. If this added roughly 2.5% to the price level, an increase in the money growth rate of, say, 5 percentage points in 1974:2 and 1974:3 would have been required to "finance" it. In total, then, this alternative policy would have raised the money *stock* of 1974:3 by about 6% by adding this much to the annual growth rate of M_1 from 1973:3 to 1974:3. A rough guess is that this would eventually have left the price level 6% higher than it was under actual policies, but that very little of this additional inflation would have occurred in 1973-1975.

A monetary policy something like this has been simulated on the MPS model by Perry (1975b), who examined the monetary policy that would have lowered the commercial paper rate to 7% by 1974:1 and held it there through 1975:1. As it turns out, this would have required a big burst of money creation in 1974:2 and a smaller acceleration in the following quarter to bring the 1974:3 money stock to a level 6.2% higher than it actually was. Thereafter, monetary growth actually could have decelerated substantially, enough to leave the 1975:1 money stock only 2.2% above its historical value.

According to the MPS model, such a policy would not have been nearly enough to stop the recession, though it would have ameliorated it. Whereas the actual decline in real GNP from 1974:1 to 1975:1 was 4.8%, Perry's alternative policy limits the fall to 3.1%.[23] The rise in the unemployment rate is .5 percentage point less under Perry's alternative monetary policy than under actual monetary policy. The inflation rate shows no adverse effects from the additional money supply as of the termination of the simulation (1975:1), though we may surmise from the long-run classical properties of the MPS model that some additional inflation is on the horizon.

Otto Eckstein (1978, Chapter 7) obtained comparable results by simulating the DRI model. According to his estimates, monetary growth of about 11% from mid 1973 to mid 1974 would have been necessary to hold the Federal funds rate at 6%. The amount of additional money creation is similar to that of Perry's simulation, and the result is that the recession is considerably muted. Eckstein, in fact, reports larger monetary effects than Perry—a real GNP about 3.5% higher in 1974 and 1975. And he agrees with the MPS model that no extra inflation would have resulted in the short run.

Those who have advocated "accommodating" the oil shock by increasing the money stock in this way often have also advocated a tax cut that would have compensated consumers for all or part of their higher fuel bills. When Perry simulated the effects of the above-mentioned monetary policy[24] *plus* a $20 billion reduction in personal taxes in 1974:1,[25] he found

---

[23] More precisely, Perry reports an increase in real GNP in 1975:1 of 1.7%. When Perry did the work reported here, the data were showing a deeper recession than they do now.

[24] With the additional fiscal stimulus, maintaining a 7% commercial paper rate requires more money than before. In particular, the 1974:3 money stock is up 7.3% and the 1975:1 money stock is up 4% (both relative to actual history).

[25] This is little more than half of the increase in fuel bills, and hence is not a full offset by any means.

much stronger effects. In particular, the drop in real GNP was limited to
about 1.5% (versus 4.8% in the actual data), and the unemployment rate
was 1.1 percentage points lower by 1975:1 under the combined fiscal-
monetary package. As a consequence, the inflation rate from 1974:1 to
1975:1 was estimated to be .5 percentage point higher.

If these models are to be believed, then, things could have been quite
a bit better in 1974–1975 under a more expansive set of monetary and
fiscal policies.[26] The calculations do, however, assume away any of the
potential adverse effects on expectations that were discussed at the end
of Chapter 5.[27]

4. Monetary Policy for the Recovery, 1975:2–1976:4

Knowing what to say about monetary policy during the first year and
a half of recovery is no easier than knowing what to say about it during
the downswing, for the usual demand function for M_1 (though not for
M_2) continued to shift downward. It is notable, however, that the Fed
consistently defended its policy of moderation in monetary growth by
insisting that velocity would increase during the upswing, as it had in the
past. While government and private forecasters were looking for both
real growth and inflation in the 5–7% range, implying growth of nominal
GNP of 10–14%, Chairman Burns was insisting that M_1 growth in the 5–
7% range would be enough to finance the recovery because of anticipated
increases in velocity. And unlike the forecasters, Burns was in a position
to influence these velocity movements by the Fed's regulatory policies.
We do not know whether his crystal ball was simply clearer than others,
or whether the Fed's actions conveniently helped his prophecy come
true; but in any case Burns' predictions turned out to be remarkably
accurate.

But the accuracy of this forecast was not apparent early in 1975. By
March, there was considerable dissatisfaction within the FOMC over the
course of monetary policy. While there was no change in the policy
directive, three members (Bucher, Eastburn, and Sheehan) dissented on
the grounds that the poor state of the economy and the slow growth in
the monetary aggregates called for a more aggressive policy stance. In
May, Chairman Burns publicly announced the Fed's ranges of tolerance
for money growth rates for the first time: 5 to 7.5% for M_1 and 8.5 to

---

[26] It should again be noted that the models would predict more inflation in 1976 and
thereafter as a result of such policies.

[27] See pages 104–105 and also Blinder (1980).

10.5% for M_2 over the year beginning in March 1975. Many in the Congress thought this would not be enough money to finance the recovery. At its May meeting, the FOMC decided to allow a temporary bulge in monetary growth in May–June 1975 to accommodate the upcoming income tax rebates, and stressed interest rate stability in its operating instructions. As a result, both M_1 and M_2 spurted briefly. Then, in June, the FOMC decided to tighten things a bit with "moderate growth" in money, though Governors Bucher and Coldwell insisted that the move was premature.

In July, Chairman Burns revised the base for computing the Fed's publicly announced growth rate targets in such a way as to permit slightly faster growth,[28] and the FOMC decided "to maintain about the prevailing bank reserve and money market conditions . . . provided that growth in monetary aggregates appears to be slowing substantially from the bulge during the second quarter." The call for "moderate growth" continued in August–October 1975, while the staff was projecting a strong rebound first in 1975:4 and then in 1975:3. At its August meeting, the Committee decided that financial markets had overreacted to its slight tightening, and raised its target ranges for monetary growth. By the October meeting, several members were expressing doubts about the vigor of the recovery, but there were no dissents.

Policy attitudes appear to have shifted by November. While its operating instructions continued to request "moderate growth," the FOMC added the rather cryptic proviso that the Account Manager should take "more than the usual account of developments in domestic and international financial markets." More specifically, it raised its short-run (internal) monetary growth targets very substantially: from 3–7% to 6–10% for M_1, and from 5.5–8.5% to 7.5–10.5% for M_2. Governor Jackson and the New York Fed's Paul Volcker objected to this change in policy, but David Eastburn of Philadelphia argued that it was too timid. In a Congressional appearance that month, Chairman Burns announced another change in the base for the publicly announced monetary growth ranges, and also increased them to 7.5–10.5% for M_1 and 9–12% for M_2 between 1975:3 and 1976:3.

The proceedings of the FOMC in 1976 were characterized by nothing if not blandness. During the entire year, the Committee's basic policy directive never changed, its short-run operating instructions had only minor changes, and there were hardly any dissents from the majority view.[29] The Fed's continuing concern was to limit the rates of monetary

---

[28] Such revisions were permitted under House Concurrent Resolution 133, the legislation that required the public announcements.

[29] Burger and Mudd (1977).

expansion to non-inflationary levels, while at the same time providing enough money to support the recovery. It was helped along in this effort, once again, by downward shifts in the demand function for M_1, which made money growth rates in the 5% range quite compatible with a steady if unspectacular expansion coupled with 5-6% inflation—and even allowed the federal funds rate to decline steadily during the second half of the year.

The short-run (internal) ranges of tolerance for M_1 growth were nearly steady for most of 1976, and then were lowered quite substantially at year end.[30] M_2 ranges, by contrast, were mostly raised as the Committee recognized the shift of money demand away from M_1 and toward M_2. The publicly announced long-term ranges of tolerance were also gradually lowered during the year, mainly for their psychological impact. As Chairman Burns stated, the Fed was anxious to demonstrate that "the growth rates of money and credit presently desired by the Federal Reserve cannot be maintained indefinitely without running a serious risk of releasing new inflationary pressures."[31]

While there was much discussion at FOMC meetings of the slowing down or "pause" in the economy, the Committee did not consider this as something it should respond to. The attention of Committee members was quite clearly on long-run, rather than short-run, stabilization and, in particular, on gradually getting the rate of growth of money down without upsetting the expansion. Monetarists were presumably quite pleased with this policy stance, while potential criticism from Keynesians was muted by the perplexities surrounding the money demand equation.

What actually happened? Monetary growth rates during the first 2 quarters of the recovery were near the high end of the Fed's ranges of tolerance, as Table 8-6 shows, but both aggregates decelerated sharply

TABLE 8-6
Monetary Growth Rates during the Recovery[a,b]

Money definition	1975:2	1975:3	1975:4	1976:1	1976:2	1976:3	1976:4
M_1	5.9	7.5	3.0	4.7	6.5	4.2	7.7
M_2	9.9	10.4	7.0	11.0	10.3	9.1	13.2

[a]*Source:* Federal Reserve.
[b]Change from average of preceding quarter at annual rates, based on seasonally adjusted data.

[30] From 5-9% at the October meeting to 2.5-6.5% at the December meeting.
[31] Statement to Congress in February 1976, as quoted by Burger and Mudd (1977).

in 1975:4. The FOMC minutes do not indicate that the Fed wanted such a precipitous drop in monetary expansion, and Goldfeld's M_1 equation shows large increases in the residual in that quarter and the next (respective annual rates of decline of 7.7 and 5.2%). So the Fed may have been taken by surprise. Growth in M_2 rebounded in 1976:1, and was relatively steady for the remainder of 1976. But growth in M_1 did not rebound as strongly, and was extremely irregular during 1976. Again, it seems advisable to ignore M_1, and look at M_2 and interest rates.

Growth rates for M_2 in Table 8-6 appear to be rather generous—they average just over 10% for the 7-quarter period. Yet it must be remembered that nominal GNP expanded at an 11% annual rate during this period, and that the forecasts of early and mid 1975 were calling for even higher growth. Given the high income elasticity of the demand for M_2 balances, this much money growth may not be overly expansive, and the FOMC certainly did not view it as such.

Nominal interest rates, my estimated expected rate of inflation, and the implied real interest rates are shown in Table 8-7. It can be seen that while nominal interest rates bounced up and down a good deal, the predominant trend was downward: from 1975:2 to 1976:4, the bill rate fell 71 basis points and the commercial paper rate fell 93 basis points. This is unusual behavior for a recovery, and suggests an extremely easy monetary policy. But it seems certain that expected inflation rates were falling rapidly during the early part of the period, and were probably drifting down slowly during 1976 as well. In fact, my series on expected

TABLE 8-7
Interest Rates during the Recovery[a]

Item	1975:2	1975:3	1975:4	1976:1	1976:2	1976:3	1976:4
Nominal interest rates							
Treasury bills	5.40	6.34	5.68	4.95	5.17	5.17	4.69
Commercial							
paper	5.92	6.67	6.12	5.29	5.57	5.53	4.99
Inflation rates							
Actual	5.7	7.2	5.3	4.9	4.3	5.3	5.4
Expected	6.91	5.69	6.07	5.41	4.99	4.54	4.75
Real interest rates							
Treasury bills	−1.51	0.65	−0.39	−0.46	0.18	0.63	−0.06
Commercial							
paper	−0.99	0.98	0.05	−0.12	0.58	0.99	0.24

[a]See footnotes to Tables 8-4 and 8-5.

inflation behaves more or less in this way. If it is to be believed, we must conclude that *real* interest rates *increased* sharply from 1975:1 to 1975:3, dropped back to roughly zero in 1975:4, and fluctuated near zero with some upward trend during 1976.[32] These real rates suggest a very restrictive monetary policy in mid 1975 followed by a moderately accommodative policy stance in late 1975 and an approximately "neutral" policy during 1976 (since a recovery would be expected to pull up the real interest rate under a "neutral" policy).

I read this evidence, with great hesitancy, as painting a picture of a central bank adhering to an "even keel" policy—not providing aggressive support for the recovery, but not acting strongly to restrain it either. But, as the man said, "Ya pays yer money, and ya takes yer choice."

5. Summary

The Federal Reserve System, and especially its chairman, Arthur Burns, has been roundly criticized for the monetary policy that it followed during 1972-1976.[33] This criticism comes both from the left and from the right, from both Keynesians and monetarists. Much of it seems justified. Nonetheless, several puzzles make the case against the Fed less compelling than is often supposed.

With hindsight, there is no question that the exuberant monetary growth rates of 1972 were excessive, even reckless. And it is at least possible that the pre-election monetary policy had a strong political flavor to it. Yet it should be remembered that things were less clear to contemporary observers, many of whom supported the expansionary policies. The relative consensus within the Federal Open Market Committee—as anti-inflationary a group as you are likely to find outside the Federal Republic of Germany—is telling in this regard.

The error in 1973 was of a far different type—turning in the right direction, but too abruptly. Of all the monetary policy episodes in the mid 1970s, this one seems to have drawn the least attention; yet it seems to have made a substantial contribution to the beginnings of the Great Recession. It also bears eloquent witness to the monetarists' incessant complaint that policy is too variable, too apt to swing from one extreme to another.

---

[32] Carlson's (1977) version of the Livingston series shows expected inflation dropping very sharply from December 1974 to June 1975, with the real interest rate rising by about .25 percentage point. Then, from June 1975 to December 1975, his expected inflation measure edges up a bit so that the real rate rises another .25 percentage point.

[33] See, for example, Pierce (1979) and Poole (1979).

The year 1974, and particularly the last half of the year, is often painted as the Fed's darkest hour since the Great Depression. As the forces of recession mounted and gathered force, the Fed was gradually tightening the monetary screws. There is little doubt that this policy assisted OPEC, nature, and the Nixon–Ford administration in engineering the worst recession of the postwar period.

But several factors are worth mentioning in this regard. First, there was an inflation phobia in this country during 1974—a phobia that was in part reflected by and in part exacerbated by the nation's political leadership. Furthermore, as I have observed several times in this book, the nature of the inflation and its causes were widely misunderstood at the time. It will be recalled from Chapter 7 that fiscal policy was also contractionary during this period, and I cannot help wondering whether the public did not get precisely the stabilization policy it wanted. Stranger things have happened in democracies.

Second, while monetarists have screamed most loudly and piously about the deceleration of monetary growth in the second half of 1974—suggesting that this was the main cause of the stunning collapse of the economy in late 1974 and early 1975—there is a fairly obvious fact that someone should point out: monetary growth rates in this country were about as stable during the period from 1973:1 through 1974:4 as they have ever been.[34] Table 8-8 offers data on the average growth rate of M_1 and its variability during the 7-quarter period starting in 1973:1 and ending in 1974:4, and compares this period with the two adjacent 7-quarter periods. The contrast is marked. (The same conclusion can be seen graphically in Figure 8-1.) If there are grounds for condemning monetary policy during this period, and I believe there are, it is not for its *variability* but rather for its *constancy*—for constant monetary growth in this case

TABLE 8-8
Money Growth Rates and Their Variability

Period	Average quarterly growth rate[a]	Highest	Lowest	Standard deviation
1971:2 to 1973:1	7.4	9.4	2.8	2.1
1973:1 to 1974:4	5.2	7.6	4.0	1.1
1974:4 to 1976:3	4.8	7.5	2.0	1.8

[a]Seasonally adjusted annual rates, in percentage points.

[34] For a similar verdict, see Modigliani (1977, pp. 14–15).

represented a steadfast refusal to accommodate even a small portion of the supply induced inflation.

I hasten to add that I do not mean to imply that relative constancy of the monetary growth rate *caused* the Great Recession. OPEC, food prices, and the end of price controls took care of that; monetary policy just let it all happen, without trying to stabilize real economic activity. Nor do I suggest that constant growth of money is always a bad policy, for it certainly is not. My point is a simple one, one that Keynesians have been making for years: adherence to fixed rules is appropriate only when nothing much is going on; when the economy is buffeted by large shocks, policy must respond or the economy will pay the price.

Third, blaming the monetary deceleration in the second half of 1974 (which really became severe only in the last months of 1974 and the first months of 1975) for the collapse of demand in the last quarter of 1974 flies in the face of everything we know about the lags in the effects of monetary policy. I know of no serious student of monetary policy who claims that the *current* growth rate of the money supply has a marked effect on the *current* growth rate of real economic activity. If we want a monetary culprit for the Great Recession, we must look to the sharp deceleration in early 1973 and the sluggish (though relatively constant) money growth rates that followed—not to the sensational but brief monetary deceleration in late 1974 and early 1975.

There has been much less criticism of monetary policy during the 1975–1976 recovery period; and even with the "wisdom" of hindsight it is hard to know what to say about this period. Monetarists were reasonably well satisfied by the moderate average growth rates of the money supply, though displeased by its variability. Keynesians, on the other hand, thought the growth rates too niggardly, but were effectively muzzled by the perplexities surrounding the demand function for money. When the *demand* for money is shifting rapidly and unpredictably downward, it is hard (and unwise) to be too self-righteous about what growth rates for the money *supply* are correct. Arthur Burns seems to have been either brilliant in anticipating or skillful in causing these shifts in the money demand function, so that what appeared *in prospect* to be a rather tight monetary policy for the recovery turned out *in retrospect* to be fairly permissive.

If I were forced to summarize the influence of the Fed on the Great Stagflation in a few words, I guess I would stress how *little* difference it made rather than how *much*. If the Federal Open Market Committee had been replaced by a fixed money growth rate rule as part of the New Economic Policy in August 1971, monetary policy would have been considerably less expansionary in 1972. That is quite clear. But thereafter, except for some sharp but brief downward "blips" in the money growth rate in 1975:1 and 1975:4, the policies actually followed were not outrageously different from what I imagine a fixed growth rate regime would have produced.[35] The slowdown in 1973, the recession in 1974, and the recovery in 1975 and 1976 all would have proceeded more or less as they actually did.[36]

It is true that whenever monetary policy departed notably from what a fixed rule would have called for, it did so in the wrong direction and made things worse than they need to have been. Opponents of discretionary policy may take solace in this, and policymakers deserve to be upbraided. Monetary policy in 1972–1976 was poorly conceived and executed; there can be no doubt about that. But the economy was suffering so many body blows during 1973–1975 that it seems to me highly unlikely that monetary policy was a major cause, never mind *the* major cause, of the Great Stagflation. The Fed was guilty of contributory negligence, not of first-degree murder.

[35] They would, of course, have differed in details. The statement is also predicated on the belief that, owing to the shifts in the money demand function during 1974–1976, truly constant money growth rates could not have been achieved.

[36] For a somewhat similar assessment, see Eckstein (1978, Chapter 7).

9

the legacy of the great stagflation

Experience is the name everyone gives to their mistakes
—Oscar Wilde

The story told in this book is, very nearly, one of how the U.S. government made the worst of a bad situation. The U.S. economy was buffeted by some severe and unavoidable supply shocks in 1973 and 1974. The authorities did little or nothing to cushion these blows, and even compounded the problems through ill-timed and ill-conceived policy actions. One way to put the message of the book into focus is to ask ourselves how things might have differed if the government either had adopted a "hands off" attitude or had pursued the kinds of policies that appear in retrospect to have been more appropriate. This I do in Section 1. Reviewing the basic arguments of the book in this way points out a host of policy errors. So the natural steps are to enumerate some of the reasons for these mistakes and to see what can be learned from them— steps that are taken in Section 2. While this book is an economic history of 1972–1976, its relevance to current policy is not hidden very deeply beneath the surface. Many of the problems and issues of 1972–1976 came back to haunt us in 1977–1979; and there is every reason to suspect that they will recur. So Section 3 offers a brief discussion of some of the events of 1977–1979, drawing parallels to the Great Stagflation, and suggesting that, unfortunately, many of its lessons have apparently not been learned.

1. Three Histories of 1971–1976

The story of the Great Stagflation has been told in great (some might say excruciating) detail here. In recapitulating that story briefly, I want simultaneously to consider two other histories of events that *never* took place. One is the story of what might have happened to the U.S. economy in those years had the government adopted a "hands off" policy. The other is the story of what might have happened had the government followed the policies suggested with such magnificent clarity by the wisdom of hindsight.

The logical place to begin is in 1971, when Mr. Nixon abandoned his steady-as-you-go policy in favor of the New Economic Policy. I have argued several times in this book (Chapters 3 and 6) that inflation appears to have been winding down in 1971, though at an agonizingly slow pace. And there seems to be every reason to suspect that this process would have continued throughout 1971 and into 1972 had Mr. Nixon never fired his guns of August. In this instance, then, a policy of doing nothing would seem to have been the best policy. Indeed, the game plan of patience that the Nixon administration pursued from 1969 until August 1971 may well have constituted one of fiscal policy's finest hours. There is a message here. It is a message that conservatives, and especially monetarists, have been trumpeting for years: doing nothing is also a policy, and sometimes it is the best policy. My estimates in Chapter 6 imply that price controls did indeed push inflation down more quickly than it would otherwise have fallen, and thus by this criterion might be considered a "success." But they also sowed the seeds of some very serious subsequent problems. Better to have done nothing.

Much the same conclusion pertains to 1972. The tremendous stimulus that the economy received from monetary and fiscal policy in 1972 was documented in Chapters 3, 7, and 8, where it was suggested that without a strong push from "stabilization" policy there would have been no runaway boom to contend with in 1973. A reasonable guess is that with a "neutral" fiscal and monetary policy (however defined), and no wage-price controls, the economy would have grown at or below its long-run trend while inflation would have either stabilized or perhaps even drifted down a bit during 1972. It is perhaps a shade optimistic, but far from fanciful, to imagine that the U.S. economy could have ended 1972 with production gradually approaching full employment levels and inflation in the 3–4% range. And the magical policy needed to achieve this miracle would have been to do essentially nothing.

Things started to go wrong in early 1973, when a series of exogenous supply shocks began to buffet the U.S. economy. Rapid increases in food prices throughout the year and in energy prices in the closing months of the year made a sharp acceleration of inflation all but inevitable in 1973, despite government policies that seem to have been very slightly anti-inflationary. My preliminary estimates of the effects of price controls on non-food non-energy prices (Chapter 6, especially Table 6-2) suggest that controls had virtually no net effect on inflation during the first half of the year, but exerted a moderate downward pull (less than 1 percentage point on the annual rate of inflation) during the second half of the year. In addition, controls on gasoline and oil prices certainly limited energy inflation in the closing months of 1973 and the early months of 1974. Thus, the acceleration of inflation from 1972 to 1973 cannot be blamed on government policies; instead, these policies served to limit the acceleration a bit.[1]

Much more significant was the government's impact on real economic activity. As mentioned several times in earlier chapters, both monetary and fiscal policy turned brusquely from stimulus to restraint in 1973. Anyone who has ever been in an automobile that was brought to an abrupt halt knows that, at best, this violent wrenching gives you an uneasy feeling in your stomach and, at worst, it puts you through the windshield. The economy got indigestion in 1973. I would argue that the monetary and fiscal policy brakes, in conjunction with the first few rounds of higher food prices, first sent the economy down the road to recession. What could have been done better? A more gradual transition from extreme stimulus to moderate restraint seems to have been called for at the time; and it did not take any great foresight to see this. Score another point for the foes of activist policy.

1974 was a bad year. Fueled by further supply shocks, the high inflation rates of 1973 soared yet higher, and were in the double-digit range for much of the year. The recession, whose origins were in 1973, deepened and lengthened in 1974, and turned into a near catastrophe in the closing months. What would have happened if the government had taken no actions, adhering instead to fixed rules? I argue that the 1974 economy would have been little different, because adhering to fixed rules is essentially what the government did. The one important exception was the dismantling of wage–price controls in March and April—a masterpiece of mistiming. While the controls program probably did only a little harm

---

[1] However, some may question whether the inefficiencies caused by Freeze II in the summer of 1973 and gasoline rationing in the winter of 1973–1974 were worth what they bought in terms of reducing inflation.

when it was initiated (by helping to boom the boom), and while it remained in effect (by causing various minor inefficiencies), it really wreaked havoc upon us when it was terminated. I argued in Chapters 5 and 6 that decontrol played a major role in stretching out the period of double-digit inflation through much of 1974. I also argued that while the 1971–1974 controls had very little effect on the *average* inflation rate over 1971 to 1974, they added considerably to the *variability* of inflation by holding down prices in 1971–1973 and spurring them on in 1974. Finally, by pushing up prices so rapidly in 1974, decontrol acted like a surrogate supply shock—thereby adding to the severity of the recession.

In the realm of monetary and fiscal policy, by contrast, nothing much was happening. With no discretionary fiscal actions to offset it, the inflationary bulge of 1973–1974 caused a substantial automatic increase in tax revenues because our tax system is not indexed. This drained consumers' purchasing power. At the Federal Reserve, the constant money growth rate rule was in its heyday. While much attention has been paid to the minor (though noticeable) deceleration of monetary growth in the second half of 1974 as compared to the first half, my own view is that while this was a poor show it was dwarfed in importance by the Fed's complete refusal to accommodate the supply shocks throughout the year. From the first quarter of 1974 to the first quarter of 1975, the *real* money supply (M_1 deflated by the GNP deflator) was allowed to decline by 7%. This produced substantial stringency in financial markets, emasculated the housing industry, and so on.

It seems to me, though apparently not to many monetarists, that we have here a clear case in which monetary and fiscal policy tenaciously adhered to a steady-as-you-go stance, and where that policy stance had disastrous effects. What might have been done better? I have argued in several places throughout the book, and especially in Chapters 5 and 8, that the government could have avoided a serious recession by pursuing a two-pronged accommodative policy. The first prong would have been a large cut in personal income taxes (say, in early 1974), designed to restore a good portion of the purchasing power that American consumers were losing to farmers, oilmen, and sheiks. This would, in fact, have amounted to not much more than taking the tax cuts of 1975 one year earlier (and, of course, making them permanent rather than temporary). The second prong of the accommodative policy would have been a substantial increase in the stock of money (or, alternatively, in its growth rate for a few quarters) in early to middle 1974, an increase sufficient to keep the two supply shocks (food and energy) from reducing the real money stock very much. My guess is that a 7–9% increase in the money supply (M_1) might have been enough.[2] Analysis in Chapter 5 suggested that such an accommodative policy might have given us some 2 to 3% more inflation in both 1974 and 1975 than we actually had. In my judgment, this would not have been too high a price to pay for avoiding the Great Recession.

Others, however, disagree vehemently with this assessment of the costs and benefits of accommodation. There is room for disagreement on at least two grounds. First, according to my estimates an accommodative policy might have brought the inflation rates of 1974 and 1975 up to about 14 and 10%, respectively (as compared to the actual values of 12 and 7%). These are very high inflation rates, and those who view inflation as exacting heavy social costs may justifiably oppose the accommodative policy on these grounds. Second, some have argued that econometric models understate the potential effects of such an accommodative policy on inflationary expectations, and worry that such a policy might have led to an uncontrollable inflationary spiral.[3]

However, with a bit more creativity fiscal policy might have accommodated the energy and food shocks, and still finessed the tradeoff between inflation and unemployment, by designing policies that were simultaneously anti-recessionary and anti-inflationary. For example, Albert Ando, among others, suggested a large reduction in payroll and excise taxes for 1974—a fiscal package that, while expanding aggregate demand, would also have had favorable cost-push effects on the price level.[4] Another possibility was a federal subsidy to states that would lower their sales taxes. While policies like these cannot be used to control the inflation rate in the long run (for example, the payroll tax eventually will be entirely eliminated), they constitute favorable supply shocks that could have been used to offset the adverse supply shocks that were buffetting the economy in 1974. This idea, however, never got a serious public airing.

In the period surrounding the trough of the recession, fiscal policy

[2] Some economists who have advocated this sort of policy have emphasized that the increase in the money stock need not have been permanent, and therefore need not have *permanently* raised the price level. In principle, I agree wholeheartedly. In practice, it is hard to see when we would have been able to shave a cumulative 7-9% off the money growth rates of 1975-1978 without seriously injuring the recovery.

[3] It should be noted that the econometric models *do* imply that a policy of accommodation would have had adverse effects on inflationary expectations simply because it would have led to more inflation. The argument mentioned in the text asserts that the models systematically underestimate this effect. See pages 104-105 and Blinder (1980).

[4] See, for example, Ando and Palash (1976).

made one more small mistake and monetary policy made one more large one. In the case of fiscal policy, the error was to undermine the effectiveness of the March 1975 Tax Reduction Act by making it explicitly temporary. Thus, while fiscal policy did better than a do-nothing policy, it seems to have done worse than might have been hoped for. In the case of monetary policy, the error was to let monetary growth (at least as measured by M_1) almost cease in the last few months of 1974 and the first few months of 1975. The quarterly data displayed in Chapter 8 (Table 8-3) conceal the fact that M_1 was virtually unchanged from November 1974 to February 1975.[5] No fixed rule, nor any concept of neutral monetary policy, would have produced such niggardly growth of the money supply around the trough of a recession.

In summary, looking at the recession period as a whole, fiscal policy seems to have performed somewhat better than what a regime of fixed rules might have achieved, but rather worse than it could have. For monetary policy, the evaluation is bleaker. A fixed growth rate rule would have produced more money in 1974 and early 1975, and thus would have eased the recession a bit. Still, except for a few months in the winter of 1974–1975, the actual policies followed were much closer to a fixed growth rate rule than they were to what advocates of an activist stabilization policy were calling for. The failure of discretionary monetary policy in 1974–1975 is thus only slightly greater than the failure that a fixed growth rule would have produced.

During the 1975–1976 recovery period policy remained more or less on an even keel—with a fairly permissive (though not aggressive) fiscal policy, and a monetary policy that defies categorization owing to the shifts in the demand for money. Some would have preferred a more vigorous stabilization effort to spur the recovery on faster; others would not have. This is certainly open to debate.

As I look back over the actual history of 1971–1976 as a whole, and compare it with the two alternative histories, one generalization seems possible. When the economy behaved more or less normally and was not being buffeted by sizeable exogenous shocks, as was the case in 1971–1972 and 1975–1976, the best policy was to leave well enough alone. Most of the discretionary policy actions of the 1971–1973 period (including wage–price controls) did more harm than good. On the other hand, when the big supply shocks hit the economy in 1973 and 1974 there were a number of fairly obvious things the government could have done, but did not do, to ameliorate the recession. We know that fixed rules would not have performed very well under these circumstances because poli-

---

[5] M_2 grew at a 6.1% annual rate.

cymakers more or less aped what these rules would have done. Thus, ironically, policy proved to be activist when it should have been passive, but turned passive just when it needed to be activist!

There seems to be a fairly obvious lesson here: Don't rock the boat if it is not already rocking, but change course when the seas get rough. This lesson would be too obvious to belabor had not so many people expended so much effort trying to convince us that it is wrong. I am reminded of something Adam Smith said in a different context:

> The proposition is so very manifest, that it seems ridiculous to take any pains to prove it; nor could it ever have been called into question had not the interested sophistry of merchants and manufacturers confounded the common sense of mankind.[6]

2. Learning from Our Mistakes

Errors abound in the 1971–1976 policy record. Why did our policy-makers commit them? As usual, answers are not simple. I begin with what was to me the biggest mistake of all—the decision, whether conscious or unconscious, to sit idly by while the stagflationary shocks of 1973–1974 pounded the economy into a deep recession. Poor forecasts undoubtedly played some role in these events, since the severity of the recession was not anticipated. But I would argue that forecasting errors were of minor import. The recession, after all, lasted a long time and neither monetary nor fiscal policy did anything to arrest it until it was over. As 1974 progressed, almost everyone outside of Washington officialdom came to recognize that we were in the midst of a serious recession. Yet nothing was done.

Two factors seem mainly to explain why policymakers were so willing to let the economy suffer through a severe recession. The first was a complete failure, and perhaps even an unwillingness, to come to grips with the nature of the 1973–1974 acceleration of inflation (see Chapter 5).

As the aggregate supply and demand analysis of Chapter 2 pointed out, there is a fundamental distinction to be made between factors that contribute to *sustained inflation* and factors that lead to *one-time adjustments of the price level*. In the first category, we find only those few factors that cause aggregate demand to grow steadily faster than aggregate supply (such as excessive money creation) or that retard the growth of aggregate

[6] Adam Smith (1937, p. 461).

supply (such as a slowdown in productivity growth, if no compensatory demand policy is adopted). To argue that any such factor was behind the inflationary burst of 1973–1974 taxes the capacity for belief. What really happened is that we experienced a series of events in the second category, each of which required a one-time adjustment of the aggregate price level. These started with the devaluation of the dollar, continued through the food price increases of 1972–1974 and the energy price increases of 1973–1974, and culminated in the dismantling of price controls in 1974. Since the necessary price level adjustments did not take place instantly, but were distributed through time, each of these factors caused a *temporary* bout of *inflation*.

Based on the public discussions of economic policy at the time, there is virtually no evidence that this distinction was understood, or even recognized. All the talk was of budget deficits and monetary growth, as if they were the root causes of the acceleration of inflation and the only way to reverse it. Now I certainly do not mean to imply, as is sometimes claimed, that it is *impossible* to use aggregate demand policy to fight an inflation caused by a constriction of aggregate supply. It is possible. And this brings me to the second major reason why the government allowed the Great Recession to run its course: the trade-off between inflation and unemployment.

The harsh fact that the government has good control over aggregate demand but virtually no control over aggregate supply (at least in the short run) implies that anything it does to ameliorate a recession is likely to aggravate inflation. This Presidents Nixon and Ford and Chairman Burns were keenly aware of. In 1974, there was a genuine fear in this country that inflation was getting out of control, that somehow our steady ''baseline'' inflation rate had climbed into the double-digit range and was heading even higher. In such an atmosphere of near panic, it would have been very difficult for the President or the Federal Reserve Chairman to convince the public that expansionary policies that threatened to drive the inflation rate higher still were appropriate—even if Messers. Nixon, Ford, and Burns had been so inclined. Plainly, they were not. Thus it was that the trade-off between inflation and unemployment combined in an unholy alliance with a basic misunderstanding of the nature of the inflation to effectively paralyze stabilization policy. My reading of the current state of economic literacy is that the alliance survives intact to the present day. It could all happen again.

Next in importance after the recession of 1974–1975, the biggest policy *faux pas* of the period seems to have been the wage–price controls program. Here it seems that the Nixon administration, and also some economists, were overly optimistic about what wage–price controls might hope to accomplish. If my preliminary estimates of the effects of controls are anywhere near correct, controls took about .5 percentage point off the inflation rates of 1971 and 1973, and about .67 percentage point off the inflation rate of 1972. Can these gains conceivably have been worth the effort and risks involved? I think there can only be one answer. And this assessment applies only to the decision to embark on controls. As I have stressed several times, the most devastating costs of the controls came when we escaped from the frying pan of controls into the fire of catch-up inflation.[7] How the Nixon administration and the Congress could have allowed the controls to lapse at such an inopportune moment is beyond my personal ability to comprehend.

The unholy alliance in this case was between popular opinion, which seems always to be craving controls (see Chapter 6), and an absence of prior experience with peacetime controls that economists might have used to estimate the likely effects of controls. This alliance was damaged by the 1971–1974 episode. Economists now have some inkling of the likely effects of a peacetime controls program, and will line up much more resolutely against it in the future. But the senior partner in the alliance is as strong as ever; the public's love affair with controls apparently has not dimmed. Again the state of economic literacy is sobering.

Finally, it is worth listing some of the lesser errors of the period and their explanations. I proceed chronologically.

The overexpansion of the economy in 1972 was assisted by what now appears to have been an inaccurately large estimate of potential GNP. To this extent, it marked a failure of economic science. However, I cannot help thinking that this overestimate was a minor factor compared to the plain fact that 1972 was an election year in which a politically astute and not highly principled President was seeking re-election.

The violent wrenching of monetary and fiscal policy toward restraint in early 1973 was in part a reaction—or rather an overreaction—to the errors of 1972, and illustrates eloquently the classic monetarist claim that discretionary policy has a tendency to go overboard. Maybe this is why the Fed apparently listened to the monetarists and followed the disastrous policy of (relatively) steady growth of the money supply in 1974. It may also have helped persuade the administration to allow a tremendous inflation induced "fiscal drag" that year, though I suspect this was more a case of simply not paying attention. After all, who could get exercised about fiscal drag while Watergate was going on?

Last, and probably also least, we have the mistake of making the 1975

---

[7] In addition to the catch-up inflation, it has been alleged (but not proven) that controls had deleterious effects on investment, and hence on aggregate supply in the long run.

tax cuts temporary rather than permanent. Since economists were divided on the importance of this issue at the time (and perhaps still are), with some urging strongly that the cuts be made permanent and others arguing that it did not make much difference, this policy error was at least as much a failure of economic science as of economic policy.

There is a general lesson here too, and it too is a very old one. The failures of economic policy during 1971–1976 were in some small part attributable to weaknesses in economic theory, gaps in empirical economic knowledge, and limits on forecasting ability. But in truth these failings played a minor role in what happened, just as they have typically played minor roles in past policy errors. The main difficulties were not in understanding what was going on, diagnosing the problems, prescribing solutions, or even forecasting the future—though each of these left room for improvement. Rather the main problem was in getting the political mechanism to respond appropriately: to hold out against controls despite the public clamor; not to overstimulate the economy when the election was in sight; not to shift gears so abruptly in 1973; to comprehend the one-shot nature of the big inflationary shocks of 1973–1974, and to educate the public accordingly; to prevent a recession that was plainly preventable; and so on.

If all of this sounds like a brief against discretionary policy, and by inference in favor of fixed rules, I hasten to point out that it is not. First, while rules would have done better in some respects, they would have done worse in others. But even more important, the years chosen for study in this book were not typical; they were selected specifically because stabilization policy was executed so poorly. On balance, I do believe that the economy would have been better off under a regime of rules during 1971–1976, though I hasten to add that a more sensible discretionary policy would have been better still, But this judgment should not be misinterpreted as applicable to the entire period since World War II. Figure 9-1 illustrates the point by showing variations in the growth rate of real GNP over the twentieth century. The reduction in the amplitude of business fluctuations since World War II, that is, since the Age of Keynes began, is marked. It seems highly unlikely that this improved performance is sheer coincidence. And it was not the adherence to "Keynesian" policies that got us in trouble in the 1970s.

3. Some Remarks on 1977–1979

The years 1977 and 1978 were very different in some respects from the years considered in this book (for example, the economy expanded

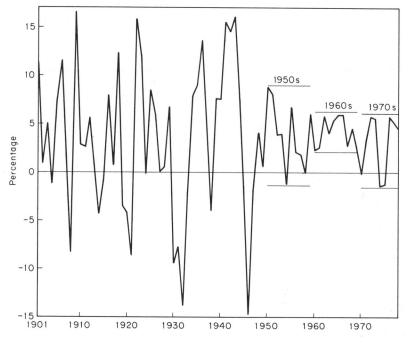

Figure 9-1. The rate of growth of real gross national product, 1901–1978. (*Sources:* U.S. Bureau of Census, 1975; U.S. Bureau of Economic Analysis, 1976; *Survey of Current Business.)*

smoothly and steadily during 1977–1978), but were quite similar in other respects (for example, the average inflation rates for 1977–1978 and for 1972–1976 were nearly equal). More to the point, a number of the policy issues that arose in 1977–1979 had parallels in the events of 1971–1976. This coincidence gave policymakers a golden opportunity to show how much they had learned from the bitter experience of the Great Stagflation. The opportunity was squandered.

The first event worthy of note was President Carter's proposed fiscal stimulus package of January 1977. The centerpiece of this package was a *rebate* of personal income taxes quite similar to the 1975 tax rebate—precisely the form of tax reduction that I argued in Chapter 7 has the weakest effects. This proposal was withdrawn in April 1977, but there is absolutely no reason to think that evidence on the relative ineffectiveness of the 1975–1976 tax cuts had anything to do with this decision. Instead, a recalcitrant Congress and an unexpectedly bouyant economy (8.9% real growth in 1977:1) combined to kill the idea. An optimist may, however, find solace in the fact that both Mr. Carter's 1978 tax cut proposal and the law that was eventually enacted did call for *permanent* tax cuts.

A second notable event was President Carter's concoction in late 1978 of a "voluntary" incomes policy whose resemblance, however, to mandatory controls was quite striking. At this writing (June 1979) it does not appear that this program is having much effect on inflation, so there hopefully will not be much "catch-up" inflation awaiting us when the program is terminated. But to a student of the 1971–1974 episode the prospects are chilling nonetheless.

What motivated Mr. Carter to opt for controls against, we may assume, the counsel of most of his economic advisers? Unlike Mr. Nixon, who ran out of patience because inflation was winding down too slowly, Mr. Carter was confronted with a sharp *acceleration* of inflation in 1978. The Consumer Price Index, which had risen 6.8% during 1977 as a whole and at only a 4.8% annual rate in the second half of the year, rose at a rapid 9.6% annual rate from December 1977 to October 1978. As inflation accelerated, public ire over inflation intensified until there was little question that inflation had once again ensconced itself as "public enemy number one."

It is interesting to examine the 1977–1979 acceleration of inflation in a manner similar to Chapter 5's anatomy of the 1973–1974 inflationary bulge, for the "special factor" nature of the recent acceleration is just as clear cut as it was in the earlier period.

If we use the CPI to measure inflation, the inflation rate rose from 6.8% during 1977 to 9% during 1978—an acceleration of 2.2 percentage points. Table 9-1 breaks down this acceleration into its major components. We see from the table that three items accounted for the lion's share of the acceleration of inflation in 1978: food prices, and in particular meat prices; costs of homeownership, where the major contributor was higher mortgage interest rates; and used-car prices. Specifically, meat prices, used-car prices, and homeownership costs together accounted for 1.8 percentage points of the total 2.2 percentage point acceleration.[8] Now, these three items are all relatively independent of movements in unit labor costs, and thus relatively independent of the economy's long-run "baseline" inflation rate.[9] Each of them recalls a "special factor" that was operative in 1974, and the case of food is almost exactly parallel to one of the major supply shocks that caused the Great Stagflation.

---

[8] The three items amounted to only 30% of the index in December 1977.

[9] For a similar appraisal of the 1978 inflationary acceleration see Congressional Budget Office (1978), Heller (1979), and, to a lesser extent, *Economic Report of the President,* 1979, pp. 38–45, 54–57. It should be noted, however, that rising mortgage rates and real estate prices in part reflected a heightened concern with overall inflation.

TABLE 9-1
Changes in the CPI and Selected Components, 1977-1978[a]

Item	Percentage change during:[b]		Acceleration	Contribution to acceleration in CPI[c]
	1977	1978		
All Items	6.8	9.0	2.2	2.2
Food	8.0	11.8	3.8	0.67
Meat[d]	7.0	20.7	13.7	0.54
Homeownership	9.2	12.4	3.2	0.731
Used cars	−4.1	13.6	17.7	0.53

[a]For 1977, data pertain to the old CPI. For 1978, data pertain to the new CPI for all urban workers (CPI-U). *Source:* Bureau of Labor Statistics.
[b]December to December.
[c]Acceleration multiplied by December 1977 relative importance.
[d]Actually includes poultry, fish, and eggs as well; but price movements in 1978 were dominated by meat prices.

The first few months of 1979 brought more of the same, only more so; and the resemblance to 1974 grew even stronger. From December 1978 to April 1979 (the last month for which data were available when this book went to press), the CPI rose at an annual rate of 13.3%—a full 4.3 percentage points above its 1978 pace. Table 9-2, which has the same format as Table 9-1, shows that this further acceleration was completely accounted for by three factors. First, beef prices accelerated yet again. Second, mortgage interest rates rose even higher. And third, the revolution in Iran and the resulting turmoil within OPEC led to rapid increases in the prices of gasoline and fuel oil. These three items, though they amount to only 19% of the index, account for the entire early 1979 acceleration of inflation.

Nor is this all that can be explained by factors reminiscent of 1973–1974. From December 1977 to December 1978, the dollar depreciated 10% against a multilateral trade weighted average of currencies.[10] According to a fairly conservative rule of thumb, each 1% depreciation of the dollar leads to a .15% increase in the Consumer Price Index over a period of 2–3 years; of this, about one-half occurs in the first year.[11] By this rule of thumb, the decline in the exchange value of the dollar might

[10] The index is reported in *Economic Report of the President,* 1979, Table B-96, p. 293.
[11] This rule is consistent with the results on the 1971–1973 devaluations of the dollar cited in Chapter 3 (see pages 28–29). It is also stated by the CEA in the *Economic Report of the President,* 1979, p. 43. A somewhat larger fraction (.21 instead of .15) is suggested by the CBO [see Congressional Budget Office (1978, p. 46)].

TABLE 9-2

Changes in the CPI and Selected Components, 1978–1979

Item	Percentage change		Acceleration	Contribution to acceleration in CPI[c]
	During 1978[a]	Dec. 1978– April 1979[b]		
All items	9.0	13.3	4.3	4.3
Food	11.8	18.8	7.0	1.27
Meat[d]	20.7	44.2	23.5	1.03
Homeownership	12.4	17.9	5.5	1.30
Financing[e]	14.7	28.0	13.3	1.29
Home heating oil[f]	6.8	42.6	35.8	.31
Gasoline	8.5	47.1	38.6	1.61

[a]December 1977 to December 1978.

[b]At annual rate, seasonally adjusted except for All items.

[c]Acceleration multiplied by December 1978 relative importance.

[d]Includes also poultry, fish, and eggs; but price movements were dominated by meat prices.

[e]Includes also taxes and insurance; but price movements were dominated by mortgate interest rates.

[f]Actually, fuel oil, coal, and bottled gas.

have added about .75 percentage point to the inflation rates of 1978 and 1979.[12]

In addition, the government chimed in with several "supply shocks" of its own: both payroll taxes and the minimum wage were raised on January 1, 1978 and again on January 1, 1979. In the case of the 1978 minimum wage hike, Crandall (1978) has used some earlier analysis by Gramlich (1976) to estimate that the 15% increase (from $2.30 to $2.65 per hour) added about .5% to the average level of wages, This helps explain why wages grew more rapidly in the first half of 1978 than in the second half, and also why nonunion wages led the way. With some lag, this increase in wages probably found its way into prices.

In sum, a variety of special factors, each suggestive of a one-time adjustment of the price level rather than an increase in the underlying steady rate of inflation, seem more than sufficient to account for the

[12] It is important to note that the contribution of devaluation to inflation is not to be *added* to the special factors discussed in the preceding paragraphs. For example, depreciation of the dollar may have been a contributing factor to the price rises for meat and used cars.

acceleration of inflation in 1978 and 1979.[13] Yet the one-shot nature of much of the 1978–1979 acceleration of inflation was not reflected in the Carter administration's response to this event. The wage–price program has already been mentioned. The President rejected suggestions to delay the scheduled increases in payroll taxes and minimum wages that took effect on January 1, 1979. The Federal Reserve, with the full blessing of the administration, embarked on a very tight monetary policy in November 1978 in order to alleviate pressure on the dollar in foreign exchange markets and to curb aggregate demand. Shortly thereafter, the President announced a correspondingly restrictive fiscal policy in his January 1979 budget message.

In a word, the 1977–1979 acceleration of inflation elicited tight money, a tight budget, and something akin to price controls. It did not elicit any creative supply-increasing initiatives (such as cutting payroll taxes). Nor was it greeted by the patient forbearance that was so lacking in 1971–1973. Finally, as of this writing (June 1979) the world seems in the midst of another "oil shock" whose dimensions are difficult to assess. There seems little indication that monetary and fiscal policy will turn accommodative if this shock proves to be as big as many fear. Such is the politics of economic policy in America.

4. In Conclusion

The economy was put through a wringer during the Great Stagflation. Suffering is good for you, my mother always told me, because you learn from it. What did we learn from the Great Stagflation? We did not learn the importance of the distinction between steady inflation and one-shot adjustments of the price level. We did not learn to steer clear of wage–price controls. We did not learn how to live with inflation as, for example, through a comprehensive system of indexing. What did we learn? A good question, but one without a good answer.

Though the prognosis sounds pessimistic, I will close on an optimistic—perhaps foolishly optimistic—note. The arguments and analyses presented in this book do not suggest that the best thing to do is to give up on stabilization policy. They do not suggest that discretion should be abandoned in favor of fixed rules. They do suggest that discretionary

---

[13] There is, however, some evidence that even the underlying rate of inflation may have increased in 1978, in part because of the slowdown in productivity growth. For a full discussion, see *Economic Report of the President, 1979.*

policy could be managed a lot better than it has been managed—with more patience, less rhetoric, and better judgment. Economic knowledge continues to accumulate and improve. For example, we now know much more about supply shocks, inflationary expectations, wage-price controls, the role of energy in the macroeconomy, and temporary income taxes than we did in the early 1970s. Though this knowledge is far from perfect, and important gaps remain, the constraining factor in the quest for better economic policy now seems to be the woefully inadequate level of economic literacy. This has often been true in the past and has sometimes—I repeat, *sometimes*—been overcome. A President who tries hard enough can raise the public's level of economic literacy, as President Kennedy did with the help of Walter Heller. Perhaps it is not too much to hope that this aspect of history may also be repeated.

references

Almon, Shirley, "The Distributed Lag between Capital Appropriations and Expenditures." *Econometrica* **33,** 1965, 178-196.

Ando, Albert, and Palash, Carl "Some Stabilization Problems of 1971-75, with an Application of Optimal Control Algorithims," in *Frontiers of Quantitative Economics,* Vol. III, M. Intriligator (ed.). Amsterdam: North-Holland, 1976.

Balbach, Anatol, and Jordan, Jerry L., "The Federal Open Market Committee in 1973." *Federal Reserve Bank of St. Louis Review* **56**(4), April 1974, 2-17.

Berndt, Ernst R., and Wood, David O., "Technology, Prices, and the Derived Demand for Energy." *Review of Economics and Statistics* **57,** August 1975, 259-268.

Blinder, Alan S., "Intergenerational Transfers and Life Cycle Consumption." *American Economic Review* **66,** May 1976, 87-93.

Blinder, Alan S., "Temporary Taxes and Consumer Spending." National Bureau of Economic Research Working Paper No. 283, October 1978.

Blinder, Alan S. "Supply-Shock Stagflation: Money, Expectations, and Accommodation," in *Development in an Inflationary World,* J. Flanders and A. Razin (eds.). New York: Academic Press, 1980 (forthcoming).

Blinder, Alan S., and Goldfeld, Stephen M., "New Measures of Fiscal and Monetary Policy, 1958-73." *American Economic Review* **66,** December 1976, 780-796.

Blinder, Alan S., and Newton, William J., "The 1971-1974 Controls Program and the Price Level: An Econometric Post-Mortem." National Bureau of Economic Research Working Paper No. 279, September 1978.

Blinder, Alan S., and Solow, Robert M., "Analytical Foundations of Fiscal Policy," in A. S. Blinder and others, *The Economics of Public Finance,* pp. 3-115. Washington, D.C.: The Brooking Institution, 1974.

Boskin, Michael J., "Taxation, Saving, and the Rate of Interest." *Journal of Political Economy* **86,** April 1978 (Part 2), S3–S27.

Bosworth, Barry, "The Current Inflation: Malign Neglect?" *Brookings Papers on Economic Activity* **1,** 1973, 263–283.

Box, G. E. P., and Jenkins, G. M., *Time Series Analysis, Forecasting and Control.* San Francisco: Holden–Day, 1970.

Bryant, John, "Relative Prices and Inventory Investment." *Journal of Monetary Economics* **4,** January 1978, 85–102.

Burger, Albert E., and Mudd, Douglas R., "The FOMC in 1976: Progress Against Inflation." *Federal Reserve Bank of St. Louis Review* **59**(3), March 1977, 2–17.

Carlson, John A., "Short-Term Interest Rates as Predictors of Inflation: Comment," *American Economic Review* **67**(3), June 1977, 469–475.

Clark, Peter B., "The Effects of Recent Exchange Rate Changes on the U.S. Trade Balance," in *The Effects of Exchange Rate Adjustments*, P. B. Clark, D. E. Logue and R. J. Sweeney (eds.). Washington, D.C.: U.S. Treasury, 1974.

Clark, Peter K. "Capital Formation and the Recent Productivity Slowdown." *Journal of Finance* **33,** June 1978, 965–975.

Congressional Budget Office, *Inflation and Unemployment: A Report on the Economy.* Washington, D.C.: U.S. Government Printing Office, June 1975a.

Congressional Budget Office, *Recovery: How Fast and How Far?* Washington, D.C.: U.S. Government Printing Office, September 1975b.

Congressional Budget Office, *Inflation and Growth: The Economic Policy Dilemma.* Washington, D.C.: U.S. Government Printing Office, July 1978.

Crandall, Robert W., "Federal Government Initiatives to Reduce the Price Level." *Brookings Papers on Economic Activity* **2,** 1978, 401–440.

Darby, Michael R., "The Allocation of Transitory Income Among Consumers' Assets." *American Economic Review* **62,** December 1972, 928–941.

Darby, Michael R., "Price and Wage Controls: The First Two Years," in *The Economics of Price and Wage Controls*, K. Brunner and A. Meltzer (eds.). Carnegie–Rochester Conference Series, Vol. 2. Amsterdam: North-Holland, 1976.

Dolde, Walter, "Forecasting the Consumption Effects of Stabilization Policies." *International Economic Review* **17,** June 1976, 431–446.

Dolde, Walter, "Temporary Taxes as Macroeconomic Stabilizers." *American Economic Review* **69,** May 1979, pp. 81–85.

Eckstein, Otto, *The Great Recession.* Amsterdam: North–Holland, 1978.

Eckstein, Otto, and Brinner, Roger, *The Inflation Process in the United States.* Study for the Joint Economic Committee, 92 Cong. 2 Sess., 1972.

Eisner, Robert, "Fiscal and Monetary Policy Reconsidered." *American Economic Review* **59,** December 1969, 897–905.

Elliott, J. W., "Measuring the Expected Real Rate of Interest: An Exploration of Macroeconomic Alternatives." *American Economic Review* **67**(3), June 1977, 429–444.

Enzler, Jared J., Johnson, Lewis, and Paulus, John "Some Problems of Money Demand." *Brookings Papers on Economic Activity* **1,** 1976, 261–280.

Fair, Ray C., "The Effect of Economic Events on Votes for President." *Review of Economics and Statistics* **60,** May 1978, 159–173.

Feige Edgar L., and Pearce, Douglas K., "Inflation and Incomes Policy: An Application of Time Series Models," in *The Economics of Price and Wage Controls*, K. Brunner and A. Meltzer (eds.). Carnegie–Rochester Conference Series Vol. 2, Amsterdam: North-Holland, 1976.

Feldstein, Martin S., and Auerbach, Alan, "Inventory Behavior in Durable Goods Manufacturing: The Target-Adjustment Model." *Brookings Papers on Economic Activity* **2**, 1976, 351–396.

Frey, Bruno S., "Politico-Economic Models and Cycles." *Journal of Public Economics* **9**, 1978, 203–220.

Gallup, George H., *The Gallup Poll: Public Opinion, 1935–1971*. New York: Random House, 1972.

Gallup, George H., *The Gallup Poll: Public Opinion, 1972–1977*. Wilmington, Del.: Scholarly Resources, 1978.

Goldfeld, Stephen M., "The Case of the Missing Money." *Brookings Papers on Economic Activity* **3**, 1976, 683–730.

Goldfeld, Stephen M., and Quandt, Richard E., *Nonlinear Methods in Econometrics*. Amsterdam: North-Holland, 1972.

Gordon, Robert J., "Inflation in Recession and Recovery." *Brookings Papers on Economic Activity* **1**, 1971, 105–158.

Gordon, Robert J., "Wage-Price Controls and the Shifting Phillips Curve." *Brookings Papers on Economic Activity* **2**, 1972, 385–421.

Gordon, Robert J., "The Response of Wages and Prices to the First Two Years of Controls." *Brookings Papers on Economic Activity* **3**, 1973, 765–778.

Gordon, Robert J., "The Impact of Aggregate Demand on Prices." *Brookings Papers on Economic Activity* **3**, 1975, 613–662.

Gordon, Robert J., "Can the Inflation of the 1970s Be Explained?" *Brookings Papers on Economic Activity* **1**, 1977, 253–277.

Gramlich, Edward M. "Impact of Minimum Wages on Other Wages, Employment and Family Incomes." *Brookings Papers on Economic Activity* **2**, 1976, 409–451.

Hall, Robert E., "Stochastic Implications of the Life Cycle–Permanent Income Hypothesis: Theory and Evidence." *Journal of Political Economy* **86**, December 1978, 971–987.

Hamburger, Michael J., "Behavior of the Money Stock: Is There a Puzzle?" *Journal of Monetary Economics* 3(3), July 1977, 265–288.

Heller, Walter W., "The Realities of Inflation." *The Wall Street Journal*, January 19, 1979, p. 10.

Houthakker, Hendrik S., and Taylor, Lester D., *Consumer Demand in the United States*. Cambridge, Mass.: Harvard University Press, 1966.

Jianakoplos, Nancy, "The FOMC in 1975: Announcing Monetary Targets." *Federal Reserve Bank of St. Louis Review* 58(3), March 1976, 8–22.

Jordan, Jerry L., "FOMC Policy Actions in 1972." *Federal Reserve Bank of St. Louis Review* 55(3), March 1973, 10–24.

Juster, F. Thomas, "A Note on Prospective 1977 Tax-Cuts and Consumer Spending." Mimeo, University of Michigan, January 1977.

Kenen, Peter B., and associates, *A Model of the U.S. Balance of Payments*. Lexington, Mass.: D. C. Heath, 1978.

Kopcke, Richard W., "The Behavior of Investment Spending during the Recession and Recovery, 1973–1976." *New England Economic Review*, November–December 1977, 5–41.

Kosters, Marvin H., *Controls and Inflation: The Economic Stabilization Program in Retrospect*. Washington, D.C.: American Enterprise Institute, 1975.

Kramer, Gerald H., "Short-term Fluctuations in U.S. Voting Behavior, 1896–1964." *American Political Science Review* **65**, 1971, 131–143

Kwack, Sung Y., "The Effects of Foreign Inflation on Domestic Prices and the Relative

Price Advantage of Exchange-Rate Changes," in *The Effects of Exchange Rate Adjustments*, P. B. Clark, D. E. Logue, and R. J. Sweeney (eds.). Washington, D.C.: U.S. Treasury, 1974.

Lanzillotti, Robert F., Hamilton, Mary T., and Roberts, Blaine, R. *Phase II in Review: The Price Commission Experience*. Washington, D.C.: The Brookings Institution, 1975.

Lipsey, Richard G., and Parkin, J. Michael, "Incomes Policy: A Reappraisal." *Economica* 37, 1970, 1–31.

Lucas, Robert E., Jr., "Econometric Policy Evaluation: A Critique," in *The Phillips Curve and Labor Markets*, K. Brunner and A. Meltzer (eds.). Carnegie-Rochester Conference Series, Vol. 1. Amsterdam: North-Holland, 1976.

Maccini, Louis "An Empirical Model of Price and Output Behavior." *Economic Inquiry* 15, October 1977, 493–512.

Maisel, Sherman J., *Managing the Dollar*. New York: Norton, 1973.

Malkiel, Burton G., "The Capital Formation Problem in the United States." *Journal of Finance* 34, May 1979, 291–306.

McGuire, Timothy W., "On Estimating the Effects of Controls," in *The Economics of Price and Wage Controls*, K. Brunner and A. Meltzer (eds.). Carnegie-Rochester Conferences Series, Vol. 2. Amsterdam: North-Holland, 1976.

Mishkin, Frederic S., "What Depressed the Consumer? The Household Balance Sheet and the 1973–75 Recession." *Brookings Papers on Economic Activity* 1, 1977, 123–164.

Modigliani, Franco, "The Monetarist Controversy or, Should We Forsake Stabilization Policies?" *American Economic Review* 67, March 1977, 1–19.

Modigliani, Franco, and Steindel, Charles, "Is a Tax Rebate an Effective Tool for Stabilization Policy?" *Brookings Papers on Economic Activity* 1, 1977, 175–203.

Nixon, Richard M., *Six Crises*. Garden City, N. Y.: Doubleday, 1962.

Nordhaus, William D., "The Recent Productivity Slowdown." *Brookings Papers on Economic Activity* 3, 1972, 493–536.

Nordhaus, William D., "Comment." *Brookings Papers on Economic Activity* 3, 1975, 663–665.

Oi, Walter Y., "On Measuring the Impact of Wage-Price Controls: A Critical Appraisal," in *The Economics of Price and Wage Controls*, K. Brunner and A. Meltzer (eds.). Carnegie-Rochester Conference Series, Vol. 2. Amsterdam: North-Holland, 1976.

Okun, Arthur M., "The Personal Tax Surcharge and Consumer Demand, 1968–1970." *Brooking Papers on Economic Activity* 1, 1971, 167–204.

Okun, Arthur M., "Did the 1968 Surcharge Really Work? Comment." *American Economic Review* 67, March 1977, 166–169.

Perloff, Jeffrey M., and Wachter, Michael L., "A Production Function—Nonaccelerating Inflation Approach to Potential Output: Is Measured Potential Output Too High?" in *Three Aspects of Policy and Policymaking: Knowledge, Data and Institutions*, K. Brunner and A. Meltzler (eds.). Carnegie-Rochester Conference Series, Vol. 10. Amsterdam: North-Holland, 1979.

Perry, George L., "The United States," in *Higher Oil Prices and the World Economy*, E. R. Fried and C. L. Schultze (eds.), pp. 71–104. Washington, D.C.: Brookings Institution, 1975a.

Perry, George L., "Policy Alternatives for 1974." *Brookings Papers on Economic Activity* 1, 1975b, 222–235.

Pierce, James "The Political Economy of Arthur Burns." *Journal of Finance* 34, May 1979, 485–496.

Pierce, James L., and Enzler, Jared J., "The Effects of External Inflationary Shocks." *Brookings Papers on Economic Activity* 1, 1974, 13–54.

Poole, William, "Burnsian Monetary Policy: Eight Years of Progress?" *Journal of Finance* **34**, May 1979, 473–484.

Roesch, Susan R., "The FOMC in 1974: Monetary Policy during Economic Uncertainty." *Federal Reserve Bank of St. Louis Review* **57**(4), April 1975, 2–13.

Sargent, Thomas J., "Rational Expectations, Econometric Exogeneity, and Consumption." *Journal of Political Economy* **86**, August 1978, 673–700.

Schnittker, John A., "The 1972–73 Food Price Spiral." *Brookings Papers on Economic Activity* **2**, 1973, 498–506.

Schultze, Charles L., "Falling Profits, Rising Profit Margins, and the Full-Employment Profit Rate." *Brookings Papers on Economic Activity* **2**, 1975, 449–469.

Shoven, John B., and Bulow, Jeremy I., "Inflation Accounting and Nonfinancial Corporate Profits: Financial Assets and Liabilities." *Brookings Papers on Economic Activity* **1**, 1976, 15–57.

Shultz, George P., and Dam, Kenneth W., *Economic Policy Beyond the Headlines*. New York: Norton, 1977.

Siebert, Calvin and Zaidi, Mahmood A., "The Short-Run Wage-Price Mechanism in U.S. Manufacturing." *Western Economic Journal* **9**, September 1971, 278–288.

Smith, Adam, *The Wealth of Nations*, Modern Library Edition. New York: Random House, 1937.

Springer, William L., "Windfalls, Temporary Income Taxes and Consumption Behavior." Unpublished Ph.D. dissertation, Princeton University, 1974.

Springer, William L., "Did the 1968 Surcharge Really Work?" *American Economic Review* **65**, September 1975, 644–659.

Springer, William L., "Reply." *American Economic Review* **67**, March 1977, 170–172.

Tobin, James and Brainard, William C., "Asset Markets and the Cost of Capital," in *Economic Progress, Private Values and Public Policy: Essays in Honor of William Fellner*, B. Belassa and R. Nelson (eds.). Amsterdam: North–Holland, 1977.

Tufte, Edward R., *Political Control of the Economy*. Princeton, N.J.: Princeton University Press, 1978.

U.S. Board of Governors of the Federal Reserve System, *Federal Reserve Bulletin*, various issues.

U.S. Bureau of Census, *Historical Statistics of the United States: Colonial Times to 1970*, Part 1. Washington, D. C.: Government Printing Office, 1975.

U.S. Bureau of Economic Analysis, *Survey of Current Business*, various issues.

U.S. Bureau of Economic Analysis, *The National Income and Product Account of the United States, 1929–1974*. Washington, D.C.: U.S. Government Printing Office, 1976.

U.S. Bureau of Labor Statistics, *CPI Detailed Report*, various issues.

U.S. Cost of Living Council, *Economic Stabilization Program Quarterly Report*, various issues.

U.S. President, *Weekly Compilation of Presidential Documents*. Washington, D.C.: U.S. Government Printing Office, various issues.

U.S. President, *Economic Report of the President together with the Annual Report of the Council of Economic Advisers*, various issues.

Von Furstenberg, George M., "Corporate Investment: Does Market Valuation Matter in the Aggregate?" *Brookings Papers on Economic Activity* **2**, 1977, 347–397.

Von Furstenberg, George M., and Malkiel, Burton G., "Financial Analysis in an Inflationary Environment." *Journal of Finance* **32**, May 1977, 575–588.

index